This book is the first to address and synthesize bank lending's full scope. Academics and practitioners will find much to stimulate their thinking in this book, from the legal and regulatory environments which govern the field to detailed sections on the lending cycle, collateral security and loan evaluation. Traditionally neglected topics like the impact of lending (which challenges lenders' social responsibilities) and Islamic finance (an important and flourishing component of modern business) are laudable and long overdue in the industry.
– *Gary van Vuuren, formerly Senior Director at Fitch Ratings, Goldman Sachs, Merrill Lynch, Standard Bank and Aviva Investors*

This is an excellent introduction to both the theory and, more importantly, the practice of lending in all its forms. Lending prudently, responsibly and, of course, profitably is far from simple, especially when markets are booming. However, as we have seen and this book clearly explains, it is essential in order to create a thriving and successful economy.
– *Liam O'Keeffe, Managing Director, Head of Special Projects London Branch, Credit Agricole Corporate and Investment Bank*

The authors' extensive practical and theoretical experience in industry and academia make them eminently qualified to write this book which serves as a definitive reference book on lending for both banking professionals and academics.
– *Prabhakar Kaza, formerly Relationship Director at HSBC and General Manager at State Bank of India*

This is an excellent book that includes qualitative and quantitative analysis of both consumer and corporate lending. I am delighted to recommend it both for academic study as well as professional practice. The authors are clearly experts in the area of bank lending.
– *Dr Sushil Mohan, Head of Economics & Finance Subject Group, Brighton Business School, University of Brighton*

Bank Lending: Principles and practice is an important contribution to the field of banking and finance as it bridges the gap between theory and practice in a concise and comprehensive manner. It should prove useful to students and practitioners who wish to gain insight and further their understanding of the subject of bank lending. The authors present a universal perspective and interestingly highlight an alternative mode of lending within Islamic Finance.
– *Asif Zaman, Senior Lecturer, Islamic Finance, Cardiff Metropolitan University*

It is hard to find good banking practice books to recommend to students. I welcome and endorse this text, which is written by academics who also have a wealth of practical experience of working in the banking industry. The book thoroughly covers how banks apply core lending principles to serve individuals, small businesses and large corporates. I have recommended this book for my courses and we will definitely be buying copies. I am happy to recommend this text for all students who are interested in banking.
– Dr Sallyanne Decker, Principal Lecturer in Banking and Finance, Accounting and Finance Department, University of Greenwich

Nirmala Lee & Vijay Lee

BANK LENDING
Principles and practice

Gosbrook

First published in 2018 by
Gosbrook Professional Publishing Ltd
20 Patrick Road
Reading RG4 8DD, UK

www.gosbrook.com

ISBN 978 1 91218 404 0 (paperback)
ISBN 978 1 91218 405 7 (hardback)
ISBN 978 1 91218 406 4 (ePub)
ISBN 978 1 91218 407 1 (PDF)

Cover and text design: Anke Ueberberg
Cover image: Matthias Hloucha

Printed and bound by Lightning Source

To our parents
Ambrose and Dhanam Azariah, and Thomas and Ranie Lee
who gave us the gift of education

Contents

List of figures *x*
List of tables *xi*
Acronyms and abbreviations *xii*
Foreword *xiv*
Preface *xv*

1 An introduction to lending concepts and principles 1

1.1 Introduction 1
1.2 An overview of the lending market 2
1.3 What is 'lending'? 4
1.4 Risk and return 6
1.5 The attributes of good lending 11
1.6 The principles of credit risk management 12
1.7 Conclusion 15

2 The legal and regulatory environment 18

2.1 The legal and regulatory framework 18
2.2 Codes of practice 29
2.3 Ombudsmen 31
2.4 Customer rights and complaints procedures 32
2.5 Treating customers fairly 32
2.6 Conclusion 34

3 Types of borrower 37

3.1 Introduction 37
3.2 Personal borrowers 38
3.3 Partnerships 39
3.4 Companies 42
3.5 Unincorporated associations 45
3.6 Conclusion 46

4 Purposes of financing 48

4.1 Introduction 48
4.2 Consumer finance 48
4.3 Business finance 53
4.4 Conclusion 60

5 Forms of lending 63

5.1 Types of lending 63
5.2 Overdrafts 64
5.3 Loans 67
5.4 Credit cards 69
5.5 Invoice discounting 71
5.6 Factoring 73
5.7 Hire purchase 75
5.8 Leasing 77
5.9 Other forms of providing finance 79
5.10 Conclusion 81

6 The lending cycle – the credit-granting process 84

6.1 The lending cycle 84
6.2 The loan application and supporting information 86
6.3 Loan documentation and covenants 96
6.4 Further advances 97
6.5 Conclusion 98

7 Loan evaluation 101

7.1 Loan evaluation tools and techniques 101
7.2 Evaluation of working capital requirements 104
7.3 Evaluation of term lending requirements 108
7.4 Credit scoring 112
7.5 Credit rating agencies 115
7.6 Conclusion 118

8 Security – general 120

8.1 Introduction 120
8.2 The attributes of good security 121
8.3 Perfecting security interest 122
8.4 The desirability of taking security 125
8.5 Conclusion 127

9 Security – specific forms 130

9.1 Introduction 130
9.2 Land and property 131
9.3 Life insurance policies 134
9.4 Stocks and shares 139
9.5 Guarantees 142
9.6 Debentures – fixed and floating charges 146
9.7 The realisation of security 148
9.8 Conclusion 152

10 The lending cycle – the monitoring and control process 156

10.1 The need for monitoring and control 156
10.2 Information sources for review 159
10.3 Detecting problem loans 161
10.4 The stages of recovery 168
10.5 Conclusion 172

11 Islamic finance 175

11.1 Introduction 175
11.2 Modes of Islamic finance 176
11.3 Some special features of Islamic finance 179
11.4 Conclusion 181

12 The impact of lending and social responsibility 184

12.1 The economic and social effects of lending 184
12.2 Responsible lending 185
12.3 Relationship lending and responsible lending 189
12.4 Conclusion 190

Appendix A: Suggested answers to case study questions 193
Table of cases 199
Table of statutes 201
Table of statutory instruments 203
Table of European legislation 204
References 205
Index 210

List of figures

1.1 The loan 5
1.2 The management of risk 11
1.3 The lender's conflicting objectives 12
2.1 The UK's regulatory architecture 20
4.1 Purposes of financing 48
5.1 Lending classifications 63
6.1 The brief lending cycle 84
6.2 The credit-granting process 85
7.1 The SWOT grid 103
7.2 Porter's Five Forces 104
7.3 The cash operating cycle 105
7.4 Financing policies 107
9.1 Realisation risk 150
10.1 The lending cycle 159
10.2 Sources of information for monitoring and control 160
11.1 *Murabaha* finance and a standard bank loan compared 177
11.2 The structure of a *sukuk* transaction 179

List of tables

4.1 Balance sheet 61
4.2 Calculating the working capital and current ratios 61
6.1 A simplified balance sheet 88
6.2 Balance sheet equation 89
6.3 Calculating the gearing ratio 91
6.4 Impact of gearing on return 92
6.5 Impact of variability on return 93
7.1 CAMPARI 101
7.2 CCCPARTS 102
7.3 PARSER 102
7.4 Knowledge of the past 102
7.5 Forecast for the future 103
7.6 The basic structure of a balance sheet 104
7.7 Components of a credit score 113
7.8 Credit rating scales 116
10.1 Balance sheet 157
10.2 Deteriorated balance sheet 157
10.3 January (1,000 cans sold for a profit of £500) 163
10.4 February (2,000 cans sold for a profit of £1,000) 163
10.5 March (4,000 cans sold for a profit of £2,000) 163
10.6 Income statements 173
10.7 Financial position statements 174
11.1 A comparison of *murabaha* and *ijara* 178
11.2 Tax implications on forms of borrowing 180

Acronyms and abbreviations

ABFA Asset-based Finance Association
ABI Association of British Insurers
ABL asset-based lending
ABS asset-backed securities
ADR alternative dispute resolution
AER annual equivalent rate
ANN artificial neural network
APR annual percentage rate
AST assured shorthold tenancy
ATM automatic teller machine
BBA British Bankers' Association
BCC British Chambers of Commerce
BCBS Basel Committee on Banking Supervision
BCSB Banking Code Standards Board
BEIS Department for Business, Energy and Industrial Strategy
BIOA British and Irish Ombudsman Association
BIS Bank for International Settlements
CAMPARI Character, Ability, Margin (or Means), Purpose, Amount, Repayment, Insurance
CCCPARTS Character, Capital, Capability, Purpose, Amount, Repayment, Terms, Security
CCJ county court judgment
CDO collateralised debt obligation
CHOICE Creating Hope and Opportunity for Investors, Consumers and Entrepreneurs (US Financial CHOICE Act of 2017)
CIC community interest company
CILA certificate of independent legal advice
CLO collateralised loan obligation
CMA Competition and Markets Authority
CML Council of Mortgage Lenders
CRA credit rating agency
CRD Capital Requirements Directive
CRD IV Capital Requirements Directive IV
CRR Capital Requirements Regulation
CSR corporate social responsibility
CVA company voluntary arrangement
CVL creditors' voluntary liquidation
Dodd–Frank Act US Wall Street Reform and Consumer Protection Act of 2010
DSCR debt service coverage ratio
EAR effective annual rate
EBA European Banking Authority
EBIDA earnings before interest, depreciation and amortisation
EBITDA earnings before interest, taxes, depreciation and amortisation
ECB European Central Bank
EFG Enterprise Finance Guarantee
EIOPA European Insurance and Occupational Pensions Authority
EPS earnings per share
ESA European supervisory authority
ESMA European Securities and Markets Authority
ESRB European Systemic Risk Board
EU European Union
FATCA US Foreign Account Tax Compliance Act of 2010
FCA Financial Conduct Authority
FICO Fair Isaac Credit Organization (or Fair Isaac and Company)
FLA Finance and Leasing Association

FOS Financial Ombudsman Service
FPC Financial Policy Committee
FRS Financial Reporting Standard
FSA Financial Services Authority
FSAP Financial Services Action Plan (EU)
FSB Financial Stability Board
FSMA Financial Services and Markets Act 2000
FV future value
GAAP Generally Accepted Accounting Principles
GDP gross domestic product
HLC higher lending charge
HMRC HM Revenue & Customs
IAS International Accounting Standard
IASB International Accounting Standards Board
ICB Independent Commission on Banking
IFRS International Financial Reporting Standards
IMF International Monetary Fund
IRB internal ratings-based
IRS US Internal Revenue Service
ISA individual savings account
ISDA International Swaps and Derivatives Association
LIBOR London Inter-bank Offered Rate
LLP limited liability partnership
LMA Loan Market Association
LOLR lender of last resort
Ltd Limited
LTV loan-to-value
M&As mergers and acquisitions
MBS mortgage-backed security
MiFID Markets in Financial Instruments Directive
MiFID II Revised Markets in Financial Instruments Directive
MiFIR Markets in Financial Instruments Regulation
MPBR more principles-based regulation
NGO non-governmental organisation
NPL non-performing loan
NPV net present value
NYSE New York Stock Exchange
OFT Office of Fair Trading
ONS Office for National Statistics
P2P peer-to-peer
PARSER Person, Amount, Repayment, Security, Expertise, Expediency, Remuneration
PBIT profit before interest and tax
PE price–earnings ratio
PIN personal identification number
plc public limited company
PPI payment protection insurance
PRA Prudential Regulation Authority
PV present value
R&D research and development
RAROC risk-adjusted return on capital
ROCE return on capital employed
ROE return on equity
ROI return on investment
ROT retention of title
S&P Standard & Poor's
SAM shared appreciation mortgage
SIFI systemically important financial institution
SIV special investment vehicle
SME small or medium-sized enterprise
SPV special purpose vehicle
SSAP Statement of Standard Accounting Practice
SVR standard variable rate
SWOT strengths, weaknesses, opportunities and threats
UAE United Arab Emirates
USP unique selling proposition
VAR value at risk
VAT value added tax
VMCR value, measure, charge, realise
WTO World Trade Organization

Foreword

For all those who are involved with and concerned about bank lending, this is a crucially important book. It fulfils a real need for a contemporary approach to the study of the principles and practice of bank lending.

Bank Lending: Principles and practice offers important insights for industry and for academia; that is to say, both for graduate and undergraduate students on the one hand and for banking industry professionals on the other. The authors have the advantage of having been first-hand bank lenders themselves in both junior and senior management levels in top international banks. Their practical banking expertise in personal and corporate lending, combined with teaching and research expertise in banking and finance as senior academics at London-based universities, makes this a definitive reference book on the theory and practice of bank lending.

The text is written in a clear, concise and comprehensive manner. Extensive use of examples highlights the underlying concepts. Every page is packed with information and insights into the principles and theory behind bank lending as well as practical suggestions and activities illustrating the application of theory in the real world. Pedagogical features such as review questions, activities, case studies and numeric exercises stimulate interest and enable effective learning.

For the learning and teaching of the principles and practice of bank lending, this text is a solid motivational tool. It is strongly recommended for any reader who wishes to acquire knowledge, understanding and expertise in the art and science of bank lending.

Professor Dean Bartlett
Head of School, Guildhall School of Business and Law
London Metropolitan University
May 2018

Preface

RATIONALE

This book is a reference text for all students of lending. It is aimed at students, as well as professionals working or intending to work in a lending-related role.

Bank lending performs a key role within the economy. Individuals, as well as small, medium-sized and large enterprises, look primarily to banks and other financial institutions to finance their personal and business requirements. As such, lending is a core skill required within the financial services industry, and lending staff are required to have a detailed knowledge and understanding of the financial and legal aspects of their roles if they are to fulfil employer, as well as customer, expectations.

The book provides students and practitioners of bank lending with an understanding of lending practices, as well as the theories that underpin these practices. It covers lending principles, the legal and regulatory framework, types of borrower, the purposes of financing, forms of lending, security, and the lending cycle, including loan granting, loan evaluation, loan monitoring and loan recovery. Modes of Islamic finance are explained and the importance of responsible lending is highlighted.

Bank lending is the art and science of creating value for bank borrowers to capture value from them in return, leading to economic growth and overall prosperity. To lend or not to lend? How to lend and to whom to lend? This text helps you to answer these questions, and to make, monitor and control lending decisions.

Lenders need to be aware of the diversity of customers that could approach them for the wide range of lending services provided in today's financial markets. A lack of understanding of the nature of the customer or of the details of the lending request can result in the lender recommending the wrong product to the customer or in the lender not being able to recover a loan because it was not aware of the legal implications of lending to that particular customer type.

The nature of lending means that, on some occasions, the lender will not be able to recover the whole debt from the customer. It is through an appreciation of the risks involved in lending and the development of an ability to reduce those risks that providers are able to make better decisions. A full understanding of the lending cycle reduces the risks. The lending cycle starts with an analysis of financial information leading to the lending decision, and includes monitoring and control, plus the ability to detect early-warning signals and, ultimately, the repayment or recovery of debt so that the cycle of lending can be continued.

A key influence on the recovery of the debt is the action taken when the original advance was agreed. Did the lender take any security, and if so, is that security realisable? Many lenders have taken court action and found themselves unable to rely on security that they previously thought would provide them with an alternative source of repayment.

In summary, the subject will provide the lender, or prospective lender, with a framework within which to operate effectively, and to lend money safely and profitably, maximising the possibility of repayment by the borrower or through suitable alternatives where appropriate.

LEARNING OBJECTIVES

On completion of your study of this text, you will be able to:

- understand the principles of good lending, including relevant law and codes of practice such as the fair treatment of customers, responsible lending and the Banking Code;
- understand the nature of different types of borrower, such as personal customers, sole traders, partnerships and limited companies, and the lending services that may be of benefit to them;
- analyse the borrowing requirements of personal and commercial customers, including the interpretation of financial statements;
- understand and apply the features and benefits of a range of lending products and services to different customer types and lending situations;
- apply the principles of security to land and property, life policies, stocks and shares, guarantees and debentures, incorporating fixed and floating charges;
- understand the principal modes of Islamic finance;
- understand the implications and application of the lending cycle, from the lending decision, through loan management, monitoring and control, to the recovery of debts; and
- recognise the importance of responsible lending as a good business model.

STRUCTURE

This text has been designed to provide the knowledge, understanding and requisite skills underpinning the effective management of lending requests made by customers, including the repayment or recovery of credit that has been extended.

The early sections provide a broad overview of the legal and regulatory environment in which lenders operate, raising awareness of the implications of making the lending decision. This is followed by an analysis of the different types of customer, of their lending requirements and of the range of lending services that can be used to satisfy those lending needs.

The general principles of security are then investigated and applied to different forms of security, whether direct or third party, and whether covering personal or corporate debts.

An overview of the lending process includes a review of the lending cycle, comprising the initial lending decision, loan management, monitoring and control, spotting any early-warning signals that the repayment of the debts could be potentially problematic, and the eventual process of debt repayment, recovery or write-off.

A section on Islamic finance introduces the reader to the modes and features of Islamic lending products.

The text concludes with an assessment of the economic and social effects of lending, and of the importance of responsible lending.

1

An introduction to lending concepts and principles

LEARNING POINTS

This chapter is an introduction to the basic concepts related to lending, including the participants and the activities involved, setting the context for further learning.

Learning areas include:

- an overview of lending;
- lending risks and the risk–return trade-off;
- the principles of lending; and
- the attributes of good lending – safety, liquidity and profitability.

1.1 INTRODUCTION

To lend or not to lend? That is the question that has confronted lenders down the ages. Lending has been an important economic activity since ancient times. From pawnbroking to mortgages to credit derivatives, lending has taken on many shapes and sizes. Today, it is one of the most challenging and significant activities contributing in large measure to the effective allocation of resources, enabling firms and individuals to achieve their goals and aspirations. Lending plays a significant role in the economy of nations. The availability of credit can determine the extent of a country's economic development.

Lending decisions may be subject to two types of error. *Not* lending could itself be a wrong decision: this is a 'type I' error, being the false detection of poor loan quality, leading to rejection of good proposals – an error that may never come to light. Conversely, a decision *to* lend may be wrong: a 'type II' error, being a failure to detect poor loan quality, leading to acceptance of proposals that should have been rejected – and an error that will come to light sooner or later. It is also possible that a decision to lend may appear to be right at the time of granting, but may turn out to be wrong in hindsight due to subsequent unforeseeable developments. Worst of all is a decision to lend for disingenuous reasons despite the correct detection of poor loan quality – an error that will become known later, but which may come to light only after the lending official has benefited through bonuses and moved on, leaving the lending organisation – and/or the taxpayer, if the bank or lending institute has to be bailed out by a government – to meet the loan losses. The complexity of the loan-granting and loan-monitoring process merits careful consideration and analysis to avoid the consequences arising from wrong decisions to lend or not to lend.

Lending is determined to a large extent by the supply and demand of loanable funds. The higher the demand or the lower the supply of funds, the higher will be the price of the loan. Conversely, the lower the demand or the higher the supply of funds, the lower will be the price of the loan. The level or tightness of bank lending standards has also been found to have an effect on the supply of credit to firms: low bank lending growth after a period of prolonged tightening, as well as high bank lending growth in a period of prolonged easing, have been noted (van der Veer and Hoeberichts, 2016). *Cheap credit* describes a scenario in which loans are plentiful and available at low cost. *Credit crunch* describes a scenario in which, due to a change in economic conditions, loans are suddenly in short supply, can be obtained only at higher prices, or (sometimes) cannot be obtained at all whatever the price. The price of a loan will also depend upon other factors such as the likelihood of the loan being repaid: the higher the risk of default, the higher will be the return required by the lender by way of compensation.

It has been said that a bank will lend you money if you can prove that you do not need it. Lending is a risky activity and the higher the likelihood of the loan being returned, the more likely a lender is to grant the loan. No lender can be absolutely sure that the money lent will be returned; hence prudent lending principles are necessary if lending is to be a successful activity.

1.2 AN OVERVIEW OF THE LENDING MARKET

A *market* is a network of connections that allows buyers and sellers to carry out their transactions. A *financial market* is a market in which financial products are bought and sold. A *credit market* is a financial market in which money is lent and borrowed.

Lord Denning famously said, in *United Dominions Trust Ltd v Kirkwood* [1966] 2 QB 431, that 'a banker is easier to recognise than to define'. Today, a banker is still not that easy to define, and lending, once thought of as the preserve of banks, is undertaken by a range of entities. Lending ranges from mainstream lending undertaken by banks and other financial institutions to social lending undertaken by individuals to friends and family, or on websites such as zopa.com.

Lending can be broadly divided into three categories:

- *commercial lending* –
  - to ultra-prime and near-prime borrowers;
  - to subprime or high-risk borrowers;
- *not-for-profit lending* –
  - by credit unions and other community-based lenders to those on low incomes;
  - by government social lending operations, which provide interest-free loans to welfare recipients and those on the lowest incomes; and

- *illegal lending* –
  - to the deprived and some of the most vulnerable sections of society, to fill a gap not supplied by other lenders, frequently to fund addictions or chaotic lifestyles and concentrated among the credit-impaired or those who have experienced credit refusals (Ellison, Collard, and Forster, 2006).

Commercial lenders can broadly be divided into the following categories:

- *mainstream lenders*, e.g.
  - banks (both domestic and foreign-owned), including retail and investment banks;
  - card issuers;
  - mutual societies, such as building societies;
  - hedge funds;
  - private equity firms; and
  - sovereign funds; and
- *specialist lenders*, e.g.
  - home credit or doorstep lenders;
  - payday lenders; and
  - pawnbrokers.

Mainstream lenders range from direct and multiproduct lenders, such as retail banks, to remote and single-product lenders, such as overseas card issuers. They offer a range of services via a range of delivery channels, including branches, telephone, automatic teller machines (ATMs), cards and the Internet.

- *Retail banks* Retail banking involves the willingness and ability to deal with a large number of customers and transactions, including small-value transactions. An example of a retail bank is Metro Bank. A retail bank is a financial institution that enables its personal and business customers to deal with retail transactions on a mass scale, e.g. current and business accounts, personal and business loans, mortgages, credit cards. Retail banks may have their own investment banking arms, and may undertake both retail and wholesale activity; such banks may be labelled as 'retail' or 'investment' depending upon their dominant activity. *Ring-fencing*, which requires a larger bank to separate its retail banking activity from the rest of its business, is one of the reforms brought in by governments to strengthen the financial system following the 2007–08 global financial crisis. For UK banks this comes into effect on 1st January 2019.
- *Investment banks* Investment is undertaken with the expectation that it will generate a return or appreciate in value in the future. An investment bank is a financial institution that assists its customers to raise money for investment in a variety of ways, e.g. raising capital, handling mergers and acquisitions (M&As), dealing in securities. An example of an investment bank is JPMorgan Chase. Investment banks are sometimes also known as

wholesale banks because they deal with fewer customers, smaller number of transactions and larger sums of money.
- *Credit card issuers* Credit card issuers comprise banks or businesses that authorise the holder to buy goods or services on credit and include remote lenders such as card issuers outside the UK. Capital One is an example of a credit card issuer.
- *Building societies* Building societies are mutually owned by their members, generally their borrowers and savers. They operate under certain restrictions, but are able to offer better prices because they do not have any shareholders who expect a return for their investment. Their traditional focus is mortgages for owner-occupied residential property. Nationwide is an example of a building society.
- *Hedge funds* Historically, hedge funds were so-called because of their investment strategies to limit and protect against risk. Now, these funds are more speculative than many other funds and aim to maximise profits, which involves exposure to a greater level of risk. These funds are highly leveraged, i.e. largely financed by debt, meaning that they borrow heavily from banks and other institutions to undertake their investment and lending activities. Some of these funds are set up by banks themselves.
- *Private equity firms* Private equity firms borrow money from banks to invest in companies and take them private. Many of them are highly leveraged, i.e. they borrow heavily from banks and other institutions. Some of these firms are set up by banks themselves.
- *Sovereign states or countries* Not only do countries or sovereign states need money for various reasons and borrow from banks, but they also lend to banks.

Lenders may also be borrowers for the purpose of undertaking their own lending operations. Lenders and borrowers are diverse. While the principles of lending will broadly remain the same for all categories, the main focus of this text will be on mainstream lending firms, such as banks, which undertake commercial lending.

1.3 WHAT IS 'LENDING'?

'Lending' may be defined as the giving of an asset with the expectation that an equivalent value will be returned at a future point of time. A loan is an asset for the lender and a liability for the borrower. To the lender, the loan is an asset that is expected to be repaid with compensation for the costs and risks of lending. To the borrower, the loan is a liability that is required to be repaid with compensation for the costs of receiving the benefits of borrowing.

A loan involves the creation of credit. When a loan is granted to a borrower, the lender is the *creditor* and the borrower is the *debtor*. A debtor is also known as an *obligor*, i.e. an entity or party that has an obligation to pay all principal and interest payments on a debt (see Figure 1.1).

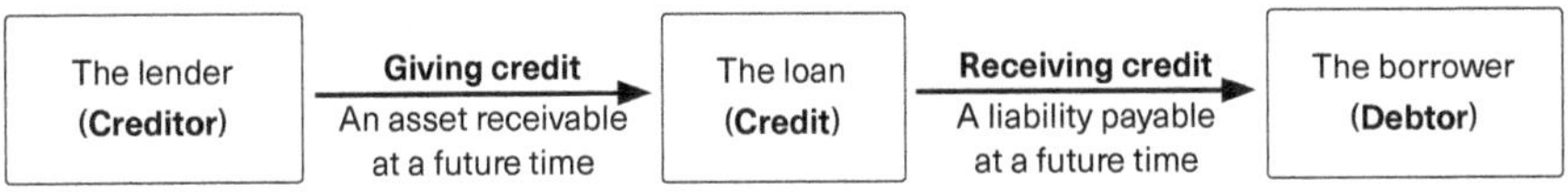

Figure 1.1 The loan

The amount of the loan is described as the *principal*. The lender will additionally have to be compensated for the costs and risks of lending, and the loan will therefore be offered at a price generally called *interest*. Interest is the charge for a loan, usually expressed as a percentage of the amount loaned. The price of the loan can also include a number of other elements such as commission, discount, fee, and so on.

Lenders are able to charge interest (or generate a return equivalent to interest) in a variety of ways. For those lenders that charge interest, this includes:

- *fixed interest*, i.e. interest rates are fixed for a specified period;
- *variable interest*, i.e. interest rates vary in relation to an underlying reference rate, such as Bank Rate (the base rate established by the Bank of England) or the London Inter-bank Offered Rate (LIBOR);
- *capped interest*, i.e. interest rates are subject to a specified ceiling;
- *simple interest*, i.e. there is no compounding of interest; and
- *compound interest*, i.e. interest is calculated on interest at periodic intervals, which was held in *Yourell v Hibernian Bank Ltd* [1918] AC 372 to be a 'usual and perfectly legitimate mode of dealing between banker and customer'.

The *standard variable rate* (SVR) is the standard rate of interest that lenders use and it is the rate to which a borrower is automatically switched when any fixed or initial offer period expires. In the UK, it is usually set at a few percentage points higher than Bank Rate, to which it is linked, meaning that it varies with changes in that rate.

The *annual equivalent rate* (AER), for savings and current accounts in credit, and the *effective annual rate* (EAR), for borrowing and overdrafts, are annualised rates of interest, including the compounding effect of charging or paying interest more frequently than once a year. The more frequently interest is applied in a year, the higher will be the effective annual interest rate. Unlike the *annual percentage rate* (APR), it does not include charges and fees. In the UK, the APR is the annualised interest rate including the effects of both interest compounding and other (non-interest) charges. (In the United States, the APR does not show the effect of compounding.)

In addition to interest, lenders charge fees to cover their expenses and generate profit, such as:

- an *arrangement fee* at the time of loan approval;
- a *valuation fee* for any valuation of assets;
- *legal fees* in relation to arranging the loan; and/or
- a *higher lending charge* (HLC), formerly known as *Mortgage Indemnity Guarantee*, i.e. a fee charged by a mortgage lender where the amount borrowed exceeds a given percentage (e.g. 80 per cent) of the value of the

property, which fee the lender uses to arrange insurance protecting itself against the risk of loan default.

Earnings from loans constitute a major part of banks' operating income and lending continues to be a core part of the business of banking despite the growth of alternative financial activities.

Gearing or *leverage* is the use of credit or borrowed funds to improve the rate of return from an investment. A high level of gearing or leverage indicates a high proportion of debt in a company's capital structure.

Loans are assets for the lender and are shown on the asset side of a lending organisation's balance sheet. Loans require the provision of more capital than some other forms of asset. The *Basel Accords* (Basel I, II and III) specify minimum capital requirements for banks, as agreed and issued by the Basel Committee on Banking Supervision (BCBS) of the Bank for International Settlements (BIS), which usually meets in Basel, Switzerland. In the past banks tried to remove loans from the asset side of the balance sheet by bundling them and converting them into securities that can be traded in the secondary market. Sold off to investors, such securities were converted to off-balance-sheet items such as collateralised loan obligations (CLOs) and collateralised debt obligations (CDOs). These were loans, such as mortgages, backed by assets, which were packaged and then sold to investors such as pension funds, hedge funds, special investment vehicles (SIVs) and other investors looking for a return from these assets. Such off-balance-sheet financing is widely considered to have caused the 2007–08 global financial crisis, during which subprime mortgages that should have been rated as 'junk' were given highly prized AAA ratings. Says Buckley (2011: 4–5): 'Not since the frog turned into a prince thanks to the kiss of a princess has a greater metamorphosis occurred . . . The transformation of frog to prince was reversed back to frog when defaults began.'

Traditionally, financial institutions have acted as intermediaries, borrowing funds from those who have surplus money and lending these funds to those who need to finance consumption or investment. *Financial intermediation* refers to the process whereby the financial intermediary borrows from savers and lends to borrowers. *Financial disintermediation* takes place when borrowers and lenders no longer rely on the financial intermediary, instead lending and borrowing directly from each other.

1.4 RISK AND RETURN

Risk can be considered the raw material for firms that undertake the business of lending. As Matthews and Thompson (2005: 183) observe, 'The business of banking involves risk. Banks make profit by taking risk and managing risk.'

Risk and return are directly related to each other: the higher the risk, the higher the return that the lender will require. Some may object to a system whereby 'to those who have, more shall be given' – but mispriced loans or low-cost loans to high-risk borrowers can lead to serious problems for lenders, as evidenced by the 2007–08 global financial crisis and subsequent credit crunch.

1.4.1 What is 'risk'?

'Risk' has been defined in various ways, depending on approach, availability of data and other factors. While we may seek to measure risk objectively where possible, there is some element of subjectivity inherent in any examination of the concept. Risk is conventionally defined as something that can be numerically estimated by multiplying two or more factors, and there are one-dimensional and multidimensional formats that attempt to explain risk by means of complex models, vectors and dendrograms. There may be significant variations from the numerical estimates when the analysis of risk is based on uncertain future outcomes rather than on historic experiences.

Some of the conceptually and mathematically linked basic elements of risk are as follows.

- *Probability* High probability (of a detrimental outcome) is considered to be high risk, while low probability is considered to be low risk.
- *Impact or severity* High impact (of an adverse consequence) is considered to be high risk, while low impact is considered to be low risk.
- *Variability, volatility or uncertainty* High levels of variability lead to uncertainty and are considered to be high risk, while low levels of variability are considered to be low risk. Probability can be considered to be a measure of variability.
- *Outcome* Variability can result in loss (a negative outcome) or gain (a positive outcome). One party's risk or problem can be the counterparty's gain. An event can cause both downside and upside risk, e.g. an increase in market interest rates can increase loan funding costs while also increasing return from loans. The goal will be to secure positive outcomes and eliminate or reduce detrimental outcomes.

Risk can be said to be the *probability* of exposure to *loss*, or 'the probability that the value of a financial asset or return will be less than its expected value' (Pilbeam, 2010: 156).

Risk is future *uncertainty* about *variability* or deviation from expected earnings or expected outcome. The greater the uncertainty or variability or volatility, the greater the risk. Risk is the volatility or standard deviation (i.e. the square root of the variance) of net cash flows of a firm (Heffernan, 2002).

Risk can be calculated as *probability* (the likelihood of the particular issue or event occurring) multiplied by *impact* (the potential harm that the particular issue or event could cause), i.e. for the Financial Conduct Authority (FCA, 2016b):

$$\text{Risk} = \text{Impact} \times \text{Probability}$$

Academics, as well as financial institutions, have developed complex multidimensional and mathematical models of risk. It is important, however, to recognise that risk models are only representations of reality. Apparently accurate mathematical models can deviate considerably from reality, and hence it is important to acknowledge the need for the uncommon characteristic of 'common sense' in the evaluation of risk and risk-related measures.

1.4.2 What are the risks in lending?

Lenders of money are risk-takers. A lender who never loses any money is being overly cautious and missing opportunities for profit, while a lender who loses money frequently is depleting the profit made on loans that are repaid.

Lending involves several types of risk, including:

- credit risk;
- interest rate risk;
- currency risk;
- country risk; and
- contagion risk.

Other risks, such as legal, operational and reputational risks, may also be involved.

Credit risk or *default risk* is one of the primary risks in lending: it is the probability of a loss occurring due to the failure of a borrower, debtor or 'obligor' to meet contractual debt obligations. The borrower may default in the repayment of the principal, or interest and fees payable, or both. The borrower in respect of a particular asset may default in full or in part on the obligations to the lender in relation to that asset. An asset or a loan may become irrecoverable in the case of outright default or delay in the servicing of the loan. Credit risk is 'the potential that a bank borrower or counterparty will fail to meet its obligations in accordance with agreed terms' (BCBS, 2000: 1). In such situations, the present value of the asset declines, thereby undermining the solvency of the lender.

Credit risk can be borrower-specific or systematic.

- *Borrower-specific* credit risk is the risk of the borrower defaulting as a result of the specific types of risk taken by that borrower.
- *Systematic* credit risk is the risk of default associated with general economy-wide or macro conditions affecting all borrowers.

Borrower-specific credit risk can be further subdivided as *stand-alone risk*, which refers to the risk of loans as independent assets, and *portfolio risk*, which measures the riskiness of the portfolio or group of loans held by the lender. Holding loans that are correlated increases portfolio risk, while holding a diversified portfolio of assets could reduce this type of risk. However, a 'lesson to be learnt is that spreading risk does not eliminate it' (Heaney, 2007: 14).

Basel II encouraged the use of credit risk management through internal ratings-based (IRB) systems, which employ internal estimates of risk components to categorise exposures. There are a number of risk components to be evaluated for measuring credit risk, which can be calculated as:

$$EL = PD \times LGD \times EAD$$

where

EL = Expected loss
PD = Probability of default
LGD = Loss given default
EAD = Exposure at default

Unexpected loss is the additional loss in atypical circumstances. The loss during a period of economic downturn, for example, is calculated by multiplying the downturn PD, LGD and EAD as laid out above. The unexpected loss is calculated by subtracting the expected loss from the total loss during the period. Of the various components, the *probability of default* is the most critical variable because, unlike the other internal risk components (i.e. EL, LGD and EAD), it could not be directly provided by supervisors (Florez-Lopeza, 2007). However, concerns about the comparability of banks' credit risk-weight models have led to proposals for moving away from IRB models towards standardised approaches.

Interest rate risk is the risk that the value of an asset will change due to a change in the level of interest rates, e.g. that the cost of funding a loan might be higher than the return from the loan.

Currency risk arises from the change in the price of one currency against another. Lenders might wish to borrow in a currency in which interest rates are low, convert it into another currency with higher interest rates and then lend in that currency. Any increase in the borrowed currency and decrease in the currency that is being lent can result in losses for the lender.

Country risk is the risk that a country is not able or willing to honour its financial commitments.

Contagion risk is the risk that difficulties experienced by one or more lenders will spill over to, or 'contaminate', other lenders or the financial system as a whole. Contagion risk can lead to, or become, systemic risk.

Systemic risk is so known because the risk affects the entire financial system rather than being limited to any particular participant(s). The turmoil in the financial markets in 2007–08, for example, is said to have resulting from contagion originating in the US subprime lending market. Because banks lend to each other and make payments to and on behalf of each other, there is a possibility that financial difficulties can be passed on from one institution or market to others. The central bank is held to be an important player in such circumstances and is required to be the *lender of last resort* (LOLR), i.e. to be prepared to lend money and offer liquidity whatever the situation – although the price of that lending will be of the central bank's choosing.

It will be relevant to note here some of the recent developments in the credit markets.

- *A rise in the number of players* While, traditionally, banks have dominated the lending arena, many new and active players have emerged today, e.g. pension funds, insurance companies, private equity firms, SIVs, special purpose vehicles (SPVs), etc.
- *A rise in the use of technology to manage risk* Computer models, while good in theory, might fail to work effectively when faced with real market crisis. Theoretically flawed computer models could accentuate risk profiles.
- *The increased repackaging and redistribution of risk* Financial institutions are able to handle greater volumes of risk by taking them off their balance sheets via securitisation and other measures.
- *Increased globalisation* This means that financial crises in one country can spread globally within a very short time.
- *Increased lack of transparency* It is not always clear who is holding the credit risk and this, in turn, can lead to a loss of confidence in the financial markets.
- *The unwillingness of organisations to recognise and acknowledge the extent of risk* This could be for diverse reasons, e.g. the dependence of personal bonuses on bank performance, and the impact of credit losses on the size of bonuses and jobs.

Lenders need to manage risk. Traditional financial strategies led to the development of standardised control systems, based on external assessments made by credit rating and other agencies. However, the globalised economic environment requires more sophisticated and adaptive credit risk management systems, which in turn might accentuate, rather than alleviate, risk. Managing lending risk is thus one of the biggest challenges that lenders need to confront if they are to manage the lending function profitably and safely.

1.4.3 The risk–return trade-off

There is a trade-off between risk and return. The potential return rises with an increase in risk. Low levels of uncertainty (low risk) are associated with low potential returns, whereas high levels of uncertainty (high risk) are associated with high potential returns. As indicated in Figure 1.2, lenders will need to manage and control risk by:

- identifying risk;
- measuring risk;
- mitigating risk; and
- monitoring risk.

Risk management strategies are discussed in Chapters 6–11, where we consider the lending cycle in detail.

Figure 1.2 The management of risk

1.5 THE ATTRIBUTES OF GOOD LENDING

A lender needs to address a number of objectives to achieve required goals. These objectives can be conflicting and contradictory, and a fine balancing act is necessary.

Some of the major objectives are as follows.

- *Safety* The lender needs to ensure that funds lent are safe and that its own financial position is sound. The lender needs to command a sound reputation in the credit markets if it is to be able to raise the funds that it requires for its lending activity. The excessive reliance of Northern Rock on borrowed wholesale funds, for example, has been cited as one of the major reasons for its liquidity problems when markets as a whole faced a credit crunch. Wholesale funds borrowed from the money markets are generally much cheaper than retail funds offered by deposits – but cheaper funds and greater profitability led to liquidity and safety problems.
- *Liquidity* Liquidity is defined as the ease with which an asset can be converted to cash. The most liquid asset is cash in hand, while an example of an illiquid asset would be a house, which might take a much longer time to sell and might not realise its full value if it has to be sold quickly. Damien Hirst's diamond-encrusted human skull may be worth £50 million, but a lender offered it as security might find it to be an illiquid asset that few investors would be interested in buying.
- *Profitability* *Profit* is the difference between revenue and costs. *Profitability* is the ability of an organisation to earn profits. The combined profits of £32 billion made by top UK banks in 2006 exceeded the gross domestic product (GDP) of Luxembourg; however, it subsequently transpired that these profits might have been earned at the cost of decreased safety and liquidity. Profitability is the measure of success of the lender in undertaking lending operations, but it is subject to also meeting the conflicting requirements of liquidity and safety, as indicated in Figure 1.3.

The lender would like the money lent to be liquid, profitable and safe. However, it may be necessary to balance one conflicting objective against the other

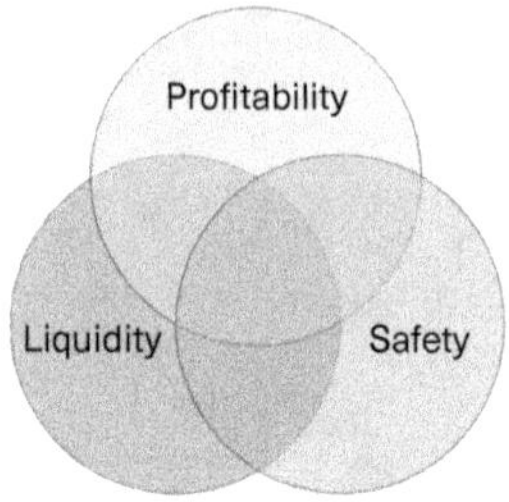

Figure 1.3 The lender's conflicting objectives

and to arrive at some kind of a compromise between them to optimise the lending activity.

1.6 THE PRINCIPLES OF CREDIT RISK MANAGEMENT

Principles may be defined as generally accepted rules for action or conduct. Lenders will wish to adopt generally accepted principles of lending that might enable them to maximise the return from lending and minimise the possibility of loss. Developing and adopting lending principles is not an exact science. Lending principles have evolved over a period of time and will continue to evolve in the future. Lenders will need to adapt these principles to suit their individual needs. Key areas, as well as key principles of credit risk management identified and developed by the Basel Committee, can be summarised as follows.

1.6.1 Areas of credit risk management

The Basel Committee sets out sound lending practices that address the following areas of credit risk management:

(i) establishing an appropriate credit risk environment;
(ii) operating under a sound credit-granting process;
(iii) maintaining an appropriate credit administration, measurement and monitoring process; and
(iv) ensuring adequate controls over credit risk.

(BCBS, 2000: 1)

In addition, it cites the role of supervisors in ensuring that banks have an effective credit risk management system in place.

1.6.2 Principles for evaluating a bank's credit risk management system

Within the areas listed above, the Basel Committee has identified 17 principles of good lending practices that can be used in evaluating a lender's credit management system.

A. Establishing an appropriate credit risk environment
Principle 1: The board of directors should have responsibility for approving and periodically (at least annually) reviewing the credit risk strategy and significant credit risk policies of the bank. The strategy should reflect the bank's tolerance for risk and the level of profitability the bank expects to achieve for incurring various credit risks.
Principle 2: Senior management should have responsibility for implementing the credit risk strategy approved by the board of directors and for developing policies and procedures for identifying, measuring, monitoring and controlling credit risk. Such policies and procedures should address credit risk in all of the bank's activities and at both the individual credit and portfolio levels.
Principle 3: Banks should identify and manage credit risk inherent in all products and activities. Banks should ensure that the risks of products and activities new to them are subject to adequate risk management procedures and controls before being introduced or undertaken, and approved in advance by the board of directors or its appropriate committee.

B. Operating under a sound credit granting process
Principle 4: Banks must operate within sound, well-defined credit-granting criteria.
These criteria should include a clear indication of the bank's target market and a thorough understanding of the borrower or counterparty, as well as the purpose and structure of the credit, and its source of repayment.
Principle 5: Banks should establish overall credit limits at the level of individual borrowers and counterparties, and groups of connected counterparties that aggregate in a comparable and meaningful manner different types of exposures, both in the banking and trading book and on and off the balance sheet.
Principle 6: Banks should have a clearly established process in place for approving new credits as well as the amendment, renewal and re-financing of existing credits.
Principle 7: All extensions of credit must be made on an arm's-length basis. In particular, credits to related companies and individuals must be authorised on an exception basis, monitored with particular care and other appropriate steps taken to control or mitigate the risks of non-arm's length lending.

C. Maintaining an appropriate credit administration, measurement and monitoring process
Principle 8: Banks should have in place a system for the ongoing administration of their various credit risk-bearing portfolios.

Principle 9: Banks must have in place a system for monitoring the condition of individual credits, including determining the adequacy of provisions and reserves.
Principle 10: Banks are encouraged to develop and utilise an internal risk rating system in managing credit risk. The rating system should be consistent with the nature, size and complexity of a bank's activities.
Principle 11: Banks must have information systems and analytical techniques that enable management to measure the credit risk inherent in all on- and off-balance sheet activities. The management information system should provide adequate information on the composition of the credit portfolio, including identification of any concentrations of risk.
Principle 12: Banks must have in place a system for monitoring the overall composition and quality of the credit portfolio.
Principle 13: Banks should take into consideration potential future changes in economic conditions when assessing individual credits and their credit portfolios, and should assess their credit risk exposures under stressful conditions.

D. Ensuring adequate controls over credit risk
Principle 14: Banks must establish a system of independent, ongoing assessment of the bank's credit risk management processes and the results of such reviews should be communicated directly to the board of directors and senior management.
Principle 15: Banks must ensure that the credit-granting function is being properly managed and that credit exposures are within levels consistent with prudential standards and internal limits. Banks should establish and enforce internal controls and other practices to ensure that exceptions to policies, procedures and limits are reported in a timely manner to the appropriate level of management for action.
Principle 16: Banks must have a system in place for early remedial action on deteriorating credits, managing problem credits and similar workout situations.

E. The role of supervisors
Principle 17: Supervisors should require that banks have an effective system in place to identify, measure, monitor and control credit risk as part of an overall approach to risk management. Supervisors should conduct an independent evaluation of a bank's strategies, policies, procedures and practices related to the granting of credit and the ongoing management of the portfolio. Supervisors should consider setting prudential limits to restrict bank exposures to single borrowers or groups of connected counterparties.

(BCBS, 2000: 3–4)

These Principles will be revisited throughout this book when each component of the lending activity is discussed. For example, the principles relating to the granting of credit will be discussed in Chapter 6, while those relating to credit administration and monitoring will be discussed in Chapter 10.

1.7 CONCLUSION

Lending is the giving of an asset with the expectation of receiving the principal plus the required rate of return at a future point of time. Lending ranges from mainstream lending, undertaken by banks and other financial institutions, to social lending, undertaken by individuals to friends and family, and via websites.

Credit risk is the possibility that a borrower will fail to meet repayment obligations in accordance with agreed terms. Risk and return are directly related to each other: the higher the risk, the higher the return that the lender will require.

Lenders need to balance a number of conflicting objectives to achieve their goals. The major objectives include safety, liquidity and profitability. Lenders will wish to adopt generally accepted principles of lending that might enable them to maximise the return from lending and minimise the possibility of loss. It is thus important for lenders to carefully note the key areas of credit risk management and the key principles of credit risk management, as identified and developed by the Basel Committee.

FURTHER READING

Ellison, A., Collard, S., and Forster, R. (2006) *Illegal lending in the UK: Research Report*, London: DTI.

Matthews, K., Murinde, V., and Zhaoc, T. (2007) 'Competitive conditions among the major British banks', *Journal of Banking and Finance*, 31, 2025–2042.

Saunders, A., and Allen, L. (2010) *Credit risk management: In and out of the financial crisis*, 3rd edn, Hoboken, NJ: John Wiley & Sons.

REVIEW QUESTIONS

1. What are the various risks that lending might entail?
2. What is 'credit risk'?
3. What is the relationship between risk and return?
4. What are the attributes of good lending?
5. What are the major areas of credit risk management identified by the Basel Committee?

ACTIVITY

Visit the website of the Bank for International Settlements (BIS) at www.bis.org

Locate and read the paper 'Principles for the Management of Credit Risk', available at www.bis.org/publ/bcbs75.pdf

CASE STUDY Turmoil in the credit markets in 2007

Financial markets were in turmoil in 2007. Liquidity had dried up; lenders were unwilling or unable to lend to one another in the manner to which they had been accustomed.

The origin of this 'credit crunch' was traced to the US subprime market, in which more than half the borrowers were reported to have lied, or been encouraged to lie, about their income. *Subprime lending* is lending offered at higher rates of interest to borrowers with poor credit histories. Lenders were less than assiduous in credit appraisal, because they felt that the loans granted would very quickly be converted into debt securities, sold off to eager investors and removed from their balance sheets. Loans were thus transferred into the hands of insurers and other investors who were motivated by the prospect of high returns, but who were not necessarily those best equipped to evaluate the risk that they were taking on.

When difficulties in the subprime market gave rise to borrower defaults, the problems were compounded by a fall in house prices and an increase in borrowing rates, which in turn trapped more borrowers in debt that they could not afford to repay.

Lenders who had considered themselves to be insulated against subprime borrower default risk found themselves nonetheless exposed to the risk via the complex interrelationships that characterise the current financial markets. Even if they had no direct exposure to these borrowers, it appeared that some of the SIVs that they had set up had been indirectly exposed by means of their investment activities.

Lenders became wary of lending to each other lest they run out of liquidity themselves.

Aggressive lenders found themselves particularly vulnerable. Northern Rock, for instance, had lent long-term funds towards mortgages and funded these mortgages by cheap short-term borrowing from the wholesale money markets. While this high-risk strategy paid off with high profits when wholesale funds were plentiful, it ceased to work when the credit markets seized up. The bank was forced to approach the Bank of England as lender of last resort. By December, the Bank of England's commitment to Northern Rock had exceeded £55 billion, indicating that the taxpayer was effectively underwriting the risks the lending banker had taken.

Northern Rock's strategy of borrowing short-term and lending long-term was highly profitable under conditions of credit boom. When funds ran dry, the bank faced insolvency. Thus it was found that *profitability had run counter to liquidity requirements.*

Banks were queuing up to announce loan write-offs and provisions for bad debts. Headlines in 2007 included:

- 'UBS AG will write off a further $10 billion [£5 billion] on losses in the US subprime lending market' (Associated Press, 10 December);
- 'Lloyds TSB reveals that bad debt linked to the US sub-prime mortgage crisis will cost it £200m' (BBC News, 10 December);
- 'Royal Bank of Scotland warns it will write off about £1.25 billion because of exposure to the US sub-prime market' (BBC News, 6 December);
- 'Canadian banks write off $2.1 billion in US subprime mortgages' (*The Bankwatch*, 17 November);

- 'Barclays calculates £1.3 billion sub-prime loss' (*The Guardian*, 16 November); and
- '[HSBC's] misadventures in the US mortgage market have forced to it to write off up to $11 billion [£5.7 billion]' (*The Independent*, 5 March).

High-risk borrowers had yielded high returns because they were prepared to borrow at high rates of interest. However, when they found themselves unable to repay the loan or interest, or both, these high yields were converted to large losses. Thus it was found that *profitability had run counter to safety in lending.*

CASE STUDY QUESTIONS

1. What seemed to be the root cause of the turmoil in the credit markets in 2007?
2. What is 'subprime lending'?
3. What was the high-risk, high-profit strategy of Northern Rock that backfired?
4. What can be the impact of poor lending decisions?
5. What are the lessons here for lenders?

Suggested answers can be found in Appendix A.

2

The legal and regulatory environment

LEARNING POINTS

This chapter enables the understanding of the legal and regulatory environment in which lending takes place.

Learning areas include:

- relevant statutes;
- codes of practice;
- the role of ombudsmen; and
- treating customers fairly.

2.1 THE LEGAL AND REGULATORY FRAMEWORK

The lending function needs to be regulated by the lending organisations themselves, as well as by independent authorities. There is evidence that competent regulators deliver economic benefit by increasing confidence in financial intermediation (Davies and Green, 2013: 206). While regulation is able to at least partially overcome market imperfections, powerful regulators can be subjected to undue influence from both politicians and the banks that are being regulated (Barth, Caprio, and Levine, 2007). Excessive regulation can curb credit development and growth, while inadequate regulation can lead to widespread loss of confidence in the credit markets due to uncurbed inappropriate behaviour. The level of competition will vary depending upon the regulatory, economic and other environmental factors. Even within the same country, competition can vary within different submarkets (Cruickshank, 2000; Matthews, Murinde, and Zhaoc, 2007). In the UK, it has been suggested that individual submarkets, such as that relating to credit cards, have deteriorated, while others, such as mortgages, have seen a strong increase in competition (Heffernan, 2002). Lending firms will have to adapt their lending strategies depending upon the level and nature of competition encountered.

It is necessary to understand the regulatory environment if we are to develop effective lending policies and practices. Consider the following trends identified in the bank lending environment.

- A blurring of organisational boundaries may have resulted in overlapping credit activities, perhaps increasing the need for more consistent regulation.

- Some non-bank originators of credit may have evaded scrutiny. There may be a need for more encompassing supervision of credit markets.
- Increased competition may have given rise to pressures on profit margins.
- Increased demand for credit may have led to unprecedented levels of debt.
- Increased borrower sophistication may have put pressure on lenders to develop increasingly complex products.
- Increased demand for complex forms of debt financing may have led to a certain opaqueness in the credit markets.
- Increased borrower range includes hedge funds, private equity firms and financial sponsors wishing to make a splash in the credit market through acquisitions and private placements.
- High levels of lending and increases in leverage levels may lead to cycles of credit boom followed by credit crunch.

As set out by Davis (2013: 7), the global regulation process comprises:

- high-level assessment and international agreements, such as the G20;
- 'thematic' analysis, overview audit and review, for example by the Financial Stability Board (FSB) and the International Monetary Fund (IMF);
- international standards and supervisory principles, such as Basel (see Chapter 1); and
- national regulation and legislation, implemented by regulators at the national level.

2.1.1 National regulatory models

There are several types of major national regulatory model in use today.

- *Tripartite models* are based on a traditional three-pillar system, comprising a central bank overseeing banks, a securities regulator and an insurance regulator.
- *Dual models* comprise a variation on the tripartite model, with some combining securities and insurance supervision under one regulator and banking under another, while others link banking and securities under one regulator and insurance under another.
- *'Twin peaks' systems* comprise one prudential regulator responsible for monitoring capital reserves, and a second 'conduct of business' regulator with responsibility for transparency and other market- or customer-transaction-related aspects of regulation.
- *Unified models* comprise a single integrated regulator that is responsible for all, or most, of the financial sector.

Regulation in the UK

The UK has adopted a 'twin peaks' system of regulation, as illustrated in Figure 2.1.

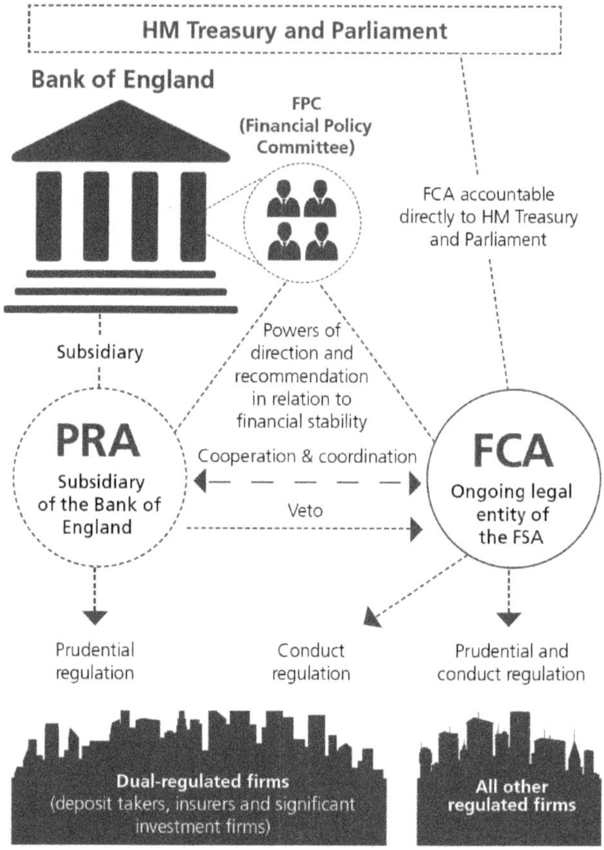

Figure 2.1 The UK's regulatory architecture. Reproduced with permission from *Financial Conduct Authority Business Plan 2013/14*, London: FCA, 2013

The main regulatory bodies in the UK are as follows.

- *Prudential Regulation Authority (PRA)* A subsidiary of the Bank of England (the UK's central bank), the PRA is responsible for micro-prudential regulation, supervising deposit-takers, insurers and others, with the statutory objective of promoting the safety and soundness of these firms.
- *Financial Policy Committee (FPC)* A body positioned within the Bank of England, the FPC is responsible for protecting the financial system as a whole and for macro-prudential regulation.

- *Financial Conduct Authority (FCA)* The FCA is responsible for conduct-of-business regulation in retail and wholesale markets, and for prudential regulation of firms not subject to the PRA's oversight.

The overall objective of the FCA is to ensure that relevant markets work well. This is supported by three operational objectives:

- to protect and enhance the integrity of the UK's financial system;
- to secure an appropriate degree of protection for consumers; and
- to promote competition in the interests of consumers.

There are other bodies that also have an impact on the lending function in the UK. For example, the Competition and Markets Authority (CMA) is a non-ministerial government department responsible for strengthening business competition, and for preventing and reducing anti-competitive activities. The CMA began operating fully on 1 April 2014, when it assumed many of the functions of the former Competition Commission and Office of Fair Trading, both of which were abolished. The CMA aims to promote competition for the benefit of consumers, both within and outside the UK, and to make markets work well for consumers, businesses and the economy.

Regulation in the European Union

Achieving an integrated market for banks and financial conglomerates is a core component of European policy in the area of financial services. The European Commission's policies on regulation in these arenas are core parts of the Financial Services Action Plan (FSAP). These policies are based on the principles of mutual recognition and the 'single passport', a system that allows financial services operators legally established in one member state to establish or provide their services in other member states without the need for further authorisation. In light of the UK's 2016 referendum vote to 'Leave' the European Union (EU), commonly known as Brexit, whether the UK will continue to benefit from the single passport system is in question at time of writing.

The major bodies within the EU system of financial supervision are:

- the European supervisory authorities (ESAs), including
  - the European Banking Authority (EBA),
  - the European Insurance and Occupational Pensions Authority (EIOPA), and
  - the European Securities and Markets Authority (ESMA); and
- the European Central Bank (ECB), including
  - the European Systemic Risk Board (ESRB).

The Capital Requirements Directive IV (CRD IV) is an EU legislative package that contains prudential rules for banks, building societies and investment firms. It is, in effect, the EU's implementation of Basel III (see Chapter 1). Basel III comprises proposals aiming to increase the prudential soundness of banks and its implementation in the EU also covers certain investments under the 2004 Markets in Financial Instruments Directive (MiFID) (Directive 2004/39/EC).

CRD IV increases the quality of capital that firms are required to hold and introduces capital buffers for some firms. It also introduces an EU-wide liquidity regime and establishes a leverage backstop position. It is made up of the 2013 Capital Requirements Regulation (CRR) (Regulation 575/2013), which is directly applicable to firms across the EU, and the 2013 Capital Requirements Directive (CRD) (Directive 2013/36/EU), which must be implemented through national law in each member state. In 2018, MiFID will be updated (MiFID II) and the accompanying Markets in Financial Instruments Regulation (MiFIR) will come into force.

Regulation in the United States

The US Foreign Account Tax Compliance Act of 2010 (FATCA) requires American persons, including individuals who live outside the United States, to report their financial accounts held outside of the United States and requires foreign financial institutions to report to the US Internal Revenue Service (IRS) about their American clients. An important piece of US legislation, the Wall Street Reform and Consumer Protection Act of 2010 (known as the Dodd–Frank Act), incorporated the 'Volcker rule', which barred proprietary trading, preventing banks from making bets for their own accounts, but allowing other types of trading to help clients to meet legitimate market needs (§619 of the 2010 Act). However, under the Trump Administration, a bill known as the Financial CHOICE Act of 2017 – CHOICE being an acronym formed from 'Creating Hope and Opportunity for Investors, Consumers and Entrepreneurs' – has passed its first hurdle towards enactment. The bill would, if enacted, repeal much of the financial regulation put in place under the Dodd–Frank Act in response to the 2007–08 global financial crisis. At time of writing, the bill is yet to be passed by the US Senate.

2.1.2 Specific legislation in the UK

Relevant law needs to be constantly kept in view by those who exercise the lending function. Some of the more important and specifically relevant statutes and statutory instruments in the UK are as follows.

Financial Services and Markets Act 2000

The effect of Part III of the Bank of England Act 1998 was to transfer the Bank of England's supervisory functions to the Financial Services Authority (FSA). The effect of the Financial Services and Markets Act 2000 (FSMA) was to constitute the FSA as a super-regulator, with powers to regulate insurance, investment business and banking through processes comprising authorisation, supervision and enforcement.

Under the FSMA, a professional firm wishing to provide mainstream financial services needs to achieve authorisation from the FSA. Subsequent to authorisation, the firm will be regulated by the FSA and has to comply with the rules and guidance embodied in the FSA Handbook.

The FSMA also established the Financial Services and Markets Tribunal (abolished in 2010 and its functions transferred to the Upper Tribunal), and created a single compensation and ombudsman scheme called the Financial Ombudsman Service (FOS).

Financial Services Act 2012

Drafted in the aftermath of the 2007–08 global financial crisis and subsequent credit crunch, the Financial Services Act 2012 created the FCA and the PRA as the new regulators, replacing the FSA.

Financial Services (Banking Reform) Act 2013

The Financial Services (Banking Reform) Act 2013 implemented further reform of the UK's financial services regulation. In particular, it gave HM Treasury and the PRA powers to implement the recommendations contained in the 2013 report of the Independent Commission on Banking (ICB), chaired by Sir John Vickers, on ring-fencing requirements for the banking sector (Edmonds, 2013).

Banking and Financial Services Act 2017

The Banking and Financial Services Act 2017 provides for:

- a licensing system for the conduct of banking or financial business and the provision of financial services;
- the incorporation of standards, principles and concepts of corporate governance in institutional systems and structures of banks and financial institutions;
- sound business practices and consumer protection mechanisms; and
- the regulation and supervision of banking and financial services.

In so doing, it repeals and replaces the Banking and Financial Services Act 1994.

Consumer Credit Acts 1974 and 2006

The Consumer Credit Act 1974 was enacted to protect non-corporate consumers and covered a range of consumer credit up to a limit of £15,000 – a figure later increased to £25,000. The limit was removed entirely under the Consumer Credit Act 2006, which amended the 1974 Act with a view to improving the protection of consumers, and creating a fairer and more competitive credit market.

Under the Consumer Credit Acts, a 'consumer' is defined as:

- a partnership of two or three persons not all of whom are corporates; or
- a person, or a body of persons not all of whom are corporate bodies and which is not a partnership.

By definition, companies are excluded from the purview of the Acts. Other exemptions include high-net-worth debtors and some businesses.

Credit agreements can take place between the creditor and debtor or between the creditor, debtor and suppliers. Credit can be extended as a fixed sum (e.g. a loan) or a running account (e.g. an overdraft), and the lender can either specify the purpose for which the credit has to be used or allow the debtor to use it for any purpose (unrestricted). There are therefore eight basic combinations of credit agreements that fall under the Acts:

- debtor–creditor, restricted use, fixed sum;
- debtor–creditor, unrestricted use, fixed sum;
- debtor–creditor, restricted use, running account;
- debtor–creditor, unrestricted use, running account;
- debtor–creditor–supplier, restricted use, fixed sum;
- debtor–creditor–supplier, unrestricted use, fixed sum;
- debtor–creditor–supplier, restricted use, running account; or
- debtor–creditor–supplier, unrestricted use, running account.

In addition, credit agreements may be cancellable or non-cancellable, modifying, multiple or credit token (a credit card, for example, is a credit token).

Some of the most significant features of the Consumer Credit Acts can be summarised as follows.

- Businesses that provide credit formerly needed to obtain a licence from the Office of Fair Trading (OFT), which was responsible for ensuring that applicants were fit to hold a licence and for monitoring their ongoing conduct. After the closure of the OFT in 2014, its responsibilities were passed on to other organisations: the FCA regulates consumer credit, while the CMA investigates unfair contract terms and uncompetitive practices.
- Consumer credit agreements need to indicate not only the rights and duties of the consumer, but also the true cost of the credit, i.e. the 'total charge for credit'.
- Consumer protection is extended to all consumer credit, with the financial limit that capped protection at loans of £25,000 abolished under the 2006 Act.
- Section 75 of the Consumer Credit Act 1974 establishes the principle of 'connected lender liability' whereby credit card issuers are liable individually and jointly with suppliers for payments for products and services between £100 and £30,000, if a consumer has a valid claim against the supplier for misrepresentation or breach of contract relating to goods or services bought with a credit card. The consumer can make a claim against the credit card issuer as well as, or instead of, the supplier. In *Office of Fair Trading v Lloyds Bank plc and others* [2006] EWCA Civ 268, the Court of Appeal held that section 75 protection will cover purchases made on a credit card abroad, as well as the UK (Saxby, 2006); this was upheld on appeal to the House of Lords (*Office of Fair Trading v Lloyds Bank plc and others* [2007] UKHL 48).

- Alternative dispute resolution (ADR) extends the FOS under the FSMA to cover licensees under the Consumer Credit Act 1974. If a consumer has complained to a consumer credit business and not received a satisfactory result, they are able to make complaints to an ADR scheme run by the FOS, which applies to all consumer credit licensees.

In addition, a new test focusing on the fairness of the relationship between creditor and debtor was brought in under the 2006 Act, to apply to all new credit agreements made on or after 6 April 2007 and also to any existing agreements that continued to exist beyond 6 April 2008. Previously, the test had been based on whether the credit agreement could be considered to be 'extortionate'; now, the court may make an order in connection with a credit agreement if it determines that the relationship between the creditor and the debtor under that agreement is unfair to the debtor because of any of its terms, or because of the way in which the creditor has exercised or enforced any of its rights, or because of any other relevant action or inaction by the creditor.

Insolvency Acts 1986 and 2000, and the Insolvency Rules 2017

The UK Insolvency Acts and Rules deal with various aspects of the insolvency of individuals, small firms and large corporations that impact on the activities of lenders. Relevant legislation includes the Insolvency Acts 1986 and 2000, and the Insolvency Rules 2017, SI 2017/369. The Insolvency Service, an agency of the Department for Business, Energy and Industrial Strategy (BEIS), is rolling out extensive changes to the insolvency industry in England and Wales.

The Small Business, Enterprise and Employment Act 2015 and the Deregulation Act 2015, which came into force on 6 April 2017, introduce various amendments to the Insolvency Act 1986.

Enterprise Act 2016

The Enterprise Act 2016 includes measures to:

- establish a small business commissioner to help small firms to resolve issues such as late payment;
- make it easier for businesses to access consistent, tailored and assured advice from local authorities, giving them greater confidence to invest and grow;
- protect and strengthen the 'apprenticeship' brand, introducing targets for apprenticeships in public sector bodies in England and establishing an Institute for Apprenticeships – an independent, employer-led body that is to make sure that apprenticeships meet the needs of business; and
- create a legal obligation for insurers to pay out on claims to businesses within a reasonable time.

Small Business, Enterprise and Employment Act 2015

Bank lenders are required to provide credit agencies with information available with them and to refer their rejected customers to other finance platforms for additional or alternative lending. Many small and medium-sized enterprises (SMEs) seeking finance tend to approach only the largest banks, the rejection rate of which could be around 50 per cent, even if the businesses are viable. The reasons for rejection may include the bank having reached the ceiling of its concentration of lending within a specific business sector or region.

The 2015 Act requires certain banks to refer their customers to alternative finance platforms if the bank has refused to provide funding. The Act also provides for certain functions to be conveyed to the FCA and to extend the remit of the FOS, to enable a complaint to be made to it about a designated credit reference agency or finance platform.

General Data Protection Regulation (GDPR)

In May 2018, the General Data Protection Regulation (GDPR) (Regulation 2016/679) came into force and was implemented domestically by the Data Protection Act 2018, which replaces the Data Protection Act 1998. The GDPR and the 2018 Act apply to all entities – including financial institutions – that control or process personal data, i.e. any information relating to an identifiable living individual. The principles require that personal data is:

> a) processed lawfully, fairly and in a transparent manner in relation to individuals;
> b) collected for specified, explicit and legitimate purposes and not further processed in a manner that is incompatible with those purposes; further processing for archiving purposes in the public interest, scientific or historical research purposes or statistical purposes shall not be considered to be incompatible with the initial purposes;
> c) adequate, relevant and limited to what is necessary in relation to the purposes for which they are processed;
> d) accurate and, where necessary, kept up to date; every reasonable step must be taken to ensure that personal data that are inaccurate, having regard to the purposes for which they are processed, are erased or rectified without delay;
> e) kept in a form which permits identification of data subjects for no longer than is necessary for the purposes for which the personal data are processed; personal data may be stored for longer periods insofar as the personal data will be processed solely for archiving purposes in the public interest, scientific or historical research purposes or statistical purposes subject to implementation of the appropriate technical and organisational measures required by the GDPR in order to safeguard the rights and freedoms of individuals; and
> f) processed in a manner that ensures appropriate security of the personal data, including protection against unauthorised or unlawful processing and against accidental loss, destruction or damage, using appropriate technical or organisational measures.
>
> (ICO, 2018)

The person whose data is processed has the following rights:

1. The right to be informed
2. The right of access
3. The right to rectification
4. The right to erasure
5. The right to restrict processing
6. The right to data portability
7. The right to object
8. Rights in relation to automated decision making and profiling.

(ICO, 2018)

2.1.3 Supranational legislation

Basel I & II

In 1988, the Basel Committee on Banking Supervision (BCBS) of the Bank for International Settlements (BIS) proposed a set of minimal capital requirements for banks. While Basel II comprises recommendations rather than prescriptive legislation, these recommendations have led to legislation in a number of countries. They became law in the UK and most other G10 countries in 1992.

Capital adequacy is a measure of a bank's financial strength and is usually expressed as a ratio of its capital to its assets. *Insolvency risk* is the risk that a bank may not have adequate capital to offset a decline in the value of its assets in relation to its liabilities. An internationally active bank needs to work within the international framework for capital adequacy published by the Basel Committee.

Mainly based at Basel in Switzerland, BIS is an international organisation that serves as a bank for central banks. Basel II is the second of the Basel Accords and the revised comprehensive framework is designed to promote the adoption of stronger risk management practices by the banking industry.

Basel II uses 'three pillars' to promote greater stability in the financial system:

- minimum capital requirements;
- supervisory review; and
- market discipline.

An important change that Basel II introduced, compared with Basel I, is that it made available a menu of approaches to calculating banks' capital needs in respect of credit risk (Taylor, 2007), i.e. to approaching credit risk:

- the standardised approach;
- the internal ratings-based (IRB) approach; and
- the securitisation framework.

Basel II is considered to be the most significant factor impacting on consumer credit scoring processes (Crook, Edelman, and Thomas, 2007). Lower credit risks are likely to be advantaged as banks move towards a more accurate pricing of risk. However, there have been unintended consequences of the way in which risk weightings work in these different approaches, including the following.

- Improved risk sensitivity could also mean that banks are more willing to lend to higher-risk borrowers at higher prices.
- Some of the credit models used might actually accentuate downturns in the business cycle by signalling the need to reduce lending to cut losses.
- It has been pointed out that large banks using IRB models tend to specialise in low loan-to-value (LTV) mortgages, while smaller banks forced to use the standardised approach tend to go for riskier high LTV mortgages (PRA, 2017).

Indeed, in this last regard, Heaney (2017) compares the higher-risk incentive for smaller banks forced to adopt the standardised approach to inept British attempts to reduce the cobra population in India during the period of colonial occupation: offering a monetary reward in return for a dead cobra resulted only in the breeding of more cobras in pursuit of that reward.

It is apparent, then, that some of the solutions under Basel II may have increased the risk incentive and hence increased credit risk in the system.

Basel III and IV

The second revision of the Basel Accords, Basel III, proposes to strengthen the resilience of the banking system by means of:

- raising the quality, consistency and transparency of the capital base, e.g. 'Tier 1' capital;
- strengthening the risk coverage of the capital framework, e.g. counterparty credit risk and operational risk;
- introducing a leverage ratio;
- introducing measures to promote the build-up of capital buffers in good times that can be drawn upon in periods of stress or within a countercyclical capital framework;
- introducing a global minimum liquidity standard that includes a 30-day liquidity coverage ratio requirement underpinned by a longer-term structural liquidity ratio; and
- reviewing the need for additional capital, liquidity or other supervisory measures to reduce the externalities created by systemically important financial institutions (SIFIs).

Basel III has, however, come in for criticism for several reasons.

- One factor relates to the delays and extended deadlines for its implementation. Many of the elements of Basel III are not yet in effect, e.g. the net stable funding ratio, which will be implemented in 2018, and the liquidity coverage ratio, which takes full effect in 2019.
- The revision builds on the existing Basel II and its reliance on credit rating agencies, whose judgement has been called into question in the aftermath of the 2007–08 global financial crisis.

- Its opaque treatment of derivatives contracts mean that some dealers remain 'too big to fail' and hence aggressively take on risk of an event that they do not believe will happen – but which can and do, as we saw as the 2007–08 global financial crisis unfolded.
- The costs of its implementation may hurt small banks and may also negatively impact on growth.
- It increases the incentives of banks to manipulate the regulatory framework.

Indeed, it has been described overall as 'inadequate', representing a significant easing of rules put in place for good reason.

As a consequence, further revision – 'Basel IV' – is already expected, the further regulatory changes anticipated including:

- requiring banks to meet higher maximum leverage ratios;
- proposing simpler or standardised models, rather than complex IRB models, for calculation of capital requirements, with a view to promoting comparability and transparency; and
- more detailed disclosure of reserves and other financial data.

2.2 CODES OF PRACTICE

Banking codes are voluntary, representing an attempt to set minimum standards for the way in which banks and other financial services providers should treat their customers.

2.2.1 Banking codes

The main codes in the UK were the Banking Code and Business Banking Code, which were superseded in 2009 and now fall within the FCA's Banking and Payments Conduct Regime.

Boards to implement banking codes were set up as independent organisations, their main roles being to:

- assist banks, building societies and other banking service providers in interpreting the Banking and Business Banking Codes;
- monitor and enforce the Codes;
- take disciplinary action where there are material breaches of the Codes;
- advocate changes when the Codes are revised; and
- promote awareness of the Codes.

The Codes contained standards relating to:

- choosing products and services that meet customer needs;
- running customer accounts;
- borrowing money;

- interest rates, charges, and terms and conditions, and how customers would be told about any changes to these;
- cards and personal identification numbers (PINs);
- protecting customer account and personal information;
- moving or closing accounts;
- dealing with financial difficulties;
- complaints procedures; and
- dormant accounts and unclaimed assets.

Similar codes in other countries have likewise been replaced by statutory financial regulation governing banking practice.

2.2.2 The Standards of Lending Practice

In the UK, the Standards of Lending Practice were established in July 2016, aiming to enhance the protections available to personal customers and small businesses.

The Standards of Lending Practice are voluntary and set the benchmark for good lending practice in the UK. Sponsored initially by the British Bankers' Association (BBA) and the UK Cards Association – both now part of UK Finance, alongside the Council of Mortgage Lenders (CML), the Asset-based Finance Association (ABFA), Financial Fraud Action UK and Payments UK – the Standards outline the way in which banks are expected to deal with their customers. The formation of UK Finance as a single body to publicly represent the British finance industry brought together into a single cross-action voice six separate lobby groups in the aftermath of the global financial crisis, as well as that of the scandals relating to the fixing of the London Inter-bank Offered Rate (LIBOR) and the mis-selling of payment protection insurance (PPI).

The Standards of Lending Practice are split into six main areas for personal customers and eight main areas for business customers, as follows.

- *Personal*
  - Financial promotions and communications
  - Product sale
  - Account maintenance and servicing
  - Money management
  - Financial difficulty
  - Consumer vulnerability
- *Business*
  - Product information
  - Product sale
  - Declined applications
  - Product execution
  - Credit monitoring
  - Financial difficulty
  - Portfolio management
  - Vulnerability

The main products to which the Standards relate are loans, credit cards, overdrafts and charge cards – although a wider range of lending products is currently under consideration for inclusion.

2.3 OMBUDSMEN

Ombudsmen are set up as an independent and impartial means of resolving certain disputes outside the law courts. Ombudsmen are complaints-handling bodies; complainants who make use of ombudsmen continue to retain the right of recourse to the courts, if necessary. The British and Irish Ombudsman Association (BIOA) has as its members various ombudsmen from the four nations of the UK (i.e. England, Wales, Scotland and Northern Ireland), the Republic of Ireland, the Channel Islands, the Isle of Man and Britain's overseas territories. The most relevant for the UK lender is the FOS.

2.3.1 The Financial Ombudsman Service

The aim of Parliament in establishing the FOS was to resolve disputes between financial services providers and their customers fairly, reasonably, quickly and informally. The Service is independent and impartial, and access is free to consumers. Each year, it deals with around half a million enquiries and settles some 100,000 disputes. On average, disputes are settled in a time frame of between six and nine months.

Consumers are not compelled to accept any decision made by the FOS and are free to take their complaint on to the courts. However, if they accept the Ombudsman's decision, it is binding both on them and on the financial services provider.

The FOS looks into complaints about most financial matters including:

- banking;
- insurance;
- mortgages;
- pensions;
- savings and investments;
- credit cards and store cards;
- loans and credit;
- hire purchase and pawnbroking;
- financial advice; and
- stocks, shares, unit trusts and bonds.

2.3.2 The Pensions Ombudsman

The role and powers of the Pensions Ombudsman have been decided by Parliament, and the Ombudsman is appointed as an independent and impartial adjudicator by the Secretary of State for Work and Pensions. While complaints about the sales and marketing of pension schemes are dealt with by the FOS, the Pensions Ombudsman investigates and decides complaints and disputes about the way in which pension schemes are run.

There is no charge for using the Pensions Ombudsman's services.

The Pensions Ombudsman's decision is final and binding on all parties to the complaint or dispute. It can be enforced in the courts and can be changed only by appealing to the appropriate court on a point of law.

2.4 CUSTOMER RIGHTS AND COMPLAINTS PROCEDURES

Complaints-handling rules are published as part of the FCA Handbook, in the section entitled 'Dispute resolution: complaints' (DISP). These rules set out the procedures and requirements that businesses must follow when handling complaints from consumers, including requirements in relation to:

- acknowledging and responding to complaints;
- the time limits for dealing with complaints; and
- record-keeping and reporting.

The rules also set out the jurisdiction and procedures for the FOS. A customer has a right:

- to be clearly informed about a firm's complaints-handling service;
- to make a complaint if they think that there are valid grounds for making a complaint; and
- if not satisfied with the firm's response,
  - to take the complaint to an independent complaints scheme, such as the FOS, or
  - to take the case to court.

2.5 TREATING CUSTOMERS FAIRLY

The FCA envisages that a move towards *more principles-based regulation* (MPBR) will offer financial services organisations greater flexibility to determine for themselves how to deliver fair treatment to their customers in a way that suits the organisations' business. In comparison with the rigidity of a prescriptive rules-based approach, the flexibility of a principles-based approach is expected to facilitate greater competition and innovation, which in turn will promote more efficient markets that will better enable consumers to achieve fair treatment.

2.5.1 Fair treatment of customers

The 'fair treatment of customers' initiative is identified as central to the delivery of the FCA's retail regulatory agenda, as well as a key part of its move towards

MPBR. Firms have an obligation under the FSMA to act fairly and to ensure that the FCA's Principles for Businesses underpin their work – especially:

- Principle 6, which requires a firm to 'pay due regard to the interests of its customers and treat them fairly'; and
- Principle 7, which requires a firm to 'pay due regard to the information needs of its customers and communicate information to them in a way which is clear, fair and not misleading' (FCA, 2014).

The initiative is described as a cultural issue in that the right organisational culture must be established to ensure fair outcomes for consumers. Through this initiative, the FCA aims to deliver the following six improved outcomes for retail consumers, originally articulated in 2006 as the FSA's TCF Outcomes and adopted in full by the FCA:

> **Outcome 1**: Consumers can be confident that they are dealing with firms where the fair treatment of customers is central to the corporate culture.
> **Outcome 2**: Products and services marketed and sold in the retail market are designed to meet the needs of identified consumer groups and are targeted accordingly.
> **Outcome 3**: Consumers are provided with clear information and are kept appropriately informed before, during and after the point of sale.
> **Outcome 4**: Where consumers receive advice, the advice is suitable and takes account of their circumstances.
> **Outcome 5**: Consumers are provided with products that perform as firms have led them to expect, and the associated service is both of an acceptable standard and as they have been led to expect.
> **Outcome 6**: Consumers do not face unreasonable post-sale barriers imposed by firms to change product, switch provider, submit a claim or make a complaint.
>
> (FCA, 2016a)

Firms are responsible for making sure that their customers are treated fairly – and those responsibilities will be enforced in the courts. In *Asset Land Investment Plc v Financial Conduct Authority* [2016] UKSC 17 in the Supreme Court, the FCA won against an illegal land bank, the Court ordering the bank to make a part-repayment of £21 million to investors to whom it had sold small plots of land at inflated prices.

2.5.2 The Unfair Contract Terms Act 1977

The Unfair Contract Terms Act 1977 requires that a contractual term needs to pass the 'reasonableness' test, section 11(1) providing that 'the term shall have been a fair and reasonable one to be included having regard to the circumstances which were, or ought reasonably to have been, known to or in the contemplation of the parties when the contract was made'. Regulation 5(1) of the Unfair Terms in Consumer Contracts Regulations 1999, SI 1999/2083, provides that '[a] contractual term which has not been individually negotiated shall be regarded as unfair if contrary to the requirement of good faith, it causes a significant imbalance in the parties' rights and obligations arising under the contract, to the detriment of the consumer'. As a 'qualifying body' under Part I of Schedule 1 to these Regulations, the FCA is empowered to challenge a firm in court about its use of any terms deemed to be unfair.

While the 1999 Regulations were replaced by the Consumer Rights Act 2015, contracts made prior to 1 October 2015 continue to be governed by the Regulations – an example of why it is imperative that lenders keep abreast of legal and regulatory developments that might impact upon their lending functions. Membership of trade bodies such as UK Finance, with the attendant benefits of networking and information flows, will help lenders to do so.

2.6 CONCLUSION

To be effective, the lending function needs to be regulated by the lending organisations themselves, as well as by independent authorities. An understanding of the regulatory environment underpins effective lending policies and practices. In the UK, that system of regulation comprises the 'twin peaks' of the PRA and the FCA.

Those who exercise the lending function need constantly to keep relevant law in view. Some of the more important pieces of legislation in the UK include the Banking and Financial Services Act 2017, the Financial Services (Banking Reform) Act 2013, the Financial Services Act 2012, the FSMA and the Consumer Rights Act 2015.

The second of the Basel Accords, Basel II, was designed to promote the adoption of stronger risk management practices by the banking industry. Proposals under Basel III to strengthen the resilience of the banking system include simpler or standardised models, rather than complex IRB models, for calculation of capital requirements, with a view to promoting comparability and transparency.

Standards of Lending Practice introduced in July 2016 seek to maintain and enhance protection for customers. The FOS was established by Parliament to resolve disputes between financial services providers and their customers fairly, reasonably, quickly and informally, and the lender has a duty to provide a formal and free complaints-handling service to customers.

The 'fair treatment of customers' initiative has been identified as central to the delivery of the FCA's retail regulatory agenda, as well as being a key part of its move towards MPBR.

FURTHER READING

Barth, J. R., Caprio, G., and Levine, R. (2007) *Rethinking bank regulation: Till angels govern*, Cambridge: Cambridge University Press.

Davies, H., and Green, D. (2013) *Global financial regulation: The essential guide*, Chichester: John Wiley & Sons.

Davis, K. (2013) 'Regulatory reform post the global financial crisis: an overview', available at www.apec.org.au/docs/11_con_gfc/regulatory%20reform%20post%20gfc-%20overview%20paper.pdf

Financial Conduct Authority (FCA) (2016a) 'Fair treatment of customers', available at www.fca.org.uk/firms/fair-treatment-customers

REVIEW QUESTIONS

1. Identify the two authorities that form part of the 'twin peaks' system of regulation in the UK.
2. Identify some of the important statutes that might be relevant to the lender in the UK.
3. Discuss the relevance of Basel for the bank lender.
4. What is the role of the FOS?
5. What is the 'fair treatment of customers' initiative?

ACTIVITIES

1. Visit the UK statute law database at www.statutelaw.gov.uk Browse the various statutes that have been covered in this section.
2. Visit the following websites and conduct in-site searches on the terms 'lending', 'credit' and similar key words:
   - www.bankingstandardsboard.org.uk
   - www.bankofengland.co.uk
   - www.bankofengland.co.uk/pra
   - www.bba.org.uk
   - www.bcsb.co.uk
   - www.fca.org.uk
   - www.financial-ombudsman.org.uk
   - www.gov.uk/government/organisations/competition-and-markets-authority
   - www.handbook.fca.org.uk
   - www.number10.gov.uk
   - www.ombudsmanassociation.org
   - www.pensions-ombudsman.org.uk
   - www.ukfinance.org.uk

CASE STUDY Connected lender liability

Lending has become global. Major card issuers such as Visa and MasterCard have developed complex networks that span the globe. Borrowers are able to use these cards in a number of countries over the world. Moreover, the World Wide Web has become a popular place to buy goods and it is difficult to determine the place of transactions when payments are effected on the Internet.

Section 75 of the Consumer Credit Act 1974 established the principle of 'connected lender liability' whereby credit card issuers are individually and jointly liable, with suppliers, for payments for products and services of a value between £100 and £30,000 if a consumer has a valid claim against the supplier for misrepresentation or breach of contract relating to those goods or services (when bought with the credit card). The consumer can make a claim against the credit card issuer as well as, or instead of, the supplier. In view of the increasing globalisation of lending in general and credit card use in particular, a question arose as to whether credit card payments made abroad would be covered by the principle of connected lender liability.

The OFT, Lloyds Bank plc and some other banks desired to clarify the grey area, i.e. to test in courts the applicability of connected lender liability to card payments made abroad. In November 2004, the High Court held that it did *not* apply. In March 2006, the Court of Appeal reversed the first-instance decision and held that it did. Saxby (2006), who researched the case, concludes that, without doubt, consumers 'will continue adding by credit card to the £12.5 billion spent in 2004 on overseas transactions'. In October 2007, the House of Lords upheld the Court of Appeal's decision.

The case has clarified that the lender is liable for any misrepresentation of breach of contract on the part of suppliers abroad when the payment of goods and services has been made by cards issued in the UK. Accordingly, a lender who has provided a credit card to a UK borrower will be liable if, for example, such a borrower uses the card abroad to pay for the hire of a defective car, which defect results in accidental damage to property – even to life.

CASE STUDY QUESTIONS

1. What is 'connected lender liability'?
2. What will be considered to be a valid claim for connected lender liability to apply?
3. What is the implication to a lender of the ruling made by the House of Lords in October 2007 in relation to the case filed by the Office of Fair Trading on connected lender liability?

Suggested answers can be found in Appendix A.

3

Types of borrower

LEARNING POINTS

This chapter examines the natures of different types of borrower.

Learning areas will include:

- individuals and sole traders;
- partnerships;
- companies;
- clubs and societies;
- trusts; and
- others.

3.1 INTRODUCTION

The lender needs to bear in mind an important principle: 'Know your customer', also known as 'Know your client', an FCA requirement throughout the lender–borrower relationship. The law requires that the lender do so to combat money laundering and other types of criminal activity.

Knowing its customer enables a lender to:

- safeguard against fraud, recognise suspicious or illegal activity, and protect against reputational and financial risks;
- avoid recommending the wrong product to the customer and provide only those lending products that are suitable;
- monitor lending activity in an effective manner; and
- avoid being in a position in which it cannot recover a loan because it was not aware of the legal implications of lending to that particular customer type.

The lender needs to understand not only the nature of the borrower, but also the industry in which they operate, including its competition, its location and many other factors.

While a number of hybrid types of customer are continually being identified, the major types of borrower can be classified as follows.

- *Personal borrowers*
  - Individuals
  - Sole traders

    - Minors
- *Partnerships*
    - Partnerships
    - Limited partnerships
    - Limited liability partnerships
- *Limited companies*
    - Public limited companies
    - Private limited companies
    - Community interest companies
- *Unincorporated associations*
    - Clubs and societies
    - Trusts
- *Others*

3.2 PERSONAL BORROWERS

Personal borrowers can borrow singly or within joint accounts. They may borrow in their own name or as a sole trader in the name of a business. They may be over the age of 18 or they may not, i.e. they may be minors.

3.2.1 Individuals

An *individual* can be defined as a person or body of persons not all of whom are corporate bodies and which is not a partnership. The terms and conditions of loans to an individual are relatively simple. The loan agreement will indicate details such as the amount of the loan, the interest payable, the repayment terms, the details of any security, and any other terms and conditions to which the loan may be subject. The borrower will indicate acceptance of the loan by signing on the duplicate copy of the loan letter and returning it to the lender.

Private individuals bear the same rights and responsibilities as sole traders.

3.2.2 Minors

According to the Family Law Reform Act 1969, a person attains the age of majority on reaching the age of 18. Someone under the age of 18 is known as a *minor*. While a minor may be able to take out a loan and that loan will be ratified as soon as the minor reaches the age of majority, any lender making a loan contract with a minor runs the risk of repudiation. A minor's debts are not always enforceable, particularly if the loans have not been given for 'necessaries' (*Coutts & Co. v Browne-Lecky and others* [1947] KB 104). Lenders therefore need to be cautious about lending to minors and will usually take the guarantee of an adult to safeguard repayment. Under section 2(b) of the Minors' Contracts Act 1987, where a minor's debt is guaranteed by an adult, 'the guarantee shall not for that reason alone be unenforceable against the guarantor'. Guarantees therefore provide some protection to the lender, allowing it to rely on the guarantor to repay a debt repudiated by a minor.

Another remedy available to lenders in the instance of a repudiating minor lies in the *doctrine of subrogation* whereby the lender is entitled to 'stand in the shoes of' a third party. A lender who has lent money to a minor to pay for a purchase will be able to stand in the shoes of the seller of the goods and exercise the rights of the seller. For example, in *Nottingham Permanent Benefit Building Society v Thurstan* [1903] AC 6, the House of Lords held that a building society could be subrogated to an unpaid vendor's lien in respect of an unlawful loan to a minor to purchase land.

3.2.3 Sole traders

Sole proprietorships are unincorporated businesses owned by a single person who has the right to profits and is liable for its debts. A *sole trader* is a person who is the sole owner of a business, regardless of whether they employ other people to help to run the business. A *sole trader* may adopt a different name for the business: Joe Smith may run Somerset Gardening Services, but the law will not distinguish between the assets of Joe Smith and those of Somerset Gardening Services. The sole trader has complete responsibility for all of the debts of the business, i.e. bears unlimited liability, unlike a limited company or limited partnership.

Some lenders are reluctant to extend credit to sole traders because they have a higher rate of bankruptcy.

3.3 PARTNERSHIPS

Partnerships are associations of two or more persons who have entered into a legal contract under which each agrees to furnish a part of the capital and labour for a business enterprise, and each shares a fixed proportion of profits and losses, and each is individually and jointly liable for the debts of the business.

3.3.1 Partnership firms

The Partnerships Act 1890 sets out the basic structure of a partnership. Some of the characteristics of a *partnership firm* are as follows.

- Section 1(1) of the 1890 Act defines a 'partnership' as a 'relation which subsists between persons carrying on a business in common with a view of profit'. Companies are specifically excluded from the definition of partnerships.
- Any two or more persons can form a partnership.

- Every partner is an agent of the firm for the purpose of the business of the firm, and can bind the firm and other partners.
- Every partner in a firm is liable jointly with the other partners for all debts and obligations of the firm incurred while they were a partner.
- Everyone who, by words or by conduct, represents themselves or 'holds themselves out' as a partner in a firm is liable as a partner to anyone who has, on the faith of such representation, given credit to the firm.
- All of the partners are entitled to share equally in the capital and profits of the business, and are required to contribute equally towards its losses.
- A partnership is dissolved:
  - if specified, on the expiration of any term;
  - if specified, on the termination of any undertaking;
  - on the occasion of any partner giving notice to the others of an intention to dissolve the partnership;
  - on the bankruptcy or death of any partner;
  - on the occurrence of any event that makes it illegal for the business of the firm to be carried on;
  - on the decree of a court that a partner is mentally incapable or of unsound mind; and/or
  - on the retirement of an existing partner or the admission of a new partner.
- In terms of liability to lenders:
  - a person who is admitted as a partner into an existing firm is not liable to the creditors of the firm for anything done before they became a partner; and
  - a partner who retires from a firm does not cease to be liable for partnership debts incurred before that retirement.
- The rights and duties of partners may be varied by the express or implied consent of all of the partners.
- The articles of partnership can vary some of the legal provisions.

Lenders need to be aware that the rule in *Devaynes v Noble* (1816) 35 ER 781 (known as *Clayton's case*) will apply when a partnership is dissolved. This case established the principle of 'first incurred, first discharged', whereby a credit to a customer's account is deemed to discharge the earliest of the debit items on the account.

In *Royal Bank of Scotland v Christie* (1841) 8 Cl & Fin 214, a partner mortgaged his personal property to secure the debts of a partnership firm. On his death, the firm was overdrawn, but the bank did not rule off the account, which continued unbroken. The surviving partners paid amounts into the account that exceeded the debit balance at the deceased partner's death and then withdrew an even larger balance. The court held that the payments into the account after the death of the partner went towards paying off the deceased partner's mortgage. Thus if the lender fails to rule off the account on one partner's death and allows the surviving partner to continue to operate the account, the lender's recourse to the deceased partner's estate may be lost.

3.3.2 Limited partnerships

The Limited Partnerships Act 1907 introduced a second form of partnership under which the liability of one or more of the partners could be limited, while also retaining general partners with unlimited liability. Some of the characteristics of a *limited partnership* can be summarised as follows.

- A limited partnership consists of one or more persons called 'general partners', who are liable for all debts and obligations of the firm, and one or more persons called 'limited partners', who contribute to capital or property, but who are not liable for the debts or obligations of the firm beyond the amount contributed.
- A limited partner cannot:
  - draw out or receive back any part of their contribution;
  - take part in the management of the partnership business; or
  - bind the firm.
- If a limited partner does take part in the management of the partnership business, they will be liable for all debts and obligations of the firm incurred while they took part in the management as if they were a general partner.
- A limited partnership will not be dissolved by the death or bankruptcy of a limited partner and the mental incapacity of a limited partner will not generally be a ground for dissolution of the partnership by the court.
- A corporate body may be a limited partner.

3.3.3 Limited liability partnerships

The *limited liability partnership* (LLP) is a type of corporate vehicle created by the Limited Liability Partnership Act 2000. The LLP structure has been adopted by a range of firms in a number of sectors. Most of the larger accountancy and legal firms are LLPs, and the form is also used by a number of medical practices and small firms.

Some of the characteristics of an LLP can be summarised as follows.

- Any two or more persons can form as an LLP. Members have the same flexibility in terms of their business structure as applies to a traditional partnership.
- Members are generally taxed in the same way as partners in a partnership.
- Unlike a company, an LLP does not have shares or shareholders or directors.
- The LLP is registered on the Companies House Register.

- Like a company, it is a legal entity separate from its members and therefore enjoys the benefit of limited liability. While the LLP is liable for the full extent of its debts, the liability of the members is limited, except to the extent that the members agree otherwise.
- Subsequent regulations broadly apply large parts of the Insolvency Act 1986 and the Companies Act 2006 to the LLP. It is subject to similar accounting and disclosure provisions.

3.4 COMPANIES

Companies, or corporations, are separate legal entities formed for the purpose of undertaking a business (*Salomon v Salomon & Co. Ltd* [1897] AC 22). Companies are owned by shareholders, who have the right to participate in the profits by means of dividends and/or the appreciation of stock, but are not personally liable for the company's debts. The day-to-day management of companies is undertaken by directors appointed by the shareholders.

Companies can be limited or unlimited, public or private. A *public* corporation is one in which anyone can buy shares, which may be traded on a stock exchange. A *private* corporation is one in which the sale of stock may be limited to stipulated persons, such as members of the principal stockholder's family.

Section 1(1) of the Companies Act 2006 defines a 'company' as 'a company that is formed and registered under this Act'. The Companies Act 2006 – the longest Act ever to have been passed by the British Parliament – repeals and restates almost all of the current Companies Acts. The 2006 Act, which affects directors, auditors, shareholders and company secretaries of private and public companies, came fully into force by October 2009. Since that time, companies have been required to disclose their registered names and numbers on company websites and order forms, and they are now allowed to communicate electronically with shareholders and others.

Companies are required to have the following documentation:

- a *memorandum of association* that regulates the affairs of the company and which states the company name, the location of the registered office, the objects of the company and the extent of its liability;
- *articles of association* that regulate the actions of the directors; and
- a *trading certificate* or *certificate to commence business.*

It is important for a lender to remember that any debts that a company incurs before its trading certificate or certificate to commence business is issued will be deemed to be pre-incorporation debts for which the company may not be liable, because it had not yet assumed a legal identity when the debts were incurred.

Before the enactment of the 2006 Act, an *objects clause* in a company's memorandum of association excluded the possibility of that company acting *ultra vires*, i.e. 'beyond its powers'. *Ultra vires* actions once carried risks for lenders, depriving them of enforceable security and the possibility of recovering their money if the company were to become insolvent. However, the Companies Act 2006 greatly reduced the applicability of *ultra vires* in corporate law and if a third party, such as a bank lender, were to act in good faith, it was not to be prejudiced by any deficiency in a company's constitution.

Under the Companies Act 2006, the position has become even simpler: with effect from October 2008, the objects clause was removed from the memorandum – as, indeed, were most of the other standard clauses. The memorandum was reduced to a simple statement that the initial subscribers wish to form a company, and agree to become members and take at least one share each. Only if the articles of association contain some specific restriction will the company be limited in its actions, for example limiting a company that is a charity to objects that are of a charitable nature. In general, the effect of the 2006 Act is to preclude the need for a lender to concern itself with whether the company has the right objects or powers in its constitution to allow it to borrow.

If, in winding up a company, it emerges that any business has been carried on with the intent of defrauding creditors or for any other fraudulent reason, the court may declare that any 'knowing parties' are guilty of *fraudulent trading* and personally liable to make such contributions as the court thinks proper. In *Re William C. Leitch Brothers Ltd* [1932] 2 Ch 7, it was held to have been fraudulent to continue to trade when directors knew that there was no reasonable prospect of the company paying its debts. More recently, in 2007, the disgraced former chief executive of Independent Insurance, which collapsed dramatically in 2001, was handed down the maximum penalty of ten years' imprisonment for fraudulent trading.

Wrongful trading takes place when the directors know, or ought to have known, that there is no reasonable prospect that the company would avoid insolvent liquidation. In *Re Produce Marketing Consortium Ltd (No. 2)* [1989] 5 BCC 569, it was held that reasonable standard of skill expected of a director will vary depending upon the size of the company.

Fraudulent and wrongful trading can lead to an individual's disqualification from being a director in a company in the future.

3.4.1 Limited or unlimited companies

A company is a *limited company* if the liability of its members is limited by its constitution. It may be limited by shares or limited by guarantee.

- If the members' liability is limited to the amount unpaid (if any) on the shares that they hold, the company is *limited by shares.*
- If their liability is limited to such amount as they undertake to contribute to the assets of the company in the event of its being wound up, the company is *limited by guarantee.*

If there is no limit on the liability of its members, the company is an *unlimited company.*

3.4.2 Public and private companies

In the UK, a company name that ends in the abbreviation 'plc' is a *public limited company*: a type of limited company in which shares may be offered for sale to the public.

A public company is a company:

- limited by shares or by guarantee and having share capital;
- whose certificate of incorporation states that it is a public company; and
- in relation to which the requirements of the Companies Acts as to registration or re-registration as a public company have been complied with.

A public company must not do business or exercise any borrowing powers unless:

- the registrar has issued it with a 'trading certificate';
- the nominal value of the company's allotted share capital is not less than the authorised minimum; and
- at least a quarter of the nominal value of the share capital has been paid up.

Thus a lender must, on no account, lend money to a public company before it has been issued with a trading certificate or a certificate to commence business.

A *private company* is any company that is not a public company. In the UK, the letters 'Ltd' after a company name indicate that it is a private *limited* company.

3.4.3 Community interest companies

The *community interest company* (CIC) was introduced by the Companies (Audit, Investigations and Community Enterprise) Act 2004. The basic legal structure for a CIC is the limited liability company. It can either be incorporated as a new company or converted from an existing company. The CIC can take one of three company forms:

- a company limited by guarantee without a share capital;
- a private company limited by shares; or
- a public company limited by shares.

A CIC's name must, however, end in Community Interest Company (CIC) and not Limited (Ltd).

Their primary purpose is to provide benefits to the community, rather than to the individuals who own, run or work in them. This core principle is set out as the 'community interest test'. A company satisfies the community interest test if a reasonable person might consider that its activities are carried on for the benefit of the community (CIC Regulator, 2016).

3.5 UNINCORPORATED ASSOCIATIONS

3.5.1 Clubs and societies

A *club* or *society* can be defined as a group of people organised for a common purpose, distinguished by mutual interests, and generally arranging to meet at regular intervals, e.g. a book club, a garden club, a badminton club. The club or society will generally:

- identify the objectives of the group;
- set out the rules of the club or society in a governing document;
- designate officers authorised to sign on its behalf;
- record minutes of committee meetings;
- have a chair, secretary and treasurer (the last being responsible for the organisation's finances, including finding a bank account); and
- appoint an auditor or independent examiner to check the accounts.

Any decision to have a bank account or to borrow will be recorded in the form of a resolution at a committee meeting.

The Charity Commission defines a club or society as a means by which people share a common interest and create a formal structure through which they can pursue that interest. Section 3 of the Charities Act 2011 stipulates that a charity must be for the public benefit if it is for a charitable purpose. The Charity Commission regulates charities of all sizes and forms.

To gain charitable status, the group has to either:

- provide relief for the poor, handicapped and/or disabled;
- assist the advancement of education;
- further the promotion of religion; or
- make another beneficial contribution to the community.

Since 23 April 2007, under the Charities Act 2007, a charity has had to be registered only if its annual income is over £5,000.

3.5.2 Trusts

A *trustee* is a person who holds legal title to an asset for the benefit of another. A *trust* is a fiduciary relationship in which one party, known as a creator, grantor, donor or trustor, gives another party, the trustee, the right to hold legal title to assets for the benefit of a third party, who will be the beneficiary of the trust.

Power to permit trustees to borrow money and/or charge trust property can be found:

- in the governing document;
- in the Trusts of Land and Appointment of Trustees Act 1996;
- in the Trustee Act 2000; and/or
- by implication.

Where trustees do not have the power to borrow and/or charge property, they can confer a suitable power on the trust by using the power of amendment for unincorporated charities or the power of amendment available to companies under the Companies Acts. In the unlikely event that the governing document specifically precludes borrowing, a scheme will be required to authorise it.

The exercise of any power of borrowing and/or charging property must be strictly in accordance with the terms of the power.

3.5.3 Others

Borrowers can take many a variety of forms. Indeed, even a country can be a borrower. A sovereign borrower might be the government itself, or a ministry in the government, or an entity owned by the government. A number of sovereign debt defaults have shaken the general belief that a country cannot default.

3.6 CONCLUSION

Lenders need to 'know their customers', who can range from individuals or sole traders, partnerships and companies, to clubs and societies, trusts and others. An understanding of the various types of borrower will enable the lender to be more effective in exercising the lending function.

FURTHER READING

Arora, A. (2014) *Banking law*, Harlow: Pearson Education.

Macintyre, E. (2016) *Business law*, Harlow: Pearson Education.

Riches, S., Allen, V., and Keenan D. J. (2013) *Keenan and Riches' business law*, Harlow: Pearson Education.

REVIEW QUESTIONS

1. Why is it important to understand the nature of the type of borrower?
2. What is the risk of lending to a minor?
3. Distinguish between partnerships, limited partnerships and limited liability partnerships.
4. Distinguish between public limited companies and private limited companies.
5. Are trusts entitled to borrow money?

ACTIVITIES

1. Look at 'The London Share Services' section of the *Financial Times*. Identify the various industry classifications of public limited companies. Select a company that interests you, telephone the CityLine number and request a copy of the company's financial statements. Go through the statements when they are received and consider how a lender might use the information available in the documents.
2. Visit the following websites, identify the key features companies, and consider how they differ from unincorporated clubs and societies:
   - www.charity-commission.gov.uk
   - www.companieshouse.gov.uk

CASE STUDY ***Kelner v Baxter***

In *Kelner v Baxter* (1866) LR 2 CP 174, the plaintiffs and the defendants were promoters of the Gravesend Royal Alexandra Hotel Company Ltd. The defendants purported to make a contract to purchase goods on behalf of a proposed hotel company. The plaintiff was to be the manager of the new company. Before the company was incorporated, the plaintiff offered to sell a stock of wine for £900, which the defendants accepted on behalf of the proposed company on 27 January 1866. The goods thus delivered were delivered to persons who purported to act on behalf of the company and the goods were subsequently consumed. On 1 February, the directors of the proposed company purported to ratify the agreement. Later, on 20 February 1866, the company received the certificate of incorporation. Subsequently, the company again purported to ratify the transaction on 11 April 1866 – just days before the company went into bankruptcy.

It was held that the 'agents' had no principal when they purported to make the contract and that the company, when it came into existence, was incapable of 'ratifying' the contract that the agents had purported to make on its behalf. Thus both of the ratifications purported to have been made on 1 February and 11 April 1866 were held to be invalid.

An action was brought against the agents and it was held that they were personally liable.

It was held that if a promoter or agent purports to act on behalf of an as-yet-unformed company, that promoter or agent will become personally liable even if they represented themselves only as an agent of the company. The company itself, having come into existence subsequent to the relevant transaction date, is unable to ratify what an agent purported to carry out in its absence.

CASE STUDY QUESTIONS

1. What is the significance of the certificate of incorporation?
2. What is pre-incorporation debt?
3. Is a company able to ratify pre-incorporation debts after it has been duly incorporated?
4. What might be the position of a lender who has lent money to a company prior to its incorporation?
5. What is the lesson for lenders that can be drawn from *Kelner v Baxter*?

Suggested answers can be found in Appendix A.

4

Purposes of financing

LEARNING POINTS

This chapter introduces particular types of lending requirement and the types of finance that can be made available to meet differing customer needs.

Learning areas include:

- forms of consumer finance, including bridging loans and house purchase;
- working capital;
- new ventures;
- business expansion; and
- the purchase of fixed assets.

4.1 INTRODUCTION

Lending can be extended for a variety of reasons. Some of the purposes of lending are illustrated in Figure 4.1.

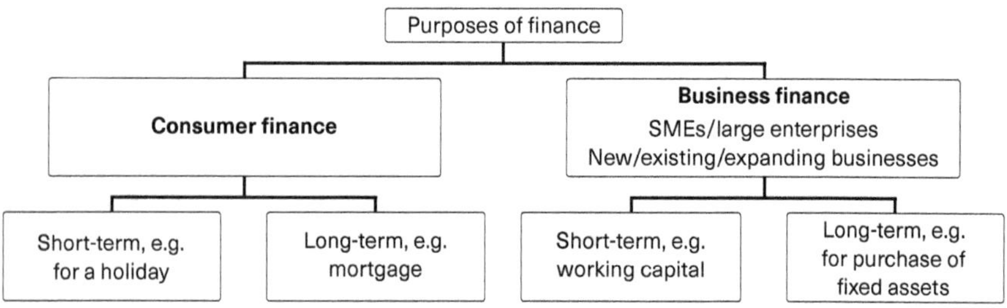

Figure 4.1 Purposes of financing

A period of a year or less is generally considered to be short-term lending, while periods in excess of a year are classified as long-term lending.

4.2 CONSUMER FINANCE

In general, *consumer finance* means finance that is extended to consumers. Specifically, it refers to finance extended to personal consumers as opposed to business customers. Consumer finance can be offered for a short term, e.g. a loan for home improvements, or for a long term, e.g. a mortgage for home purchase. We will now examine some of these examples.

4.2.1 Home improvement loans

As the name suggests, home improvement loans are offered for home improvements and are aimed at owners of residential property, as well as leaseholders with lease periods that extend well beyond the planned date of repayment of the loan. Care must be taken to ensure that appropriate planning and other permissions are in place.

Some of the specific purposes of home improvement loans include:

- additions or extensions to structure, e.g. additional baths, skylights, attics, basements, garages;
- repair or replacement of structural damage;
- other structural alterations;
- repair of termite damage or preventative treatment against termites and other types of pest infestation;
- improved functional and other modernisation, e.g. remodelled bathrooms and kitchens;
- elimination of health and safety hazards, such as asbestos and lead-based paint surfaces;
- changes to enhance aesthetic appeal, e.g. a covered porch, stair railings;
- reconditioning or replacement of plumbing, sewerage, heating, air conditioning and electrical systems;
- improvements to, or repair of, roofing, gutters and drainage;
- replacement of flooring, tiling and carpeting;
- energy conservation improvements, e.g. double glazing, loft insulation, solar heating systems;
- landscape work and site improvement, e.g. patios, terraces, driveways, walks, fencing, clearing undergrowth and removal of trees that pose a safety hazard;
- improvements for accessibility purposes, e.g. remodelling kitchens and baths for wheelchair access, lowering kitchen cabinets, installing wider doors and exterior ramps, related fixtures such as new cooking ranges, refrigerators and other appliances;
- preservation of historic homes; or
- installation of fire and other safety equipment.

4.2.2 Bridging loans

A *bridging loan* serves to bridge a gap in the form of interim financing until the way is cleared for longer-term financing to be obtained. It is usually taken out to meet a temporary cash shortfall, such as that which may arise when buying a property or business.

A bridging loan will usually involve lending a large sum of money over a short period (generally not more than six months) at higher interest rates to compensate for the higher risk that arises because the borrower may effectively have to service two or more loans at the same time. The loan amount will depend upon the valuation of available security, i.e. the equity available in the assets being financed. The loan-to-value (LTV) ratio will generally be lower than that for standard mortgages – typically, not more than 65–70 per cent. Fees will generally be a percentage of the sum borrowed. A longer-term loan will usually form the principal source of repayment of the interim bridging loan.

There are two major types of bridging loan:

- *closed bridging,* whereby the loan is for a defined period, i.e. when the date on which the funds for closing the loan will become available is known in advance, such as when the date of completion on the sale of a property has been fixed; and
- *open bridging,* whereby the loan is open-ended and the closure date is not known, which type of loan will be charged a higher rate of interest to compensate for the higher risk.

Some of the purposes for offering bridging finance include:

- bridging the gap between the purchase of a new home and the sale of the old home, i.e. to buy a second property before the first property has been sold;
- buying a property at auction;
- buying a home needing renovation before it is habitable and thus able to be mortgaged;
- temporarily financing a home overseas; or
- enabling property developers to work on a project while approval for the plan is awaited.

Bridging loans are also used in venture capital and corporate finance to finance interim needs, e.g. between successive financings, or immediately prior to an initial public offering.

4.2.3 Mortgages

A *mortgage* is a legal agreement conveying conditional ownership of assets as security for a loan. Most commonly, it is a term used to refer to a loan secured by a mortgage of fixed assets. The person offering the mortgage is the *mortgagor* and the institution lending money against the security of the mortgage is the *mortgagee.* Mortgages are generally extended to owners of residential property, as well as to leaseholders with lease periods that have at least 70 or 80 years remaining to run. Mortgage payments are generally required to be made at monthly intervals.

Traditionally, the standard mortgage repayment term has been 25 years, but the impact of longer working lives has resulted in some lenders, such as Nationwide, Halifax and Leeds Building Society, extending their maximum term length to 40 years and offering their loans to persons up to 70 years old. The cost of homes in the UK is such that lenders are commonly allowing people to borrow up to 4.5 times their annual income, leading to predictions of another financial crisis in the making.

Some of the purposes for granting mortgage loans include:

- purchase of residential property for owner occupation;
- purchase of residential property for letting and rental income;
- purchase of commercial property for rental income;
- structural extensions and alterations to existing property, e.g. building another floor or self-contained annex;
- release of equity in the property to fund income during retirement; and
- consolidation of existing debt, with a view to reducing interest costs and/or monthly outgoings.

There are various types of mortgage loan.

- A *repayment mortgage* is one that is repaid by a regular monthly payment that combines interest on the capital with an element of capital repayment. Because interest payable will be much higher at the start of the loan, when the principal outstanding is higher, than towards the end, when most of the loan has been paid off, the lender calculates equalised (known as *equated*) monthly instalments that even out the repayment obligations of the borrower over the lifetime of the mortgage.
- An *interest-only mortgage* or *endowment mortgage* is one under which only interest is paid during the life of the loan, the principal being repaid in one lump sum from the proceeds of a separate investment in an endowment fund, an individual savings account (ISA) or a similar investment vehicle. It is estimated that approximately a fifth of all outstanding residential mortgages in the UK are interest-only. Many borrowers with an interest-only mortgage are thought not to have a repayment vehicle in place to pay off the principal at the end of the mortgage term, and a significant proportion either have no plan or are unaware of having to repay the principal (Citizens Advice, 2015).
- *Consolidation loans* usually convert a number of unsecured loans into one loan, secured by residential property.

The lender needs to be able to assess the suitability of a mortgage to the needs of the client. The impact of various features of repayment and interest-only mortgages on that decision can be summarised as follows.

- *Investment risk* In recent years, many homeowners who took out interest-only mortgages with an endowment fund as the repayment vehicle have faced unexpected financial problems when the average growth rate of the endowment fund proved insufficient to cover the mortgage capital.
- *Life insurance* Should an endowment policy be taken out for repayment of the principal, life insurance will be built into the product; a repayment mortgage is likely to require a separate life insurance policy be taken out.
- *Amount of interest paid* The outstanding balance of an interest-only mortgage does not decrease over time and therefore more interest is paid over the life of such a mortgage than over the life of a repayment mortgage.
- *Impact of interest rate risk* An increase in interest rates will normally cause a greater change in the interest outgoings under an endowment mortgage than a repayment mortgage, while simultaneously causing downward pressure on the value of the investment portfolio.
- *Tax implications* Because interest could be set off as expenses in buy-to-let or business mortgages, the tax relief available in these cases was higher than for residential purchase – but this benefit is being phased out.

Lenders are being required to tighten up criteria for *buy-to-let* borrowers – in particular, to 'portfolio landlords' with four or more mortgaged buy-to-let properties. Lenders are required to assess affordability based on the entire mortgaged property portfolio even if the landlord is arranging finance for only a single property. Landlords are required to have higher levels of rent relative to their mortgage costs and new mortgages need to undergo stress-testing to ensure the viability of the buy-to-let business.

A *second mortgage* is a type of subordinate mortgage made while an original mortgage is still in existence. In the event of default, the original mortgage will have priority, i.e. the proceeds from the sale of the property will be first applied towards the first mortgage. Any remaining proceeds will then be applied to the second mortgage. A second mortgage is thus subordinate to the charge on the property created by a first mortgage, but senior to subsequent charges. In view of the increased risk, the interest rate charged for the second mortgage is likely to be higher and the amount lent will be lower than granted under a first mortgage.

Second mortgages are commonly offered for meeting large expenditures that may otherwise be difficult to finance, such as:

- the purchase of a second home or a buy-to-let property;
- home improvements;
- funding a child's education; or
- consolidating debt and paying off other sources of outstanding debt, which may carry higher interest rates.

A *sale-and-leaseback scheme* involves a lender purchasing property from a borrower and leasing it back to the former owner as its tenant, potentially on an assured shorthold tenancy (AST) basis. Property Rescue, National Property Buyers and other such companies promote such 'sell and rent back' schemes as arrangements that allow a homeowner needing to release the value of their home, but not wanting to move, to 'maintain stability' in their life. While assurances that the 'home cannot be repossessed by your building society or mortgage company' are technically accurate, this is because the borrower no longer owns the property and is no longer responsible for mortgage repayments. It is likely, however, that the sale-and-leaseback company may have financed its purchase of the property from the homeowner by means of a loan – and in the event of the sale-and-leaseback company itself going into insolvency, that lender will have the power to evict the tenant.

4.3 BUSINESS FINANCE

Business finance is finance offered by lenders to businesses (as opposed to personal customers). Those businesses may be either small or medium-sized enterprises (SMEs) or large enterprises.

Loans to businesses can be structured depending upon the requirements of the borrower, including:

- currency requirements, i.e. whether they are domestic or foreign;
- time periods, i.e. whether short-term or long-term;
- interest rate requirements, i.e. whether variable or fixed; and
- repayment terms, i.e. whether in a lump sum from a defined source or in instalments, in which latter case payments can be equated, front-ended (higher at the start of the loan) or back-ended (higher towards the end of the loan) depending upon the timings of cash flows.

4.3.1 New ventures

Lending to new ventures involves a high level of risk in comparison with lending to well-established businesses. New ventures face an uncertain future, carry a higher risk of failure and have limited borrowing options. Lending can take the form of bank loans, supplier credit or venture capital.

While creditors might focus more on past history when considering extending loans, venture capitalists (which might include banks and bank subsidiaries) might be more interested in future potential and will usually take a stake in the business in the form of equity capital.

Venture capital is capital extended to new start-up business ventures and it has become synonymous with risk capital. Venture capital has a number of distinctive features, as follows.

- Venture capital is extended by a range of lenders, such as wealthy individuals (sometimes known as 'business angels'), private equity firms, or banks, subsidiaries of banks and other financial institutions that pool such investments.
- Venture capitalists may offer a mix of debt capital and share capital, thereby acquiring a proportion of the equity.
- In addition to finance, venture capitalists may also extend managerial and technical support to the venture, and acquire a say in company decisions.
- Because of the highly speculative nature of their investments, venture capitalists expect a high rate of return. In addition, they often wish to obtain this return over a relatively short period of time – usually of between three and seven years.

Ruhnka and Young (1987, 1991) construct a venture capital model that identifies five sequential stages in the venture capital financing process.

- At the *seed stage*, the business approaches the lender for finance and persuades the lender to participate in the new business venture.
- At the *start-up stage*, the business idea is developed, business plans are presented, management teams are formed and market research is evaluated.
- The *second stage* sees the business idea converted to products and marketed to consumers, some sales achieved and the venture aiming to break even.
- At the *third stage*, the business aims to expand its market share.
- During the *bridge stage* or *pre-public stage*, the investor seeks exit strategies, such as mergers and acquisitions (M&As), which might be a prelude to an initial public offering on the stock exchange.

4.3.2 Expansion of existing business

Lenders will also be approached for finance for the purpose of funding the expansion of existing businesses. Expansion allows a business to meet the demands of a larger customer base, to increase its sales volume and to increase profits, providing a greater return to the entrepreneurs.

Expansion may be required for a number of reasons, including targeting new market segments, diversifying into new products or services, opening new locations domestically and/or internationally, starting new distribution methods (e.g. Internet sales), franchising or licensing, forming partnerships and alliances or engaging in M&As, or bidding for new contracts.

An existing business that plans to expand will have more borrowing options than a new venture, because a business that has been around for some time will have had the opportunity to build up a good financial track record, credit history and reputation. Moreover, the business might have been able to plough its own profits back into the business and may also be in a better position to command forms of finance such as invoice discounting and factoring (see Chapter 5). Lenders will be more willing to lend to an existing well-established business rather than a new venture with an uncertain future.

Nonetheless, potential lenders need to examine the viability of any expansion plans. Some of the areas at which they will need to look include:

- the business's history and its reputation;
- market analysis and target markets;
- financial results and growth that have proven the viability of the business idea, i.e.
  - financial statements for the past three years,
  - current financial indicators,
  - personal financial statements of the promoters, partners or principals, to demonstrate net worth outside of the business,
  - statements of debts and accounts receivable, and
  - tax returns for the past three years;
- the business's operating plan, including
  - current operating facilities and equipment, and
  - plans for expansion, such as any new space, new production facilities and infrastructure, or new information technology;
- a marketing plan and sales forecast;
- the CVs of members of the management team and key personnel, and any additional staffing requirements; and
- the details of loan requested, including
  - its amount,
  - its purpose,
  - the period (term), and
  - details of the security to be offered.

4.3.3 Working capital requirements

Working capital is capital or cash available for conducting the day-to-day operations of a business. The *working capital ratio* of a business is calculated as its net working capital or net current asset or current assets *less* current liabilities, i.e.:

Working capital = Current assets – Current liabilities

The *current ratio* is a measure of the working capital of a business:

Current ratio = Current assets ÷ Current liabilities

While a current ratio of more than 1 (i.e. >1) is generally considered to be comfortable, much depends on the nature of the company and the industry within which it functions. Thus a supermarket that is able to convert stock into cash very quickly might be 'comfortable' even if the current ratio is less than 1 (i.e. <1).

The *liquidity ratio* is a measure of the liquidity position of a business. Also known as the *acid test* or *quick ratio*, it measures the relationship between current assets *less* stock and current liabilities:

Liquidity ratio = (Current assets – Stock) ÷ Current liabilities

Examples of *current assets* include cash, short-term investments, accounts receivable or trade debtors, stock or inventory, and prepaid expenses.

Examples of *current liabilities* include short-term debt, accrued expenses and accounts payable or trade creditors.

Trade credit has been found to be an important source of funding for businesses that have no recourse to bank lending (Mateut, Bougheas, and Mizen, 2006).

When current assets are more than current liabilities, the working capital ratio is positive and the business is seen as able to repay its obligations. Conversely, when current liabilities exceed current assets, the working capital is negative and the business is seen as unable to repay its obligations.

A comparison of these ratios over time will indicate whether the business is doing well or declining. A working capital or current ratio that declines over time could signal problems for the business. Some of the reasons could be that:

- sales are declining and hence accounts receivable are declining;
- debtors include a high proportion of bad debts that will not repaid and hence the amount of debtors is consistently high;
- debt collection processes are inefficient and hence the level of debtors is increasing;
- there is no demand for the product and hence the amount of finished goods held as stock is increasing;
- inefficient production processes may also result in increasing stock levels; and/or
- the business is unable to pay its debts on time and hence the level of creditors is high or is increasing.

Whatever the reason, when a business is unable to pay its debts as and when they fall due, it is exposed to the risk of bankruptcy.

The purpose of short-term financing will be to meet the working capital requirements of a business to enable it to run its day-to-day operations, including the payment of inventory costs and wages to employees. The *working capital cycle* or *cash operating cycle* is the period between first buying raw material to commence production and the final collection of cash from the debtor or the purchaser of the product.

Ways of managing the working capital cycle include:

- reducing the stock-holding period for raw materials and finished goods;
- improving the efficiency of the production process;
- collecting debts more efficiently;

- reducing the period of credit offered to debtors; and
- negotiating for an increase in the period of credit offered by creditors.

Any borrowing taken to finance production will be repaid when the finished products are sold and debtors pay their dues, which will usually be within a period of less than a year. If something goes awry, however, businesses need liquid working capital to bridge the shortfall and allow them to continue to run smoothly. A severe shortage of liquidity can even result in bankruptcy if the business is unable to pay its own debts as and when they fall due for payment.

The lender needs to recognise the importance of forecasting working capital requirements to ensure that the business is effectively able to meet its short-term financial obligations. Forecasting is vital to the management of cash, and enables both the lender and the borrower to:

- predict expected inflows and outflows of cash;
- ascertain when possible cash surpluses or shortages might occur, especially in industries with seasonal peaks and troughs;
- plan ahead;
- arrange lending or borrowing;
- forecast future sales, and the amount and timing of cash receipts; and
- prepare a number of budgets for different eventualities, e.g. a more optimistic forecast, a more probable forecast or the worst possible forecast.

Lenders of short-term funds will want to see steady growth potential and reliable projected cash flows, demonstrating the business's ability to repay the borrowing commitments. However, even a small change in a company's working capital can have a significant impact on cash flows.

The effective management of working capital plays a vital role in providing both cash flow and finance for the increased holding of stock that might be needed for sales growth. A supply chain manager, for example, may have a primary goal of ensuring that there is no shortage of stocks of raw materials – but carrying excess inventory levels will lead to higher costs and adversely impact profitability. Working capital management influences both the risks and expected returns of a business: too much working capital will mean reduced profitability, while too little will involve an increased risk of disruption to the production processes. This risk–return trade-off underscores the importance of forecasting for working capital requirements. For the lender, the available security will usually be in the form of current assets, such as stock and debtors, and therefore the rate of interest will be higher for operating loans reflecting this relatively weaker security position.

There are a variety of forms in which short-term finance can be extended, including:

- overdrafts;
- short-term loans;
- trade and expense credit;

- bills of exchange;
- promissory notes or commercial paper;
- inventory loan;
- letters of credit;
- short-term eurocurrency advances;
- short-term leasing and instalment credit; and
- factoring and invoice discounting.

We look at some of these in more detail in Chapter 5.

4.3.4 Requirements for purchasing fixed assets

A *fixed asset* may be defined as any tangible asset that is expected to have a useful life of more than one year. Unlike short-term working capital requirements, which need to be financed over periods of less than one year, purchase of an asset that can be used for a number of years will require lending over a longer period.

Longer-term lending may be required for financing the purchase of fixed assets or large capital equipment, large-scale construction and other projects, the expansion of facilities, infrastructure or production capacity, or a change in company control or an acquisition.

The period over which an asset can be used is known as its *useful economic life*. *Depreciation* is the decline in the value of an asset over time as a result of age, wear and tear, obsolescence, and other reasons. The total amount that will be depreciated over the useful economic life of a fixed asset can be calculated as:

Depreciation = Cost of the fixed asset – Residual or salvage value

Various methods are used to allocate the total amount to be depreciated between each accounting period of the asset's useful economic life.

The widely used *straight-line method* of depreciation is based on the principle that each accounting period of the asset's life should be allocated an equal amount of depreciation and it is calculated as

In the straight-line method:

$$D = (C - R) \div N$$

where:

D = Depreciation
C = Cost of the asset
R = Residual value of the asset
N = Useful economic life of the asset (usually in years)

Alternatively, the *reducing balance method* allocates a high annual depreciation charge in the early years of an asset's life and then reduces the annual depreciation charge progressively as the asset ages. A fixed annual depreciation percentage is applied to the written-down value of the asset; thus depreciation is calculated as a percentage of the reducing balance. This method will be more appropriate in the case of assets that yield higher benefits in the early years, the value of which declines as the asset ages.

The lender needs to be aware that the depreciation calculation can be subjective. The lender also needs to be aware of any changes in the method of calculating depreciation and other charges, because these can have a considerable impact on the stated profits of the company.

Efforts targeted at the management of fixed assets include:

- maintaining an up-to-date record of fixed assets purchased and disposed;
- developing clear policies for the budgeting and authorisation of purchases of fixed assets;
- using a fixed asset system with acceptable capitalisation policies;
- using a consistent policy for depreciation charges and asset activity;
- linking an automated capital project tracking system to purchasing and accounts payable systems;
- conducting physical inventories of fixed assets; and
- bar-coding assets.

The forms of long-term finance can be grouped as debt or owed funds and equity-based finance.

- *Debt or owed funds*
  - Subordinated debt, e.g. loans by a company's own directors subordinated to the claims of other lenders
  - Preference shares
  - Convertible stock, i.e. bonds or preference shares that can be converted to ordinary shares
  - Debentures, whereby debt is secured by the assets of the borrower
  - Secured and unsecured medium-term notes
  - Bonds
  - Derivatives that facilitate preferred types of borrowing, e.g. interest rates swaps, currency swaps and interest-only futures
  - Term loans or mortgages
  - Leasing and hire purchase finance
- *Equity-based*
  - Ordinary shares or own funds
  - Retained profits

Some of these forms of finance will be considered in detail in Chapter 5.

4.3.5 Short-term or long-term lending?

Lenders need to exercise their discretion as to whether a particular purpose warrants short-term or long-term finance. Traditionally, short-term lending has been considered appropriate for short-term requirements, such as working capital needs, while long-term loans have been extended for long-term requirements, such as the purchase of fixed assets. However, lending requirements do not always fall into neat categories, with some asset requirements fluctuating with seasonal variations and a large proportion of current assets actually required on a long-term basis, for example the requirement for a minimum amount of stock to prevent shortages adversely impacting on the production process.

Given the 'permanent' nature of a large proportion of current assets, it is generally considered to be prudent to fund a proportion of net current assets with long-term finance. The lender can consider several options in this regard: some permanent current net assets might be financed by long-term credit; all permanent and some fluctuating current net assets might be financed by long-term credit; or all activities might be funded by long-term credit. Alternatively, short-term credit can fund a proportion of fixed assets. While this latter strategy can be highly risky, as evidenced by the difficulties experienced by Northern Rock at the outset of the 2007–08 global financial crisis, it can be highly successful in other situations.

Short-term finance is usually cheaper for the borrower than long-term finance, because the probability of things going wrong in the short term is lower and the lender is able to link lending prices more closely to the cost of borrowing. However, short-term finance might be higher risk, because renewal might not be possible when required and the cost of borrowing might rise in the short term. For the borrower, then, there is a trade-off between the cost and risk of short-term debt.

4.4 CONCLUSION

Lending can be extended to meet a variety of purposes, ranging from the installation of a washing machine in a neighbourhood property to the construction of a dam across the Bio Bio River in Chile. The general rule of thumb has been that long-term assets should be financed by long-term funds and short-term assets by short-term funds, i.e. that the term of lending should match the useful economic life of the asset being financed, but the rigorous application of this rule may not always be appropriate. Conclusions that a lender might draw about the ideal lending package may vary and the lending decision needs always to take into consideration the risk–return trade-off for individual borrowers.

FURTHER READING

DeAngelo, H., DeAngelo, L., and Wruck, K. H. (2002) 'Asset liquidity, debt covenants, and managerial discretion in financial distress: the collapse of LA Gear', *Journal of Financial Economics*, 64, 3–34.

Rouse, N. (2014) *Applied lending techniques*, 3rd edn, Cranbrook: Global Professional Publishing.

REVIEW QUESTIONS

1. Examine some of the purposes for which the following types of lending can be extended: home improvement finance; bridging finance; mortgage finance.
2. Examine the importance of forecasting for working capital requirements.
3. What are the sources of finance for purchasing current and fixed assets?

ACTIVITY

Let us examine the change in BT's working capital ratio between 2005 and 2007.

Table 4.1 Balance sheet

	As at 31 March 2007 (£m)	As at 31 March 2006 (£m)	As at 31 March 2005 (£m)
Cash and short-term investments	1,105	2,399	4,946
Receivables	3,380	2,916	2,423
Inventory	133	124	106
Prepaid expenses	922	686	423
Other current assets	275	292	1,423
Total current assets	**5,815**	**6,417**	**9,321**
Accounts payable	3,717	3,466	2,921
Accrued expenses	519	488	719
Short-term debt	2,203	1,940	4,261
Other current liabilities	3,178	3,586	4,203
Total current liabilities	**9,617**	**9,480**	**12,104**

Source: BT

Table 4.2 Calculating the working capital and current ratios

Ratio	2007	2006	2005
Working capital (Current assets – Current liabilities)	-3,802	-3,063	-2,783
Current ratio (Current assets ÷ Current liabilities)	0.60	0.68	0.77

The results of these calculations raise interesting questions for the lender. The company's working capital ratio is negative throughout the period and that position has worsened over the three years. This will require further investigation and analysis, as well as a comparison with other companies in the same industry.

The example is fascinating because while the results might ordinarily discourage a lender, we know that BT has survived. In fact, the negative picture was explained at the time as resulting from huge spending on bids for licences to run third-generation (3G) mobile phone services at the height of the dot.com frenzy, when inflated prices were being paid for assets in telecoms and information technology.

CASE STUDY LA Gear

LA Gear was a company that manufactured fashion footwear in the 1980s. It designed glamorous workout shoes and casual footwear, and used well-known models to market its products. Its rise was meteoric. In 1988, it was ranked number three on *BusinessWeek*'s list of best small companies. In 1989, it was the top performing company on the New York Stock Exchange (NYSE) and was valued at more than US$1 billion. The company was able to cater successfully to the demands for fashion 'excess' of the 1980s.

The company failed to predict the more austere lifestyle trends of the early 1990s and suffered massive losses. The company was able to fund operating losses by selling its marketable assets. By managing its working capital and selling excess inventories, and despite strict loan covenants and large losses, the company was able to survive for several years largely because of the liquidity of its asset base. That highly liquid asset structure enabled LA Gear to meet its debt obligations despite falling revenues.

Although, in the case of LA Gear, the high degree of asset liquidity could not save it from eventual collapse in 1998, DeAngelo, DeAngelo and Wruck (2002) concluded that such asset liquidity is beneficial and is able to give a company management time in which to implement a successful turnaround. A high degree of asset liquidity – particularly the ability to liquidate working capital – might enable a company to survive financial difficulties for a considerable length of time.

CASE STUDY QUESTIONS

1. What was the primary reason for the decline in LA Gear's sales in the 1990s?
2. Why is it necessary for a lender to have a good knowledge of the industry in which a borrowing company operates?
3. Why was the company able to survive for a number of years despite heavy losses?
4. What is the significance of having asset liquidity in times of financial distress?

Suggested answers can be found in Appendix A.

5

Forms of lending

LEARNING POINTS

This chapter aims to emphasise the importance of matching products with needs, and to assess the features and benefits of a range of secured and unsecured lending products.

Learning areas include:

- overdrafts;
- loans;
- credit cards;
- invoice discounting and factoring;
- hire purchase and leasing; and
- other forms of finance, such as equity finance.

5.1 TYPES OF LENDING

It is important to match lending products to the needs of individual consumers. Borrowers need to be targeted with the right products and the lender needs to be flexible in a number of areas to match borrower requirements, including:

- loan size;
- loan availability;
- repayment terms;
- delivery methods;
- seasonality and time of requirement;
- level of security; and
- form of lending.

Lending can therefore take a range of forms, which forms can vary in nature and complexity. Figure 5.1 illustrates some of the ways in which lending can be classified.

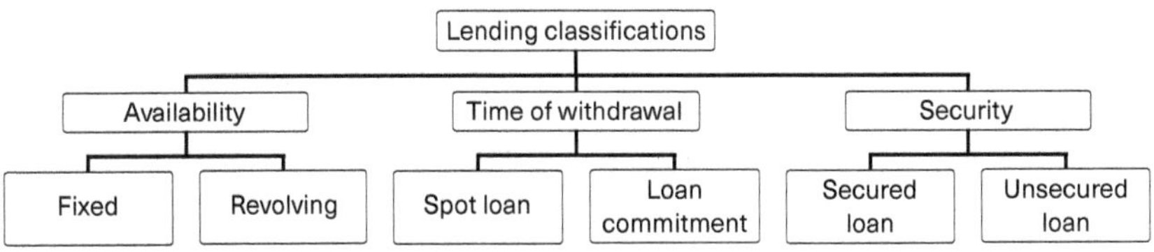

Figure 5.1 Lending classifications

Successful lending requires the successful matching of lending products with consumer needs. The lender therefore needs to be aware of the various forms in which lending can be extended.

- *Fixed and revolving credit* *Fixed credit* is granted for a fixed amount and reduces when loan repayments are made, whereas *revolving credit* retains its credit limit when repayments are made. Revolving credit is a credit line that is available to a borrower on a revolving basis: loan withdrawals and loan repayments can be made as often as required within the stipulated credit limit, and the availability of credit is dependent upon credit repayments.
- *Spot loan and loan commitments* A *spot loan* is withdrawn immediately in full, whereas a *loan commitment* can be withdrawn as and when required in instalments over a stipulated time period.
- *Secured and unsecured loans* A *secured loan* is backed by security such as land or shares, whereas an *unsecured loan* is not backed by any specified security. A secured lender has first claim on the specified security in the event of default or insolvency, whereas an unsecured lender has only a general claim on the assets of the borrower in the event of default or insolvency. Because unsecured loans involve a higher degree of risk to the lender, these loans will attract a higher rate of interest charges and fees to compensate the lender for the higher amount of risk involved.
- *Single-payment loans and instalment credit* A *single-payment loan* is repaid in one lump sum, whereas *instalment credit* is repaid over more than one instalment.

Depending on the size and other relevant features, a loan can be given by a single lender or a syndication of lenders. A *syndicated loan* is that given by a group of lenders rather than a single lender.

These types of lending can be structured to suit the needs of a variety of borrowers, ranging from an individual who requires a small personal loan to a large corporation requiring a syndicated loan that involves the participation of many lenders.

5.2 OVERDRAFTS

An *overdraft* is a revolving loan commitment and can be secured or unsecured. An overdraft is a credit facility whereby a lender allows a borrower to withdraw funds over and above the amount deposited, i.e. to borrow up to or over a specified limit, subject to the payment of interest and other charges.

Overdrafts are usually permitted on a current account. The funds in a current account are repayable on demand and current accounts are therefore also known as on-demand accounts. A *current account* is a transactional or running account in which the account holder is able to deposit funds and withdraw the funds deposited as and when required. In some countries, such as the United States and Canada, it is known as a *checking account* because the funds in the account can be paid out or withdrawn by using cheques (spelled 'checks' in American English). Methods of withdrawing or paying out funds from these accounts include using an electronic debit card via an automatic teller machine (ATM), contactless or app payments. Direct debits and standing orders can be set up on a current account whereby funds can be automatically paid out to designated parties at regular intervals as required.

Overdrafts are granted to a variety of customer types, such as individuals, partnerships and corporations. Although an overdraft is regarded as short-term finance, many customers operate a core overdraft on an almost permanent basis. This is known as hard-core debt and is indicative of a customer in financial difficulties, so a meeting should be arranged to re-establish the customer's requirements. An overdraft generally is a regulated consumer credit agreement for unrestricted-use, running-account credit, as defined under section 10 of the Consumer Credit Act 1974.

5.2.1 Features

- An overdraft is a credit facility generally granted on a running current account.
- It might be an *agreed overdraft* according to prior arrangement or an *unauthorised overdraft* allowed by the lender when the account holder issues a payment that is in excess of the amount of credit available in the account. In *Cuthbert v Robarts Lubbock and Co.* [1909] 2 Ch 226, it was held that when a customer draws a cheque in excess of the amount available in the account, that cheque is deemed to be a request for credit, and if a bank allows the excess payment, the customer is deemed to have borrowed money from the bank. Unauthorised overdrafts are usually subject to higher fees and interest.
- An overdraft is a loan commitment whereby the borrower is able to draw funds as and when required. Thus the borrower can avoid making use of the limit altogether if they prefer.
- It is a revolving credit whereby any repayments restore the limit available for future withdrawals.
- It is generally unsecured unless the lender has entered into a prior arrangement whereby security is obtained. An unsecured overdraft limit will therefore be charged higher interest and fees than a secured facility.
- As indicated in Chapter 3, a credit item in the account is deemed to discharge the earliest of the debit items, according to the rule in *Devaynes v Noble* (1816) 35 ER 781 (known as *Clayton's case*). In that case, there was a substantial debit balance in a partnership's account when one of the partners died, but the firm continued to run the account as a going concern. Eventually, the firm became insolvent, but Clayton, a surviving partner, was unable to recover money due to him from the

deceased partner's estate because it was held that subsequent credits had gone to towards extinguishing the liability of the deceased partner's estate towards the partnership firm. The rule applies the 'first in, first out' approach to determine the effect of payments from an account, i.e. payments are presumed to be appropriated to debts in the order in which the debts are incurred.

- An overdraft is generally repayable on demand unless otherwise specified. However, the lender's right to immediate repayment cannot unduly prejudice the legitimate rights of the borrower (Arora, 2014). In *Rouse v Bradford Banking Co.* [1894] AC 586, it was held that if a bank has agreed to give an overdraft, but intends to withdraw that overdraft, it cannot refuse to honour cheques or other drafts (provided that those cheques or drafts do not exceed the agreed limits of that overdraft) that were drawn and put into circulation before it gave notice to the borrower that the overdraft is to be withdrawn or the limit is to be lowered. Thus the lender is required to give the borrower reasonable notice to make repayment (*Joachimson v Swiss Bank Corporation* [1921] 3 KB 110; *R.A. Cripps and Son Ltd v Wickenden* [1973] 1 WLR 944). The debtor is not in default unless and until they have been given an opportunity to arrange for the 'mechanics of payment' that might be needed to repay the debt; however, the lender is not required to extend any further time to the borrower for raising money if the money is not available for making payment (*Bank of Baroda v Panessar* [1987] Ch 335). As a consequence, where a borrower who has received a demand for the repayment of an overdraft informs the bank that they do not have sufficient funds to repay in full, the lender can treat the customer as being in default and can take immediate legal action.
- Where a lender has the right of setting off an overdrawn account against the credit balance in another account held by the same person, the lender can recover the whole or part of the overdraft without having to make a prior demand for repayment (*Garnett v M'Kewan* (1872) LR 8 Ex 10).

5.2.2 Advantages

- The lender is able to generate income in the form of interest and fees. Because overdrafts are generally unsecured, the lender charges higher interest charges and fees to compensate for the increased level of risk involved. Lenders charge even higher fees and penal rates of interest when limits are overdrawn without prior arrangement (i.e. unauthorised overdrafts).
- The rate of interest will usually be linked to an underlying base rate and will vary with the reference rate. Thus the lender is able to adjust the rate whenever the general rate of interest or the cost of funds undergoes a change. The lender is also able to reserve the right to change the rate even if the reference rate has not changed or to effect a change that is higher than the change in the reference rate.

- In larger overdraft agreements, the lender is able to levy non-utilisation fees on the amounts of the facility not being used.
- The lender is able to verify the borrower's creditworthiness at periodic intervals to ensure that it has not deteriorated. Overdrafts are generally renewable annually, and there is an opportunity to review the conduct of the account at periodic intervals and to take timely action. The onus is on providers to monitor, assess and take action, abiding by the principle set out in the FCA's Banking Conduct of Business sourcebook (BCOBS) that they 'must pay due regard to the interests of ... customers and treat them fairly'.
- Unless there is a prior arrangement whereby the overdraft has been granted for a fixed period, the lender can demand repayment at any time. Overdrafts are generally repayable on demand and the lender retains the right to call up the overdraft subject to giving a reasonable time to the borrower to repay the debt.
- The lender is able to generate high volumes of lending in the form of overdrafts because they are an extremely popular form of borrowing. The reasons include their ease of use and flexibility, the ease and speed with which they can be accessed, and because interest is usually payable only on the outstanding balances and not on the entire limit.

5.2.3 Disadvantages

- Because overdrafts are generally unsecured, there is a higher risk of non-recovery of dues in the event of credit default, i.e. the loss in the event of default may be higher.
- Interest is generally payable only on the amount drawn by the borrower.
- Being a credit commitment, the lender will find it difficult to predict its usage and income flow. Unexpected withdrawals can be a source of increased liquidity risk and may make liquidity management more difficult for the lender.

5.3 LOANS

A *loan* is usually made available on a fixed (rather than revolving) and spot (rather than commitment) basis, and can be secured or unsecured. A loan falls within the definition under section 11 of the Consumer Credit Act 1974 of 'a regulated consumer credit agreement for restricted or unrestricted use fixed sum credit'.

5.3.1 Features

Loans are offered for specified amounts for specified periods. The lender cannot seek repayment prior to expiry of the period unless there has been some default, e.g. in payment of periodic interest. Similarly, the borrower will be generally unable to repay in full in advance of the expiry date without incurring early redemption penalties. In the absence of a specified period, the lender will need to give the borrower a notice of repayment specifying a reasonable period for paying back the loan (*Buckingham and Co. v London and Midland Bank* (1895) 12 TLR 70). Where a loan is advanced for a specified purpose and the loan agreement does not deal with repayment, the lender cannot withdraw the loan before the purpose is achieved (*Williams and Glyn's Bank Ltd v Barnes* [1981] Com LR 205). It is therefore important that lenders specify a repayment period in such a way that it does not give rise to any ambiguity. Loans can made available in the short term for periods of a year or less, or for longer terms ranging up to 25 years. Short-term loans can be made to fund short-term purchases, such as televisions and washing machines, while long-term loans, such as mortgages, can fund home purchases and corporate projects.

5.3.2 Advantages

- The lender is able to generate income in the form of interest and fees. In addition to interest, the lender is able to charge an initial arrangement or commitment fee and other fees, and also to obtain some protection against unanticipated loan closures in the form of early redemption fees.
- Interest is paid on the full amount of the outstanding loan and the lender is not faced with a situation in which an agreed credit facility is unutilised or underutilised.
- Because loans are generally secured against a fixed charge on the asset being financed, the risk is lower and lenders are able to compete for business by charging competitive rates of interest.
- Lenders are able to reduce risk even further by requiring the borrower to take out insurance, such as key person cover (a type of life insurance policy on the life of a key employee).
- The lender is able to arrange for legally binding covenants before agreeing to a loan, for example requiring the borrower to keep the overall gearing or debt below a certain level. If the covenants (conditions) are breached, the bank will be entitled to immediate repayment.
- The lender is able to lend a fixed sum of money for a definite period, and is therefore able to anticipate earnings and make funding arrangements for a definite period.
- The loan will be generally repaid in accordance with the stipulated repayment programme and the borrower will be unable to access that portion of a loan which has been repaid unless they apply for a new loan.
- The lender is able to generate high volumes of lending in the form of loans, because these are an extremely popular form of borrowing. The reasons include the following.
  - The term of a loan can be matched to the life of any asset to be purchased.
  - Loan repayments can be tailored to match the cash flow of the project.

- Interest rate on loans can be fixed, allowing borrowers to forecast interest costs with a greater degree of certainty.

5.3.3 Disadvantages

- Some lending practices, such as the requirement to take out payment protection insurance (PPI), have given rise to negative publicity.
- There is always a risk that the borrower might fail to make repayments in accordance with the agreed programme or breach any of the covenants and that the security available might not cover the recovery costs.
- The security obtained might prove to be defective for legal and other reasons, and hence be unavailable to the lender.
- Some loan products carry particularly high risk. Among mortgages, the following products have been identified as higher-risk products and areas:
  - equity release products, whereby the equity in an asset (most commonly, a home) is released to the borrower(s) subject to repayment being made from the sale of the property on their death;
  - the subprime sector, in which loans are extended to borrowers with poor credit histories;
  - interest-only products, where no provision has been made for the repayment of the principal; and
  - self-certification products, though under FCA rules lenders must verify the claims made by borrowers in relation to their income and sources of repayment.

These higher-risk products are characterised by a combination of product complexity, potential customer vulnerability and lock-ins. Lenders are required to be particularly careful to ensure that they clearly explain the risks and features of products to customers, and that customers have obtained appropriate advice.

5.4 CREDIT CARDS

A *credit card* is a revolving loan commitment that is usually unsecured.

5.4.1 Features

Some of the main features of a credit card are as follows.

- A credit card is a plastic card that can be identified by a magnetic strip and/or chip issued by a lending institution, authorising the holder to buy goods and services on credit up to a specified limit.
- A credit card involves a 'debtor–creditor–supplier' agreement, i.e. there are at least three parties to credit card lending: the card issuer; the card holder; and the supplier, who accepts the card in payment for goods and services supplied.

- Under a four-party structure, the independent merchant acquirer is added to this framework. A *merchant acquirer* is an intermediary that recruits new suppliers willing to accept the issuer's card. Under this arrangement, the merchant acquirer accepts payment for the products or services on behalf of the merchant, and undertakes to pay the supplier and the card issuer.
- A credit card is issued for a specified credit limit.
- A period of interest-free credit is usually specified, beyond which interest will become payable at a specified rate.
- Subject to prior arrangements, the borrower will have the option of either paying off the entire credit balance within the interest-free credit period or paying a minimum required amount of the debt and paying interest on the remaining amount at the specified rate.
- There is usually a sub-limit for cash withdrawals and interest is payable from date of any such withdrawal.
- A credit card provides revolving credit, which allows card holders to make purchases and repayments as often as required within the stipulated credit limit.
- Lenders' income from credit cards arises from three sources:
  - any arrangement fee charged;
  - the interest on balances outstanding beyond the interest-free period; and
  - fees paid by merchants who supply the goods paid for by credit cards.
- There are more than 300 brands of credit card in the UK and lenders offer a variety of incentives.
  - *Balance transfer cards* offer special interest rates for a specified balance-transfer period or for the life of the balance amount transferred from another card provider. Other variations are an initially low rate for purchases, and a combination of purchases and balance transfers.
  - *Loyalty reward cards* offer rewards, such as air miles, for card usage.
  - *Cashback cards* offer cashback on purchases, usually as a fixed percentage of amount spent.
  - *Ethical cards* undertake to donate a percentage of the card spend to charity.

5.4.2 Advantages

- Lenders are able to charge high rates of interest and fees, and these rates do not seem to deter borrowers.
- Credit cards have facilitated quick and easy payments, and their use has therefore skyrocketed, increasing lenders' earnings.
- Credit cards appeal both to borrowers who wish to avoid or minimise interest payments by making early settlement on debts, as well as to those who wish to take advantage of the maximum credit periods on offer.

- Lenders receive commission from merchant suppliers on every credit card transaction.
- There is scope for increased automation and reduced paperwork.

5.4.3 Disadvantages

- Not all merchants, particularly internationally, accept credit cards, although the number of those that do not is decreasing.
- Increased automation has resulted in some loss of contact with the borrower, leading to less knowledge of the customer and an increase in moral hazard (see Chapter 10).
- High charges and hidden costs have attracted adverse publicity.
- While lenders are able to earn high interest when repayments are limited to the small amount specified as the minimum requirement each month, this has led to long-term indebtedness and has increased costs for borrowers in the form of compounded interest, resulting in further adverse publicity.
- There is also a negative public perception that credit cards involve a hidden cost, in that merchants who accept credit cards must build the cost of transaction fees into their prices, thereby increasing the cost for all purchasers, including customers using cash and other forms of payment.
- As discussed in Chapter 2, the issuer of a credit card becomes jointly and severally liable for misrepresented or defective goods sold by a supplier under of the principle of 'connected lender liability' established by section 75 of the Consumer Credit Act 1974 (FOS, 2003).

5.5 INVOICE DISCOUNTING

Invoice discounting is usually made available on a revolving basis as a line of commitment and is secured by an assignment of book debts. Subject to an overall credit limit, submission of new bills for discounting will increase the outstandings, while payment of invoices on due dates will reduce the outstandings.

Invoice discounting is a form of secured lending, i.e. *asset-based lending* (ABL) or *debtor finance*. These are forms of lending that provide an advance against outstanding invoices or accounts receivable. Invoice discounters (and factors) take an assignment of their client's book debts, thereby assuming legal title to the debt and its proceeds. Additionally, collections are received into blocked accounts. The ruling in *Re Brumark Investments Ltd* [2001] UKPC 28 regarding the proper characterisation of security interest over a company's assets (see Chapter 10) is therefore unlikely to affect the security held by invoice discounters and factors.

Sometimes, in addition to bills receivable, the lender might require further security in the form of personal guarantee or stocks, or machinery or property. In such cases, the rate of interest will be lower to reflect the reduced level of risk.

5.5.1 Features

An *invoice*, or *bill*, is a document prepared, or 'drawn up', by the *drawer* (a seller of goods or services) and submitted to the *drawee* (the buyer) for payment. Invoices are assets representing underlying trade transactions. An invoice furnishes the details, such as date, seller, buyer, quantities, prices, freight and credit terms, of a transaction. The invoice represents money receivable by the seller from the buyer at a future date, which is dependent upon the credit terms of the transaction.

While it might be necessary to offer a period of credit to the buyer to secure its order, this delays the realisation of the proceeds of the sale. The seller might therefore wish to offer the invoice to a lender as security for a loan. Alternatively, the seller might be willing to accept a reduced amount of the invoice from the lender in exchange for immediate receipt of cash. That proportion of the invoice which remains unpaid is known as the *discount*. The discount represents the difference between the face value of the invoice and the reduced, but immediate, amount advanced by the lender.

EXAMPLE

A seller might discount an invoice for £1,000 payable after three months with a lender for £980. This means the seller will receive an immediate cash amount of £980 and the lender will receive the full amount of £1,000 after three months – the £20 difference being the discount, or return for the lender, over the loan period of three months.

In this case, the effective interest rate works out to be 8 per cent annually, i.e. the rate of interest is 2 per cent over the three months and hence 8 per cent over a year.

Sellers offer invoices at a discount because of their need for cash flow to ensure the continued conduct of business. Thus invoice discounting will have three parties to the transaction:

- the seller (drawer), who originates the invoice;
- the buyer (drawee or acceptor), who has an obligation to pay the invoice at a future date; and
- the lender (discounter).

Some other characteristics of this type of finance are as follows.

- Lenders will usually retain a margin and extend advances from 70 per cent of the debtors' ledger value up to 85–90 per cent. Higher levels of finance will be available where additional security is on offer.
- Lenders are usually required to provide short-term finance of between 30 and 90 days, depending on the period of credit extended by businesses to secure orders. On average, invoices take up to 60 days to be paid. Invoice discounting provides immediate cash and facilitates cash flow.
- While borrowers are able to raise finance on debts, they continue to be responsible for chasing the debts, and hence charges are usually lower

than in forms of financing such as factoring, in which the factor company takes on the task of following up on bill payments.

5.5.2 Advantages

- Invoice discounting can be undertaken by a bank directly, rather than through a subsidiary, as might have to be the case in relation to factoring and some other forms of finance.
- Lending is made available only for genuine trade transactions and thus is secured.
- Recourse to the customer is available in the event of non-payment of the bill, and the lending is therefore relatively safe and low risk.
- Lenders are able to achieve increased volumes of this type of lending, because it is popular among customers. This is because:
  - it improves cash flow by making cash immediately available;
  - charges are comparatively low because the lending is secured; and
  - the borrowers are able to choose the bills that they might wish to discount.
- When lenders are short of liquidity themselves, these discounted invoices held in their books can be rediscounted with other financial institutions to obtain cash.

5.5.3 Disadvantages

- There is a risk of non-payment of the invoices on the due dates.
- The financial soundness of the acceptor needs to be examined in addition to the soundness of the drawers of the invoice.
- It will not be cost-effective to discount bills for small amounts.
- Some bills – particularly those drawn and accepted by smaller or private companies – are not resaleable.

5.6 FACTORING

Factoring, like invoice discounting, is usually made available on a revolving basis as a line of commitment and is secured by an assignment of book debts.

5.6.1 Features

In its simplest form, the factor company merely takes over the administration of the sale ledger as a form of service to a business. Factoring, as a form of lending, takes place when a factoring company or lender provides finance to the seller of goods by purchasing or taking over title to the accounts receivable of a business. Factoring is a form of debtor finance or accounts receivable financing, like invoice discounting, but with some added features.

In addition to benefiting from the receipt of immediate cash from the factor or lender, the seller also passes on the task of debt collection to the factor company. The factor or lender takes over title to the debts, retains a fee and passes on the remaining value of the invoice collected to the business.

Like invoice discounting, there are usually three parties involved in factoring:

- the seller (drawer), who originates the invoice;
- the buyer (drawee or acceptor), who has an obligation to pay the invoice at a future date; and
- the lender (factor).

Factoring can be with recourse or without recourse. In the case of *without-recourse factoring*, the receivables are bought by the factor without recourse to the seller, which means that if any of the debts are not paid, the factor will have to bear the loss and will not have recourse to the seller. In the case of *recourse factoring*, the factor is able to have recourse to the seller if payment of the factored invoices is not received within a certain specified period. The lender will charge a higher fee for non-recourse factoring because the risk of loss resulting from non-payment is much higher.

5.6.2 Advantages

- Factoring is popular with many businesses, because it improves cash flow and allows the business to focus its attention on its core operations rather than spending time and resources on debt collection.
- The factor or lender is able to earn income in the form of fees from the accounting services offered and from factoring debts due. Many businesses are interested in this form of finance because they benefit from the acceleration of cash flow, obtaining cash from the factor equal to the face value of the sold accounts receivable *less* the factor's fee. Non-recourse factoring yields an even higher level of income.
- The factor is able to earn fees from ancillary business, such as providing advice on trading terms in export markets, handling correspondence in the language of the overseas debtor, providing assistance with the resolution of disputes, offering protection against exchange risk, etc.
- The factor is able to build up a detailed database of information about the creditworthiness of companies with which its clients have dealings. This will help it to assess the creditworthiness of new and existing clients, and also serve as a source of income should it be used to advise clients about the potential creditworthiness of their trading partners.
- Factoring is considered off-balance-sheet financing, in that it is not a form of debt or a form of equity. This enables a factor to extend this form of finance to a borrower even in circumstances in which it would be inappropriate to extend traditional bank and equity financing. In the case of some new or undercapitalised companies, it might be the only form of finance that can be extended.

5.6.3 Disadvantages

- Factoring can create an unfavourable image of the lender as an unsympathetic debt collector, in contrast with the more favourable image of the seller as a sympathetic trade partner. Factoring can discourage some potential buyers, who would prefer to deal with the seller directly rather than via a factor, thus harming the financial standing of the seller.
- Factoring may impose constraints on the way in which a seller might like to do business. Factors may want to pre-approve potential buyers, causing delays in trade transactions.
- Sellers might also be put off by the high cost of factoring, which are usually higher than those of overdrafts. Smaller companies may even find the charges prohibitive.
- Factoring is perceived to be inflexible. Sellers might be put off by the fact that they cannot choose which invoices to sell to the factor and will have to pay factoring charges for sound debts, while remaining exposed to debts that are less safe.
- Factors might be able to take only customers who sell on credit for fairly large amounts at a time. It might not be viable to take on smaller transactions.
- Non-recourse factoring can give rise to the risk of bad debts and losses.

5.7 HIRE PURCHASE

As noted in Chapter 4, fixed assets have a useful economic life spread over a number of years and it will be appropriate to spread the repayment of loans over the period of the life of the asset for which the lending is undertaken. The most common forms of medium-term finance for investment in capital assets are *hire purchase* and leasing.

Hire purchase and leasing are usually made available on a fixed and spot basis, and are secured by the asset that is required to be purchased with the finance. Those assets commonly include:

- plant and machinery;
- business cars and other vehicles;
- office equipment and tools; and
- computer hardware and software.

5.7.1 Features

Under a hire purchase agreement, the borrower or hirer or user chooses the equipment required and the lender buys it on their behalf. The user is able to avoid the immediate cash outflow required to purchase the asset, instead paying for the cost of the asset in instalments over the period of the hire purchase. The main difference between hire purchase and leasing is that, under hire purchase agreements, ownership will ultimately pass to the user of the asset after all of the payments have been made. Consequently, hire purchase is more similar to a straight loan, with the user of the asset gaining the benefit of capital allowances. Capital allowances can be a significant tax incentive for businesses.

The difference between hire purchase and a straight loan, however, is that, under hire purchase, the repayment instalments are equated as in a mortgage. As a consequence, the timings of the interest payments, as well as repayments of the principal, will differ from those on a straight loan.

The user of the asset is normally responsible for its maintenance.

5.7.2 Advantages

- The lender is able to generate income in the form of fees.
- Interest is paid on the full amount of the initial loan, even though the balance outstanding will decline over its term. Because of the way in which interest is calculated, the true interest is roughly double that of the quoted rate (Pike and Neale, 2006).
- Because loans are secured against a fixed charge on the asset being financed, the risk is comparatively low. In addition, lenders will require the hirer to put down a deposit for hire purchase, or to make one or more payments in advance under a lease. It may be possible for the business to 'trade in' other assets that they own as a means of raising the deposit.
- Lenders are able to reduce risk even farther by requiring the borrower to take out insurance to cover the asset.
- In most cases, the payments are fixed throughout the period of the hire purchase or lease agreement, and the lender is therefore able to anticipate earnings and make funding arrangements for a definite period.
- The lender is able to match the repayments with the expected revenue and profits generated by the use of the asset.
- Hire purchase offers both the lender and the borrower the opportunity for tax trading. If the business is profitable, it can claim its own capital allowances through hire purchase or outright purchase rather than opt for leasing.

5.7.3 Disadvantages

- If the lender has not made appropriate arrangements to fund the finance over the fixed-rate period, any increase in interest rates might lead to a rise in funding cost and hence to potential losses.
- Many businesses cannot afford the costs of hire purchase, which is a relatively expensive form of financing fixed assets.
- Because many manufacturers of fixed and other assets offer hire purchase facilities at the time of purchase, the opportunities for this type of lending activity are decreasing.

5.8 LEASING

A *lease* is defined as a rental agreement between the owner of an asset (the *lessor*) and the user of the asset (the *lessee*). It is based on the realisation that it is the use, rather than the ownership, of assets that generates revenue. The lessee has the right to use the asset during the term of the lease and also the obligation to make specified payments over that term. The lessor or the lender who leases out the asset has the right to receive payments during the lease term and to the residual value of the asset after that term has expired.

5.8.1 Features

As with hire purchase, the lessee is able to avoid immediate cash outflow for purchase of the asset, the cost of the asset being paid for in instalments over the period of the lease. The main difference from hire purchase is that, under leasing, the ownership never passes to the user of the asset. Ownership continues to remain with the lessor at all times, and the lessor claims the capital allowances and passes some of the benefit on to the lessee by way of reduced rental charges. The lessee is able to deduct the full cost of lease rentals from taxable income, as a trading expense.

There are a variety of types of leasing arrangement, including the following.

- An *operating lease* is a short-term agreement for renting an asset. The agreement is cancellable during the contract period and the asset is returned to the lessor well before the expiry of its life. Such leases are entered into mainly for convenience and to avoid the risk of obsolescence in respect of assets such as computers, which tend to become outdated very quickly. Maintenance of the asset is the responsibility of the lessor.
- A *finance lease* is a long-term, non-cancellable agreement for renting an asset for virtually its full economic life. The asset is usually selected by the lessee and is bought by the lessor for the specific purpose of leasing it out to the lessee only. The lessee is usually responsible for maintaining and insuring the asset.

In fact, a finance lease is nothing more than a way of financing the purchase of an asset. Under the UK's Statements of Standard Accounting Practice (SSAP), a 'lease' is defined as a facility that 'transfers substantially all the risks and rewards of ownership to the lessee' (SSAP 21). Until a few years ago, leasing was off-balance-sheet financing, which means that gearing ratios and return on investment (ROI) ratios would appear to be better than they actually were. However, with the introduction of SSAP 21, all financial leases were required to be capitalised and the present value of lease rentals payable to be shown as a liability on a company's balance sheet. It is therefore no longer accurate to say that leasing improves gearing and other ratios. Accounting standards such as SSAP 21 require that appropriate disclosure is made and that the substance of the transactions is transparent. Indeed, this is a dynamic area with which lenders are advised to keep up to date: in 2019, the International Financial Reporting Standards (IFRS) will introduce a new standard on leases (IFRS 16).

5.8.2 Advantages

- Under leasing agreements, the lender or lessor is able to generate income in the form of lease rentals and fees.
- Because the lender retains ownership of the asset at all times, the risk is comparatively low. In addition, lenders will require the lessee to make one or more payments in advance under a lease. Because the lessor retains legal title to the assets, the credit assessment is usually less rigorous, and finance can be released fairly quickly and with fewer restrictions than other forms of finance such as loans and debentures.
- Lenders are able to reduce risk even farther by requiring the borrower to take out insurance, to cover the asset.
- In most cases, the payments are fixed throughout the lease agreement, and the lender is therefore able to anticipate earnings and make funding arrangements for a definite period.
- The lender is able to match the repayments with the expected revenue and profits generated by the use of the asset. There is a lot of flexibility in structuring the lease rentals. Depending on the cash flow needs of the lessee, the lease payments can be *front-ended* (i.e. larger payments in the beginning of the lease period) or *back-ended* (i.e. increasing payments over the lease period).
- Leasing offers both the lender and the borrower the opportunity for tax trading, particularly if the lessee is not in a tax-paying position or pays corporation tax at the small companies' rate. One of the important incentives for investment in assets is the capital allowance, which is deducted from a firm's taxable income; however, if the lessee is tax-exhausted (i.e. there is no further scope for deducting anything from taxable income), capital allowance has to be carried forward, deferring the advantage of the tax deduction and reducing the present value of the benefit. Even if the lessor is not tax-exhausted, differences in tax status can offer scope for tax trading: the lessor can pass on a part of the tax benefit to the lessee through reduced lease rentals.

5.8.3 Disadvantages

- If the lender has not made appropriate arrangements to fund the finance over the fixed-rate period, any increase in interest rates might lead to a rise in funding costs, leading to potential losses.
- Many borrowers – particularly those who are generating healthy profits – are concerned that the asset does not become the outright property of lessee and that they will be unable to use the capital allowances, as in the case of hire purchase or outright purchase.

- Disposal of assets at the end of the leasing period may be difficult if the lessee does not want to continue use.
- Because many manufacturers of fixed and other assets offer leasing facilities at the time of purchase, the opportunities for this type of lending activity are decreasing.
- Many businesses are unfamiliar with this form of finance.

5.9 OTHER FORMS OF PROVIDING FINANCE

5.9.1 Equity finance

Participating in the equity of a company can be an alternative to lending as a way of providing finance. *Equity* is the ordinary share capital of a company. *Equity finance* is the provision of finance in the form of equity or ordinary share capital in a company. Equity finance is share capital invested in a business for the medium-to-long term in return for a share of the ownership and an element of control of the business. Equity finance is also known as *venture capital* or *risk capital*, indicating the high risk of providing this form of capital to new business ventures (see Chapter 4). The provider of such finance will be a part-owner, rather than a lender, and will have a right to participate in the future profits of the business. Banks, private equity firms and business angels are known to provide equity finance to upcoming business ventures, and often also share in the management and control of the business.

Advantages

- Lenders can widen the range of their product offering by making funds available in the form of equity finance.
- There is the potential for high returns. Equity finance can be used for high-growth businesses that are eventually floated on the stock market or sold for a high price, resulting in rich rewards for the equity investors.
- Equity finance provides an alternative source of funding, especially where other forms, such as bank loans, cannot be made available. In certain circumstances, equity finance might be more appropriate than other forms of finance, for example a borrower with a high level of debt who does not qualify for additional lending, or a business that does not have enough cash to pay loan interest because available cash needs to be allocated to its core activities or to fund growth.
- As part-owners, equity investors have a vested interest in the profitability and growth of the business, because they will be better able to realise their investment through floating on the stock market or sale if the business is doing well. In addition to funds, they consequently have an incentive to bring with them other valuable resources, such as skills, contacts and experience, and can assist with strategy and key decision-making. The business can also benefit from the discipline provided by the close scrutiny and evaluation of potential investors.

Disadvantages

- The funding is committed to the business and its projects, and cannot be recalled, as can be a loan.
- Arranging equity finance is demanding and time-consuming. The business will be required to submit comprehensive information, which will need to be scrutinised. Ongoing management time will need to be set aside to study the information for monitoring purposes.
- Equity finance is high risk. Shareholders rank much lower than creditors in the order of liquidation and the probability of losing the investment is high. It is because equity investors share in the risks the business faces that equity finance is often referred to as risk capital.
- No interest is receivable, as it is from loans. Unlike lenders, equity investors do not normally have rights to interest or to be repaid at a particular date. Their return is usually in the form of dividend payments, which depend on the growth and profitability of the business. Dividends need not be paid unless the business is earning profits.
- There might be long delays before any return is available on the money invested.
- There can be legal and regulatory issues to comply with when arranging finance.
- Equity investors may find small companies to be unviable. As long ago as 1979, the Committee to Review the Functioning of the Financial Institutions pointed out that small businesses find it difficult to raise venture capital (Wilson, 1979). If a firm's management team is largely restricted to family members, it may find it more difficult to attract equity finance because of the potential difficulties faced by external shareholders in monitoring and controlling the activities of the owner-managers.
- Many companies are reluctant to obtain equity finance because:
  - they will be subject to varying degrees of influence over the management of their business and making of major decisions; and
  - their share in the business will be diluted by the introduction of additional equity.

5.9.2 Enterprise Finance Guarantee

Some small or medium-sized enterprises (SMEs) may be unable to obtain conventional loans because they do not have assets to offer as security. The British Business Bank, owned by the UK government and independently managed, works with more than 80 partners, such as banks, leasing companies, venture capital funds and web-based platforms, to facilitate lending to smaller businesses. Through the Enterprise Finance Guarantee (EFG), the British Business Bank provides security to lenders by guaranteeing 75 per cent of any losses that the lender may suffer if the borrower subsequently defaults. This enables lenders to provide more finance for smaller businesses.

Support under the EFG extends to a range of business finance products, such as term loans, revolving facilities (including overdrafts), invoice finance facilities and asset finance facilities.

To be eligible for support via the EFG, the small business must:

- be UK based, with turnover of no more than £41 million per annum
- operate within an eligible industrial sector (a small number of industrial sectors are not eligible for support)
- have a sound borrowing proposal and robust business plan, but inadequate security to meet a lender's normal requirements
- be able to confirm that they have not received other public support of state aid beyond €200,000 equivalent over the previous three years

(British Business Bank, undated)

The EFG covers loans to fund the future growth or expansion of a business, with amounts ranging from £1,000 to £1.2 million. Finance terms are from three months up to ten years for term loans and asset finance, and up to three years for revolving facilities and invoice finance.

Despite the guarantee under the scheme, some banks (such as RBS) have admitted that a number of small business borrowers were led to believe that it was they who would be backed in the event of default rather than the bank (Riding and Haines, 2001). In many cases, banks have not been repaid more than 25 per cent of the loans from businesses in default, i.e. the maximum that customers were allegedly led to believe they would have to pay back.

While there is continuing debate as to whether or not government intervention in the credit market is warranted, research has shown that loan guarantees seem to make positive contributions. Loans that support the expansion of small enterprises may convey significant benefits to the borrowing firms and, through job creation and retention, to the rest of society (Riding and Haines, 2001).

5.10 CONCLUSION

The lender needs to consider a range of factors, such as loan size, loan availability, repayment terms, delivery methods, time of requirement and type of security, if it is to achieve the best match of borrower requirements to form of lending. In addition to traditional forms of lending such as overdrafts, loans, credit cards, invoice discounting, factoring, hire purchase and leasing, new and hybrid forms are continuously evolving in response to developments in the legal, accounting and other areas.

For many years, countries developed their own accounting and other standards, but standards are becoming increasingly global. For example, IFRS 9, IFRS 15 and IFRS 16 (collectively, the 'new standards') to be published by the International Accounting Standards Board (IASB) in 2018–19 have implications that extend far beyond the accounting function, being likely to affect every aspect of a business –from financial reporting to compliance with debt covenants. Lenders need to keep abreast of developments to make use of new opportunities as they arise, as well as to ensure that old forms of lending continue to be compliant with current requirements.

FURTHER READING

Financial Ombudsman Service (FOS) (2003) 'Credit cards: equal liability under section 75 of the Consumer Credit Act 1974', *Ombudsman News*, available at www.financial-ombudsman.org.uk/publications/ombudsman-news/31/creditcards-31.htm

Sathye, M., Bartle, J., Vincent, M., and Boffey, R. (2003) *Credit analysis and lending management*, Chichester: John Wiley & Sons.

Saxby, S. (2006) 'Court of Appeal increases UK consumer protection for overseas credit purchases', *Computer Law and Security Report*, 22, 181–182.

REVIEW QUESTIONS

1. How are overdrafts different from loans? Examine the distinguishing features.
2. Examine the benefits of invoice discounting and factoring as forms of debtor finance.
3. Distinguish between hire purchase and leasing.
4. Distinguish between debt finance and equity finance. When might equity finance be appropriate?
5. Examine the main features of the ELG scheme administered by the British Business Bank.

ACTIVITIES

1. Visit the website of the Financial Ombudsman Service (FOS) at www.financial-ombudsman.org.uk/publications/ombudsman-news/31/creditcards-31.htm, and read some of the complaints received and settled in relation to credit cards under the principle of 'connected lender liability'.
2. Visit the British Business Bank at http://british-business-bank.co.uk/ourpartners/supporting-business-loans-enterprise-finance-guarantee/ and read the guide *Understanding the Enterprise Finance Guarantee*, which explains the scheme in greater detail for lenders.

CASE STUDY Mr J's gold watch

Consider the following case study:

While on holiday in Turkey, Mr J bought a gold watch. He said he was told it was an expensive designer brand and he paid £1,000 for it, using his credit card.

However, shortly after he returned home, the watch stopped working. Mr J eventually got the watch repaired at a cost of £65. However, the repairer told him it was a fake and worth very much less than he had paid for it. Mr J then asked his bank to refund the difference between the amount he paid for the watch and the amount the repairer said it was worth.

> When the bank refused to meet his claim, Mr J came to us. He said he had been told that under section 75 [of the Consumer Credit Act 1974] he was entitled to a refund from his credit card company.
>
> [...]
>
> There was no evidence to support Mr J's allegation of misrepresentation on the part of the retailer in Turkey. None of the documents he was given when he bought the watch described it as a designer-make. The UK repairer confirmed that the watch was made of 18 carat gold and it was specified as such in the sales documents. So there did not appear to have been any breach of contract. Even if the transaction had happened in the UK, section 75 would not have applied. However, the firm agreed to meet the cost of the repair.
>
> (*Ombudsman News* 31, FOS 2003)

CASE STUDY QUESTIONS

1. What is the principle dealt with by section 75 of the Consumer Credit Act 1974?
2. What was Mr J's allegation?
3. Was Mr J's claim, as recounted by the FOS, valid?
4. Was the claim rejected because the transaction had taken place in Turkey?

Suggested answers can be found in Appendix A.

6

The lending cycle – the credit-granting process

LEARNING POINTS

This chapter examines the life cycle of a lending facility and the credit-granting process.

Learning areas include:

- the lending cycle;
- loan application;
- loan documentation; and
- further advances.

6.1 THE LENDING CYCLE

The word 'cycle' is derived from the Greek *kyklos*, meaning 'circle' or 'wheel', indicating a succession or recurring sequence of events. Thus 'lending cycle' refers to a succession of events that needs to be seen in its entirety to be understood: the life-cycle of the loan from granting to termination through either repayment or recovery (see Figure 6.1).

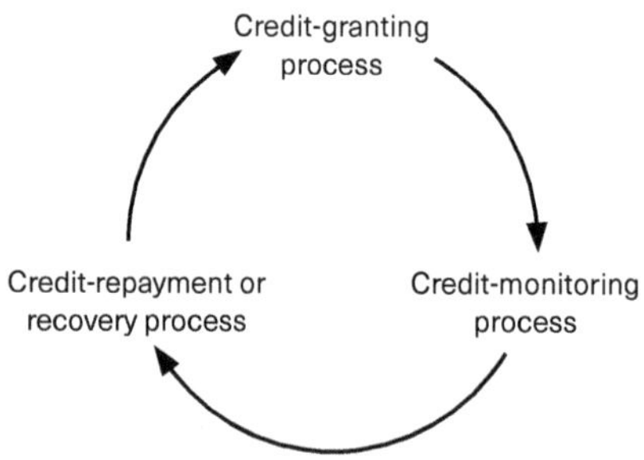

Figure 6.1 The brief lending cycle

In its briefest form, the lending cycle consists of:

1. the credit-granting process;
2. the credit-monitoring process; and
3. the credit-repayment or recovery process.

The first of these stages, the credit-granting process, is discussed in this chapter; the second and third stages are covered in Chapter 10.

6.1.1 The credit-granting process and principles

Lenders, as well as brokers, market loan services with a view to generating the interest of loan prospects and eventually converting that interest into loan applications. The credit-granting process is the first stage in the lending cycle and it consists, in turn, of a series of stages, as follows.

1. Lead generation (at which stage the lender attempts to attract the interest of potential borrowers)
2. Loan application (submitted by entities wishing to borrow)
3. Loan evaluation (of these applications by lenders)
4. Loan decision (approval or rejection)

These stages comprise the loan-origination process, or credit-granting process, whereby loans are granted to interested applicants whom lenders consider to be creditworthy (see Figure 6.2).

Figure 6.2 The credit-granting process

As we saw in Chapter 1, the key principles relating to the credit-granting process are that a lender should:

- be operating within a framework of sound, well-defined credit-granting criteria;
- establish overall credit limits for individual borrowers, for groups of connected borrowers and for types of exposure, e.g. for a particular industry;
- establish guidelines for approving new credit limits, renewing or amending existing credit limits, and mitigating risk and ensuring fairness.
- have a thorough understanding of the loan proposal, including of the borrower, of the purpose, of the structure of the credit, and of the source of repayment;

Bank lenders are also expected to consider the current state of the economy and expected changes to the economy over the term of the loan (García-Céspedes and Moreno, 2017).

6.1.2 Primary security – the borrower

For the lender, the *primary security* for a loan is the borrower's integrity and intention to repay the loan. A loan given purely against the primary security of the borrower, without any security in the form of assets, is a *clean* or *unsecured loan*. A loan that is additionally secured by assets such as shares or property (referred to simply as *security* or *collateral*) is a *secured loan*. Security is considered to be an insulation against default. Any tendency among borrowers to default wilfully, known as *moral hazard*, is discouraged by the presence of adequate security. However, it will not be good lending practice to grant a loan based purely on the strength of security without taking into account the borrower's integrity, intentionality and ability to repay the amounts borrowed.

In this chapter, we deal with primary security, i.e. the borrower's creditworthiness, while Chapters 8 and 9 deal with various aspects of security in the form of assets.

6.2 THE LOAN APPLICATION AND SUPPORTING INFORMATION

6.2.1 The loan application

Other than for some forms of lending such as overdrafts, which credit facilities lenders are able to offer without any formal application, the prospective borrower is generally required to submit an application on a prescribed form. Application forms are carefully drawn up, with the assistance of legal teams, so that they comply with legal and regulatory requirements. While many application forms are standardised, the format of the application forms will differ depending upon the nature of the credit facility sought. Applicants are required to collect the relevant form from a branch office or download it from the Internet and submit the completed form to the lender, along with supporting documentation to prove their identity and financial status.

6.2.2 Supporting information

To originate good-quality loans, lenders need to collect relevant and timely information about the prospective borrower, and about the activity for which the loan is sought. Information can be either hard or soft.

- *Hard* information is the information available from financial statements and other published sources.
- *Soft* information is the information gained about a borrower through ongoing relationships.

Soft information will be particularly important in lending to small and new private firms, because these firms may lack a track record and may not report financial information in a consistent manner. Soft information is used in conjunction with financial and other hard data when making credit decisions (Gonzalez and James, 2007).

Lenders themselves, as well as brokers and intermediaries, will have incentives to overstate both the value of assets being financed, as well as the borrower's ability to repay. Lenders need to gear reward systems towards loan safety and not only loan size. If a loan officer is rewarded based only on the size of the loan granted, the temptation to inflate the loan size will be strong. Skewed incentives will tend to generate skewed behaviour. Reckless and lax lending behaviour can be often attributed to skewed incentives. The FCA has recognised that some firms have inadequate systems and controls to manage the risks of staff incentives and are producing guidelines to counter this (FCA, 2017a).

Lenders need to be wary about incorrect information and fraudulent loan applications. Among the fraudulent practices that have been detected or suspected by lenders are:

- fraudulent documentation in relation to bank statements, utility bills, wage slips, passports, driving licences, etc.;
- false employment or income details;
- inconsistent information relating to the same applicant, i.e. various applications made with different incomes or details either to the same lender or to other lenders within a group; and
- links between different loan applicants, e.g. shared bank accounts and shared addresses.

Banks need to safeguard against fraud committed by various entities in the bank lending process.

- Bank executives may be party to insider dealing and fraud, leading to lax lending, which may perpetuate housing boom and busts.
- Frauds may be perpetrated by a borrower in collusion with a seller. For example, a seller may sell a house for an inflated price to a 'man of straw', who could disappear after obtaining a mortgage for the purchase, to later share the proceeds of the fraud with the seller, leaving the lender with an asset worth less than the loan.
- Frauds may be perpetrated by both the borrower and the lender. For example, the lender may encourage the borrower to lie about the income to take on an unaffordable mortgage so that the lender can show an increase in business and (at least temporary) profits.
- Frauds may be perpetrated by the investment banker to make huge profits converting (suspect) loans into mortgage bonds, later offloading them before their true value becomes known.
- Frauds may perpetrated by the bond insurer who fails to inform investors about the true quality of the bonds.
- Frauds may be perpetrated by the rating agency by awarding a higher-than-justifiable rating to the customer who pays for it.

Lenders need to be alert to fraud, and must seek further information or verification of details furnished in application forms and other documents both to deter fraud and to ensure that the information provided is accurate.

The sources of information available to lenders include customer interviews and other interactions, and they can be internal or external.

- *Internal* information is that held within the lender's own databases.
- *External* information is that available from published records and statements.

Lenders need to use the information that they gather from these sources to assess borrower creditworthiness and borrowing requirements.

In Chapter 4, we examined new ventures, business expansion, cash flow forecasts and forms of business finance. Lenders require business forecasts to be backed by reliable data. Projected business growth needs to be evidenced by orders, contracts and historical data.

Based on the information, lenders will need to carry out various types of credit analysis, such as:

- business plans;
- cash flow forecasts;
- long-term earnings potential;
- broad-based analysis of the products and management, the industry and the competitive strength of the business within the industry; and
- sensitivity analyses that test the effects of unfavourable developments in sales volumes, profit margins, asset turnover rates, etc.

6.2.3 Interpreting financial statements

After gathering information, a lender needs to be able to interpret that information. Figures, such as sales, profits and total assets, need to be understood in perspective. A lender needs to evaluate the performance of the borrowing business, comparing it with its own past performance, as well as with that of its industry competitors.

Financial statements enable the lender to investigate the position, performance and prospects (Pike and Neale, 2006) of a borrower.

- The *position* of the business at a point in time is examined by looking at the *statement of financial position* or *balance sheet*, which is a statement of the assets of the business and how these assets have been financed, i.e. by owned capital and by liabilities owed to others (Table 6.1).
- The *performance* of the business over a period of time is examined by looking at the *income statement* or *profit and loss account*, which is a statement of income and expenditure, and the resulting profit or loss.
- The *prospects* of the business are examined by looking at the *financial statement* of cash inflows and outflows, and the change in the cash position over a period of time, as well as the *cash flow forecast* showing expected cash receipts and payments for the following year.

Table 6.1 A simplified balance sheet

Assets		Liabilities
Current assets		Current liabilities
Fixed assets		Long-term debt
Other assets		Shareholders' funds
Total assets	=	**Total liabilities**

The *balance sheet equation* can be represented as in Table 6.2.

Table 6.2 Balance sheet equation

Assets		Capital, reserves and liabilities
Current assets – Current liabilities = Net current assets (Net working capital)		Long-term debt
Fixed assets + Intangible assets		Shareholders' funds
Net assets	=	**Capital employed**

Using ratios

Comparative ratio analysis will help the lender to identify and quantify the borrower's strengths and weaknesses, and to understand the risks to which the borrower might be exposed. In this section, a prior knowledge of accounting ratios and methods of calculations is assumed, and a detailed analysis of financial statements is outside the scope of this text. However, for the purposes of ready reference, we now summarise some of the main ratios used for interpreting financial statements: the profitability, activity, liquidity, investor and gearing ratios. Many of these ratios appear under slightly different names, which often have more than one definition.

- *Profitability ratios* help the lender to assess the performance and profitability of the borrower, the adequacy of profits earned and whether profits are increasing or decreasing. Some of the main ratios are as follows.

  Gross profit margin (%) = (Gross profit ÷ Sales) × 100

  Net profit margin (%) = (Profit before interest and tax (PBIT) ÷ Sales) × 100

  Return on capital employed (ROCE) (%) = (PBIT ÷ Long-term capital) × 100

  Turnover Growth (Fall) (%) = (Change in turnover ÷ Starting turnover) × 100

- *Activity ratios* or *Asset turnover ratios* help the lender to assess the efficiency of the use of the assets in terms of sales achieved:

  Fixed asset turnover = Sales ÷ Fixed assets

  Asset turnover = Sales ÷ (Fixed assets + Current assets)

  Stock turnover = (Average value of stock ÷ Cost of sales) × 365

  Creditor repayment rate (days) = (Trade creditors ÷ Cost of sales) × 365

  Debtor recovery rate (days) = (Average trade debtors ÷ Credit sales) × 365

  The lender needs to note the period of credit allowed to debtors: too little credit makes it difficult to achieve a satisfactory level of sales, while too much credit reduces the liquidity of the business and makes it more dependent on lenders (Marriott, Edwards, and Mellett, 2002).

- *Liquidity ratios* help the lender to assess the availability of liquidity to meet debt obligations as and when they arise (see Chapter 4):

  Current ratio = Current assets ÷ Current liabilities

  Quick ratio = (Current assets – Stock) ÷ Current liabilities

- *Investor ratios* help the lender to assess the return available to investors in the business:

  Earnings per share (EPS) = Earnings ÷ Number of equity shares

  Price–earnings ratio (PE) = Current share price ÷ EPS

  Dividend cover = EPS ÷ Dividends per share

  Return on equity (ROE) = PBIT ÷ Shareholders' funds

- *Gearing ratios* calculate the proportionate contributions of owners and creditors to a business. The debt–equity ratio indicates the level of outside debt in relation to ordinary share capital:

  Debt–equity ratio = Debt ÷ Equity

- *Interest cover* assesses the borrower's ability to meet interest commitments:

  Interest cover = PBIT ÷ Interest payable

Finance for businesses can take the form of *debt* (owed capital) or *shares* (owned capital). Shares may be *ordinary* shares or *preference* shares (classified by lenders as debt, rather than shares, because these usually carry fixed rates of interest and have priority of repayment, thus behaving like debt rather than shares).

Debt has priority in relation to repayment because creditors need to be repaid before the owners. Also, creditors need to be paid interest before the owners can be rewarded with any dividends. Debt is therefore less risky and hence debt-holders will be satisfied with a lower rate of return than the shareholders. Debt also introduces an element of tax savings, because tax is payable only on profits after interest, unlike dividends, which are paid out on after-tax profits. Shareholders are the ultimate risk-bearers and have voting rights that give them a say in how a business is run. For the investor or lender, debt yields interest and shares yield dividends, on both of which income tax is payable, while shares might also appreciate in value, which value is subject to capital gains tax.

When a business has a high proportion of debt in its capital, it is described as being *highly geared* or *highly leveraged*. Gearing enhances the impact of a rise or fall in profits. A rising profits scenario will result in rising returns to shareholders because interest payable on debt is fixed and the excess profits go to reward the shareholders. Conversely, in a falling profits scenario, shareholders will face increased losses – and even the risk of the business going bankrupt if the interest and debt cannot be serviced as envisaged.

Generally, lenders will be more willing to extend finance when the level of debt in relation to equity decreases. Gearing ratios help the lender to assess risk. The prudent lender will want to examine total borrowing in relation to the equity base. For this reason, the lender often finds it useful to extend the definition of debt to include loans from directors and bank overdrafts, i.e. any debt for which interest is payable.

EXAMPLE

Let us look again at BT over a three-year period (2005–07).

Table 6.3 Calculating the gearing ratio

	As at 31 March 2007 (£m)	As at 31 March 2006 (£m)	As at 31 March 2005 (£m)
Total debt	10,300	13,665	15,384
Total equity	4,238	1,555	45
Debt–equity ratio (Debt ÷ Equity)	2.43	8.79	341.87

Source: BT

The results of this calculation raises an interesting insight for the lender. A lender would normally view the horrendous picture in 2005 – probably the consequence of borrowing for the acquisition of 3G licences (see Chapter 4) – as totally unacceptable. Yet lenders who were not deterred from lending to BT would have welcomed the remarkable recovery staged by the company, which achieved a sharp decline in the proportion of debt to equity over the three years to reach an acceptable ratio in 2007.

Loans or debt finance will be normally cheaper than equity for at least two reasons: first, unlike dividends, interest is payable regardless of whether there are any profits; and second, in the event of insolvency, the creditors will be paid first and the owners will receive any remaining equity last. Because debt is less risky than equity, holders of debt will be satisfied with a lower return. However, as borrowing increases, both equity holders and lenders might require higher returns to compensate for the higher gearing and higher risk. Thus both lenders and borrowers would attempt to achieve a balance between the owed capital and owned capital in the capital structure.

Business risk and financial risk

Business risk is the variability of operating profit (PBIT), which in turn depends upon a number of factors, such as the variability of demand for the products, the selling price and the input costs, and the percentage of fixed costs in the cost structure. *Operating gearing* is the mix of the variable costs and fixed costs. A business with a larger percentage of fixed costs is said to have a higher degree of operating gearing and this provides a measure of business risk of the borrower.

Financial risk is the variability of net profit available for distribution to shareholders, i.e. the additional risk borne by the equity holders as a result of using debt in the capital structure. *Financial gearing* is a company's mix of equity and debt capital. A business with a large percentage of debt is said to have a high degree of financial gearing and this provides a measure of its financial risk. The higher the borrowing, the higher the interest payments that must be paid before any remaining earnings can be paid out to equity shareholders as dividends. Hence financial risk enhances the level of risk over and above the inherent business risk.

There is a trade-off between operating and financial gearing. If there is a high degree of operating gearing, then – unless sales are very stable – it is better to avoid financial gearing and vice versa. Thus a lender would not like to see a business having high levels of both business and financial risk.

The importance of financial gearing can be highlighted with a simple example.

EXAMPLE

Suppose an individual buys a property for £100,000 and the value of the property rises to £120,000 after one year (if then sold). Let us consider how the return would be different if they were to use borrowed money to fund the purchase rather than their own money on the basis of two different strategies.

- *Strategy A* The individual uses £100,000 of their own money to buy the property.
- *Strategy B* The individual meets 90 per cent of the investment cost with a mortgage loan, with interest at the rate of 10 per cent, i.e. £10,000 equity and £90,000 loan.

Table 6.4 Impact of gearing on return

Strategy A	£
Value of investment after one year	120,000
Recovery of capital invested	(100,000)
ROE	20,000
Percentage ROE (20,000 ÷ 100,000)	20%
Strategy B	**£**
Value of investment after one year	120,000
Less 10% interest on loan of £90,000	(9,000)
Less Repayment of loan	(90,000)
Recovery of capital invested	(10,000)
ROE	11,000
Percentage ROE (11,000 ÷ 10,000)	110%

The investor's ROE has increased from 20 per cent to 110 per cent simply by changing the way in which the investment was financed (although note that the return on total capital employed is still 20 per cent).

But return and risk go hand in hand. Let us look at the impact of variability on that example.

EXAMPLE

Suppose a stagnant property market results in the investment generating no surplus, but simply giving back the original investment of £100,000 after one year. The results under each strategy would be as follows.

Table 6.5 Impact of variability on return

	Strategy A £	Strategy B £
Value of investment after a year	100,000	100,000
Less Interest on loan	–	(9,000)
Less Repayment of loan	–	(90,000)
Recovery of own capital invested	(100,000)	(10,000)
ROE	0	(9,000)
Percentage ROE	0 ÷ 100,000 = 0%	–9,000 ÷ 10,000 = –90%

Under Strategy A, the investor would just break even, but Strategy B would result in a whopping negative return of –90 per cent. Given the two possible states of the economy, the ROE varies from 20 per cent to 0 per cent (a variation of 20 percentage points) under Strategy A, but from 110 per cent to –90 per cent (a variation of 200 percentage points) under Strategy B, i.e. the variability of outcome (the fundamental measure of risk) is much greater under Strategy B.

These examples demonstrate, then, that while investors can hugely increase their return by gearing up, they simultaneously increase the financial risk of their investment. This interplay of return and risk is a fundamental feature of finance, and is something of which lenders need to be very aware. The huge impact of gearing on investor return can, for example, encourage housing market bubbles caused by investors jumping on the bandwagon and making geared property investments with 90 per cent (or even 110 per cent) mortgages – a strategy that may yield rich dividends when the market is rising, but can result in disaster for both investor and lender if the market falls. It was consequently unsurprising that lenders such as Northern Rock, who were happy to consider loan-to-value (LTV) ratios of up to 125 per cent, ran into difficulties when the 2007–08 global financial crisis began to bite.

What is an acceptable level of gearing?

The impact of gearing on ROE is also affected significantly by taxation, since the use of debt capital generates a tax shield that equity capital does not. Gearing can therefore create significant extra value for a business – but since the use of debt increases the financial risk, there will come a point at which further increase in debt will begin to destroy value rather than create it.

The optimum level of gearing will vary from industry to industry and from firm to firm. Business risk is a key factor in determining it, since financial risk is merely an enhancer of business risk; companies with high business risk should aim to reduce their financial risk and vice versa. It thus becomes a matter of judgement for the financial manager and the lending banker.

This dilemma is acknowledged by what is referred to as the *trade-off theory of capital structure*, which recognises that target debt ratios vary from firm to firm because there is a trade-off between increased return and increased risk for a geared firm. Companies with relatively low business risk and substantial taxable income can aim for higher debt ratios; less profitable companies with high levels of business risk should mainly rely on equity financing.

6.2.4 The limitations of financial statements

Lenders use financial ratios to look at past performances, as well as to make predictions for the future, based on those past trends. It is important to note the following while using ratios for analysing company performance.

- Ratios can be expressed in a number of different ways, e.g. as a ratio, a fraction, a percentage, etc.
- Ratios can be calculated in a number of different ways.
- It is important to be consistent in the method of calculating ratios; otherwise, the results will not be meaningful.
- By themselves, ratios may not convey much meaning; comparisons will need to be made with those of previous years or those of similar companies in the same industry to obtain more meaningful data.

Lenders also need to recognise that financial statements and accounting ratios, while providing useful information about a business, are subject to a number of limitations.

- The figures in financial statements are likely to be at least several months *out of date* and so will not provide a true picture of the current financial position.
- Financial statements are *summarised versions* of accounting records. The process of summarising could have led to a loss of important information that might have been relevant to the user of that information.
- *Inflation* renders comparisons of results over time misleading. What appears to be an improvement in performance may prove to be the opposite when figures are adjusted for inflation.
- Financial statements are based on *year-end results*, which may not always reflect the position during the course of the year. Seasonal businesses may choose the best time of the year to produce financial statements so as to show better results.
- Financial statements can be *distorted by large, one-off transactions*. It is important to ask for and analyse additional information that might throw light on the implications.
- Too much importance should not be attached to *individual ratios*: some ratios might indicate good performance, while others may signal the

opposite. It is important to study a range of financials, understand the interplay of the ratios and adopt a balanced view that takes into account any conflicting messages conveyed by financial statements.

- On their own, ratios *are not definitive*, i.e. cannot indicate whether a result is 'good' or 'bad'. A high current ratio could be 'good' in that it indicates high liquidity, but 'bad' in that it might indicate overstocking leading to decreased profitability.
- It may be *inappropriate to draw 'rule of thumb' conclusions* about the desirability of certain ratios. A current ratio of 2:1 or a debt–equity ratio of 2:1 may be the norm in one industry, yet the norm may be entirely different for another. For example, supermarkets with a high turnover of stock might be able to manage with a much lower current ratio than can an engineering firm.
- Meaningful inter-firm comparisons may not be possible even within the same industry, *because every business is unique*, with its own unique set of strengths and weaknesses.
- Even after accounting for intangible assets, *not all of a firm's gains or losses are captured by financial statements*. For example, the arrival or departure of a key staff member may have a significant impact on the profitability of a business, but no impact on the financial statements.
- The choice of *different accounting policies* may distort inter-year, as well as inter-firm, comparisons. For example, International Accounting Standard (IAS) 16 allows assets to be depreciated at historical cost or revalued; a business may prefer to continue depreciation at historical cost, because revaluation might increase the depreciation charge and result in decreased profits. Different depreciation methods and estimates will report different net income figures in the income statement and different value of assets in the balance sheet. Further, changes in accounting policy may vitiate any comparison of results between different accounting periods.
- *Creative accounting* involves the manipulation of financial numbers, usually within the legal framework, but aiming to misrepresent the true financial state of a business. An example is overstating income by making inadequate provision for bad debts or depreciation. In his book *Accounting for Growth*, advertised as 'the book they tried to ban', Terry Smith (1996) actually named British companies that use creative accounting practices and massage corporate results to make them look better (and consequently lost his job as head of UK company research at UBS Phillips and Drew).
- *Window-dressing* is similar to creative accounting, but sometimes includes illegal activities undertaken to camouflage the true state of affairs. Financial ratios can be manipulated or window-dressed and therefore need to be treated with caution.

In summary, then, financial statements and ratio analysis are useful, but lenders need to be aware of these limitations and make adjustments as necessary. Only when used with skill and care, it is possible to gain useful insights from these tools into the position, performance and prospects of a borrowing business.

6.3 LOAN DOCUMENTATION AND COVENANTS

6.3.1 Loan documentation

Loan documentation is a very important stage in the lending process. An incorrectly or inadequately documented loan may not be enforceable. Not only do lenders need to be able to obtain the relevant documents in a timely and appropriate manner (because delay in obtaining certain documentation may invalidate the lender's claim), but also the documents need to be:

- accurately drawn up, in consultation with qualified solicitors and in strict compliance with legal requirements;
- appropriate to the lending activity and loan customer (different activities and customers requiring different clauses);
- executed by authorised signatories; and
- appropriately recorded and retained for reference in case of need.

Some of the more frequently used documents are as follows.

- The borrower's application for the grant or renewal of credit facilities
- A corporate borrowing resolution or partnership agreement
- A subordination agreement
- The borrower's and guarantor's financial information and/or statements
- Credit reports
- The loan agreement (signed by the borrower and lender)
- A facility letter advising the grant of credit
- Evidence of perfection of security interest
- Existing and paid-off promissory notes
- Insurance policies
- Loan review or renewal documents
- Correspondence

6.3.2 Loan covenants

A *loan covenant* is a condition with which the borrower must comply to adhere to the terms in the loan agreement. If the borrower does not act in accordance with the covenants, the loan can be considered to be in default and the lender has the right to demand repayment. Lenders attach covenants to loans as a way of ensuring that borrowers operate in a financially prudent manner and repay the debt. Borrowers, meanwhile, like to negotiate flexible covenants that give them freedom to make decisions and take risks that might benefit them. Setting out loan covenants in a clear manner will benefit both lenders and borrowers, and ensure that both parties are aware of their duties and obligations.

There are two types of covenant in most loan agreements, as follows.

1. *Affirmative covenants* require the borrower to perform certain activities in accordance with the loan terms. Examples relate to:
   - repayment of the principal and interest at stipulated intervals;
   - compliance with legal, regulatory and accounting requirements;
   - regular submission of financial statements;
   - prompt payment of taxes, licences and fees; and
   - arranging for up-to-date insurance.
2. *Negative covenants* impose restraints on certain borrower activities. Some examples include limitations on the borrower's freedom to:
   - incur more debt;
   - increase salaries and bonuses;
   - pay large dividends;
   - purchase new assets; or
   - effect changes in management.

Covenants can be operational or financial. *Operational covenants* can require borrowers to maintain their physical assets to certain minimum standards, meet minimum disclosure requirements, engage only in permissible business activities and maintain a minimum level of insurance.

Financial covenants can stipulate ratios that the borrower is required to stay above or below. The method of calculating such ratios might be more stringent than those stipulated by accounting standards, e.g. minimum equity, minimum working capital and maximum debt to equity (leverage requirements), minimum quick and current ratios (liquidity requirements), or minimum return on assets and ROE (profitability requirements).

Loan covenants attempt to achieve a variety of objectives, such as cash flow control, balance-sheet control, and trigger recall or restructuring of the loan (Hempel and Simonson, 1999).

A rise in competition and the resultant increase in power of borrowers has led to what have been called *covenant-lite loans*, which were 'light' on covenants that were otherwise used to safeguard against borrower default. Lenders need to ensure, however, that they resist the instinct to herd with other lenders and recognise the need to stipulate rigorous covenants at all times.

6.4 FURTHER ADVANCES

6.4.1 Reasons for further advances

There are various reasons as to why a borrower might approach a lender for a *further advance*. Existing loan facilities may be due to expire, and the conduct and character of the borrower, as well as the performance of the account, may justify renewal of the facility for a further specified period. Alternatively, the borrower may be experiencing an increase in borrowing requirements, stemming from expansion of its existing business, such as increased turnover or new technologies, or from new investment activities, such as new products or new markets.

Additional reasons may relate to:

- the availability of increased capital or security, increasing the eligible loan amount;
- the borrower's need for a different interest rate structure, e.g. moving from a fixed to a floating rate of interest;
- the borrower's need for different loan products, e.g. a credit card borrower requesting an overdraft;
- an improvement in the borrower's credit rating, which might induce the borrower to seek enhanced facilities; or
- a desire to consolidate loans.

6.4.2 Loan consolidation

Borrowers may approach the lender for *loan consolidation* to save on interest and other costs by reducing overall borrowing. The lender might need to charge early redemption fees to safeguard against loss on account of early loan closures. Alternatively, the borrower may be seeking to lower its monthly payments. A longer repayment period could facilitate a reduction in outgoings for a borrower faced with a shortfall in liquidity.

In all cases, the lender needs to assess the viability of the loan and the ability of the borrower to meet repayment obligations.

6.5 CONCLUSION

The lending cycle commences with the credit-granting process, which involves scrutiny of the loan application, the gathering of information, data analysis and loan evaluation. It then moves through the evaluation of security, at which we look in Chapters 8 and 9, and is followed by the credit-monitoring and credit-repayment or recovery processes (Chapter 10). These last processes lead to the generation of funds for the granting of further credit – and so the cycle continues.

FURTHER READING

Caouette, J. B., Altman, E. I., Narayanan, P., and Nimmo, R. (2008) *Managing credit risk: The great challenge for global financial markets*, 2nd edn, Chichester: John Wiley & Sons.

Marriott, P., Edwards, J. R., and Mellett, H. (2012) *Introduction to accounting*, London: Sage.

Pond, K. (2017) 'Credit appraisal', in *Retail banking*, 4th edn, Reading: Gosbrook, 116–28.

REVIEW QUESTIONS

1. What are the main components in the lending cycle?
2. What are the limitations of financial ratio analysis?
3. Why might a borrower approach a lender for further advances?

ACTIVITY

Examine any loan agreement you might have entered into (e.g. a credit card or mortgage agreement) and read the clauses. Are there any clauses that you had not noticed before? What are the implications for the lender and borrower?

If you have not entered into any loan agreement, collect or download a sample loan agreement form and scrutinise the document for any restrictive or affirmative clauses.

CASE STUDY *Titford Property* and *Williams and Glyn's Bank v Barnes*

In *Titford Property v Cannon Street Acceptances Ltd*, unreported, 22 May 1975, the loan agreement contained the following clause: 'All moneys due by you, whether by way of capital or interest, shall be payable on demand and you shall have the right to repay all moneys due without notice.' However, a letter from the bank to the customer said:

> We have pleasure in advising you of the terms and conditions upon which we are prepared to provide an overdraft facility in the maximum sum of GBP 248,000 for a period of 12 months to assist you in the purchase and development of the under mentioned freehold premises.

Thus the loan agreement and the facility letter contained contradictory clauses.

It was held by Goff J that 'where a bank allows an overdraft for a fixed time for a specific purpose . . . , that time is binding on the bank', because otherwise the customer would be in the 'disastrous position' of being unable to meet his liabilities, which were incurred on the basis of faith in the bank's promise to lend money.

In *Williams and Glyn's Bank Ltd v Barnes* [1981] Com LR 205, Gibson J stated that: 'Bankers . . . regard repayability on demand as a universal or normal attribute of overdrafts, but there is nothing to suggest that they regard that attribute as overriding an agreement to the contrary.' However, in this case, it was held that the bank had expressly reserved the right to withdraw the overdraft facilities at any time and that there was no contradictory statement upon which the customer could rely. Accordingly, the bank was entitled to immediate repayment once a proper demand had been made, because the bank had done nothing to remove its right for immediate repayment as had been the case in *Titford Property*.

CASE STUDY QUESTIONS

1. Which were the two items of loan documentation that were found to have contradictory clauses in *Titford Property*?
2. What was the contradiction in these two documents?
3. What is the common conclusion about the nature of overdrafts reached by both *Titford Property* and *Barnes*?
4. Why was the overdraft granted in *Titford* held not to be repayable on demand?
5. What is the lesson here for lenders?

Suggested answers can be found in Appendix A.

7

Loan evaluation

LEARNING POINTS

This chapter looks at the analysis of a lending proposal.

Learning areas include:

- loan evaluation tools and techniques;
- evaluation of short-term working capital requirements;
- evaluation of long-term lending requirements;
- credit scoring; and
- credit rating agencies.

7.1 LOAN EVALUATION TOOLS AND TECHNIQUES

Credit evaluation is important for ensuring loan quality, because accumulation of bad debts can lead to insolvency. Accordingly, lenders use a variety of tools and techniques to evaluate a loan proposal. These tools include loan evaluation mnemonics such as CAMPARI, CCCPARTS and PARSER, as well as context analysis using frameworks such as SWOT and Porter's Five Forces.

7.1.1 Loan evaluation frameworks

Lenders use loan evaluation frameworks or checklists to evaluate a credit application. These canons of lending or loan criteria are expressed in the form of mnemonics for easy recall. Mnemonics such as CAMPARI (see Table 7.1), CCCPARTS (see Table 7.2) and PARSER (see Table 7.3) are used by a number of lending banks.

Table 7.1 CAMPARI

C	Character	Integrity, history and background (primary security)
A	Ability	Managerial and technical competence and business viability
M	Margin (or Means)	Varyingly interpreted as the percentage of loan-to-value (LTV) of the asset (or profit potential or resources generated by the business)*
P	Purpose	Purpose for which the finance is required
A	Amount	Evaluation of amount of loan required and how it will be drawn down, proportional to customer contribution and resources

Continued on next page

Table 7.1 CAMPARI *cont.*

R	Repayment	Sources from which and period over which loan will be repaid
I	Insurance	Security offered

* The lower the LTV, the higher the margin available to the lender. The higher the borrower's stake in the business, the lower the risk faced by the lender.

Table 7.2 CCCPARTS

C	Character	Integrity, history and background (primary security)
C	Capital	Borrower's stake in the business
C	Capability	Managerial and technical competence and business viability
P	Purpose	Purpose for which the finance is required
A	Amount	Evaluation of amount of loan required and how it will be drawn down, proportional to customer contribution and resources
R	Repayment	Sources from which and period over which loan will be repaid
T	Terms	Terms and conditions and loan covenants
S	Security	Security offered

Table 7.3 PARSER

P	Person	Integrity, history and background (primary security)
A	Amount	Evaluation of amount of loan required and how it will be drawn down, proportional to customer contribution and resources
R	Repayment	Sources from which and period over which loan will be repaid
S	Security	Security offered
E	Expertise	Managerial and technical competence and business viability
	Expediency	Advantageous on account of other business or income that may accrue
R	Remuneration	Profit potential generated by the business

The checklists indicate that lending decisions are largely based on two types of information: knowledge of the past (see Table 7.4) and a forecast for the future (see Table 7.5).

Table 7.4 Knowledge of the past

Factor	Information required
Person(s)	Background Managerial skills Technical skills
Past financial record	Capital structure or gearing Working capital or liquidity Fixed asset or investment Profitability Solvency

Table 7.5 Forecast for the future

Factor	Information required
Proposal and its risk	Amount or limit of loan Purpose for which it is sought Period for which it is required Security available
Projections and probability of repayment	Repayment programme Interest and other charges Projected sales and profit Cash forecasts and budgets

These checklists are built into credit scoring and other systems devised for determining loan quality and probability of its repayment.

7.1.2 SWOT analysis

In addition to loan evaluation frameworks that focus largely on internal factors, it is also important to undertake context analysis that focuses on the entire environment of a business, both internal and external. One kind of context analysis, known as *SWOT analysis*, allows the business (and the lender) to gain an insight into its *strengths* and *weaknesses*, and also the *opportunities* and *threats* posed by the market within which it operates (hence the acronym).

SWOT analysis provides a framework for assessing a business or business idea, and it is useful for both lenders and borrowers for reviewing the position and direction of a business proposition. Lenders use the framework to assess:

- a borrower's position in the market;
- the viability of a business proposal;
- the effectiveness of business planning;
- the product, pricing strategy, distribution method or promotion method;
- mergers and acquisitions, and proposed partnerships; and
- a variety of business ideas and strategies.

SWOT analysis is usually presented as a grid comprising four headings under each of which relevant issues and questions are examined (see Figure 7.1).

Strengths	**Weaknesses**
Unique selling proposition (USP) Resources	Reputation Liquidity
Opportunities	**Threats**
Niche market Research & Development (R&D)	Political climate Economic uncertainty

Figure 7.1 The SWOT grid

It can be accompanied by *PESTLE analysis*, which examines the external *political, economic, social* and *technological, legal* and *ethical or environmental* factors that might have an impact on the marketing environment of a business.

7.1.3 Porter's Five Forces

Lenders will also find Porter's 'Five Forces' model useful for analysing the competitive position of a business venture (Figure 7.2).

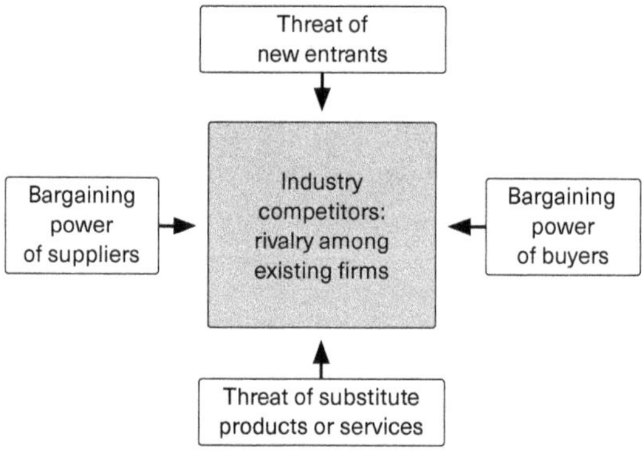

Figure 7.2 Porter's Five Forces (adapted from Porter, 1980)

7.2 EVALUATION OF WORKING CAPITAL REQUIREMENTS

In Chapter 4, we highlighted the difference between short-term lending to meet working capital needs and long-term lending to help to meet fixed asset and other long-term capital investment requirements. It is, however, important not to confuse working capital requirements with the term 'net working capital', which is usually defined as the difference between current assets and current liabilities.

The basic structure of a balance sheet can be presented as in Table 7.6.

Table 7.6 The basic structure of a balance sheet

Assets		Liabilities
Current assets		Current liabilities
Fixed assets		Term liabilities
		Equity
Total assets	=	**Total liabilities and equity**

Net working capital is usually defined as:

$$\text{Net working capital} = \text{Current assets} - \text{Current liabilities}$$

Since the two sides of a balance sheet are equal:

Current assets + Fixed assets = Current liabilities + Term liabilities + Equity

Rearranging this basic balance-sheet equation:

Current assets – Current liabilities = Term liabilities + Equity – Fixed assets

Thus net working capital represents the difference between current assets and current liabilities (Current assets – Current liabilities) – but, equally, it represents the surplus of long-term sources of funds (Term liabilities + Equity) over long-term uses of funds (Fixed and other non-current assets).

Lenders would not normally expect the current liabilities of most businesses to exceed their current assets. This means that some part of the investment in current assets must normally come from non-current liabilities, i.e. long-term financing through term liabilities and equity. The portion of current asset investment that is met from long-term finance in this way is what net working capital really is. One of the most common reasons for loan default by borrowing companies is loss of liquidity resulting from the diversion of short-term finance (current liabilities) to long-term investment, resulting in a contraction of net working capital. Long-term investment generally takes time to generate cash flows, whereas short-term finance becomes due for repayment very quickly – and this maturity mismatch can cause serious difficulties for both borrower and lender.

Cash is the life blood of a business and the cash-to-cash cycle of a manufacturing business can be simply depicted as in Figure 7.3.

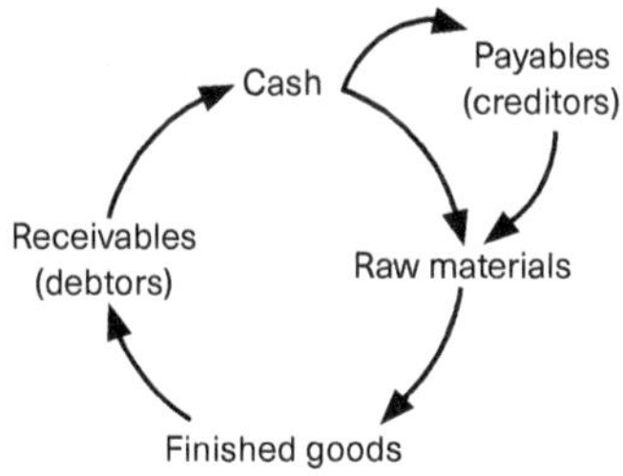

Figure 7.3 The cash operating cycle

A firm's basic working capital requirement consists of its investment in various current assets; in the case of a manufacturing firm, these would be mainly raw materials, work-in-progress, finished goods and receivables. Short-term sources of finance are essentially intended to fund this investment in current assets and are therefore meant to be liquidated by conversion of the current assets back into cash in the course of the cash conversion cycle. Consequently, short-term sources of finance are the *current liabilities* of the firm, which, by definition, are those liabilities that are liquidated in the course of the firm's current operating cycle.

7.2.1 Assessing a borrower's working capital financing policy

A firm's *working capital financing policy* is the mix of short-term and long-term financing that it intends to use to cover the net working capital investment. A firm's level of current assets fluctuates, depending on seasonal and cyclical factors, and other exigencies. However, as long as the firm is in business, there is a minimum level of current assets below which the level will not normally fall, save in exceptional circumstances. This minimum level represents a permanent investment in current assets, the fluctuations that take place over this level being considered to be fluctuating current assets.

- Since the permanent current assets are effectively a long-term, rather than short-term, investment, a *matching* financing policy (see Figure 7.4a) seeks to finance this investment from long-term sources. Long-term financing would therefore be used not only for the fixed assets, but also for the entire permanent current assets.
- Depending on the nature of the business and the speed of its cash conversion cycle, a firm may adopt a more *aggressive* financing policy (see Figure 7.4b) by financing only a portion of the permanent current assets from long-term sources and accruals – the remaining portion being financed from short-term source. Because the yield curve is usually upward-sloping, short-term finance is generally less costly than long-term finance – so an aggressive financing policy will usually have a positive impact on return. But, from the perspective of a lender, such a policy may be risky, because the pressure to repay short-term finance can cause liquidity problems and may result in the firm running out of cash and defaulting on its debt.
- A more *conservative* approach (see Figure 7.4c) would use long-term finance for the whole of the permanent current assets and also a portion of the temporary current assets. Such a policy is less risky, because there is reduced danger of running into liquidity problems – but it is likely to have an adverse impact on return because long-term finance is generally costlier than short-term finance.

When evaluating working capital loan applications lenders need to be aware of these conflicting considerations and assess the viability of the borrower's financing policy, taking account of the nature of the industry and the financial position of the borrower.

Long-term debt has longer repayment schedules, so servicing the repayment obligation is more comfortable. In the case of short-term debt, temporary liquidity problems may cause repayment difficulties. This is why the reckless financing of long-term assets with short-term funds is often a recipe for disaster.

Lenders need to be very aware of the risks of excessive use of short-term finance, which can deplete a borrower's net working capital, resulting in a liquidity crisis. As was evident in Figure 7.3, the ability of a firm to meet its current liabilities depends on its ability to convert assets into cash. If there is any bottleneck in the cash-to-cash cycle – for example because raw materials are not available as a

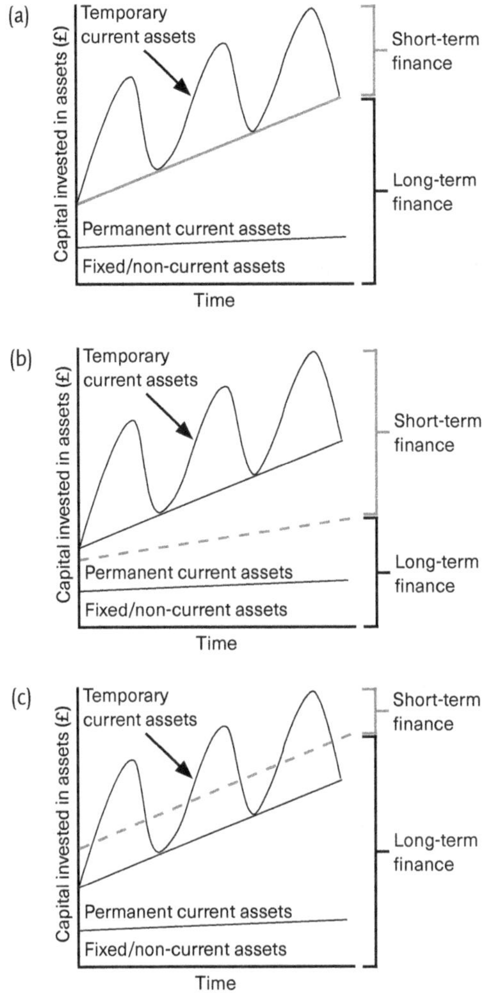

Figure 7.4 Financing policies: (a) matching financing policy; (b) agressive financing policy; (c) conservative financing policy

result of inefficient purchase management, an accumulation of work-in-progress because of production problems, a sluggish movement of finished goods because of a slump in demand, or a delay in collecting receivables because of poor credit control – the process of converting assets into cash will be disrupted, leading the firm to experience difficulty in meeting the current liabilities.

Since a firm's ability to meet its current liabilities depends on the conversion of its current assets into cash, it is generally the case that the greater the availability of current assets in relation to current liabilities, the greater is a firm's liquidity or short-term solvency. A declining current ratio indicates that current liabilities are rising at a faster rate than current assets and is the main symptom of the common malaise known as *overtrading*, which is discussed in Chapter 10.

7.3 EVALUATION OF TERM LENDING REQUIREMENTS

An overdraft is generally a short-term uncommitted facility, and there is no obligation on the lender to renew the arrangement and continue the loan facility. Banks also offer committed facilities that are available for agreed periods of time. The most common type of committed facility is the term loan, which can be granted for very long periods of up to ten years or even more (e.g. a mortgage) – although it is unusual for the maturity of a term loan to exceed five years. Because of the long period of the bank's commitment, term loans are subject to more detailed scrutiny and a more rigorous process of due diligence than short-term uncommitted facilities. Apart from the length of the commitment, the amounts required by borrowers for long-term capital investment tend to be large, and errors in investment appraisal can be very costly for both borrower and lender.

The purpose of investment appraisal is to estimate whether the proposed investment would create sufficient value to provide an adequate return to the investor after repaying all of the loan capital with interest. A term loan application is therefore generally accompanied by a business plan, which sets out the rationale and detail of the proposed investment, and the cash flows that are expected to be generated over the life of the term loan facility that is being sought.

The investment appraisal process can be broadly split into three steps.

1. The cost of the project has to be estimated. This should include the working capital requirement and a provision for contingencies such as inflation, exchange rate movement, etc.
2. The next step is to project the estimated cash inflows, including the scrap or salvage value of the investment at the end of its life and recovery of working capital, if any. These estimates will be based on sales forecasts and cost estimates, which need to be carefully vetted.
3. The information is then analysed on the basis of one or more decision rules, some of which may involve assessing the riskiness of the projected cash flows.

Any form of investment appraisal involves comparing the required investment with the cash inflows expected from the investment.

7.3.1 Net present value

Net present value (NPV) is theoretically the soundest method of appraising investments, being based on the important concept of the *time value of money*. Money has a time value because it can be invested to earn a return over time.

EXAMPLE

Suppose you have £1,000. This is the present value of your money now, i.e. at T0. Now assume that you invest this £1,000 at a rate of 6 per cent per annum (which can be expressed as $6 \div 100$, i.e. 0.06).

One year later, you will have

$$£1,000 + (£1,000 \times 0.06)$$

or

$$(£1,000 \times 1) + (£1,000 \times 0.06)$$

Because 1,000 is a common factor, this can be expressed as:

$$£1,000 \times (1 + 0.06), \text{ i.e. } £1,000 \times (1 + \text{Rate of interest})$$

Since $1 + 0.06 = 1.06$, the amount one year later will be:

$$£1,000 \times 1.06 = £1,060$$

If invested for two years, it would be:

$$£1,000 \times 1.06 \times 1.06 = £1,000 \times 1.06^2 = £1,123.60$$

If invested for three years, it would be:

$$£1,000 \times 1.06 \times 1.06 \times 1.06 = £1,000 \times 1.06^3 = £1,191.02$$

Thus the future value of £1,000 at 6 per cent is:

$£1,000 \times 1.06 = £1,060$ after one year
$£1,000 \times 1.06^2 = £1,123.60$ after two years
$£1,000 \times 1.06^3 = £1,191.02$ after three years

and so on . . .

Future value (FV) is the amount to which the *present value* (PV) of an investment will grow over a number of time periods (n), given a particular rate of interest (r).

$$FV_n = PV \times (1 + r)^n$$

In other words, to find the future value of a present sum of money, the present sum of money should be multiplied by the *future value interest factor*, i.e. $(1 + r)^n$.

Rearranging the equation:

$$PV = \frac{FV_n}{(1+r)^n}$$

or

$$PV = FV_n \times \frac{1}{(1+r)^n}$$

To find the *present* value of a sum of money to be received in the future (i.e. its value at T0), it should be divided by $(1 + r)^n$ *or* multiplied by the *present value interest factor*, i.e.

$$\frac{1}{(1+r)^n}$$

The higher the values of r (the interest rate) and n (the number of periods), the *lower* will be the *present* value.

But why do we want to identify the present value of future cash flows?

The answer is that one way of evaluating an investment is to compare the rate of return it offers with what could have been obtained if a different investment had been made at the same level of risk (i.e. the *opportunity cost*).

What if the *rate* of return on an investment is not known and what is known is only what *amounts* (i.e. cash flows) will be received back in return for making the investment?

In this scenario, the investment is being made in the *present*, but the cash flows will be received back in the *future*. Because of the time value of money, future cash flows are not comparable with a present cash flow (i.e. the original investment). To make them comparable, the *present value* of the future cash flows has to be found.

EXAMPLE

An investment of £1,000 today would get back £1,200 after three years. If the opportunity cost is 9 per cent, we can appraise this investment in two different ways.

- We can calculate the *future value* of £1,000 invested at the opportunity cost of 9 per cent:

  $$£1{,}000 \times 1.09^3 = £1{,}295$$

  The opportunity cost is greater than £1,200, so the investment is not worthwhile.
- We can calculate the *present value* of £1,200 received three years from now, *discounted* at the opportunity cost of 9 per cent:

  $$£1{,}200 \div 1.09^3 = £926.62$$

  This is less than the original investment of £1,000, so the investment is not worthwhile.

Calculating the present value is useful when evaluating investments that generate multiple cash flows over many future periods: the present values of all future cash flows can be added up and compared with the investment.

Many investments generate several periodic cash flows instead of a single cash flow at the end. To find the present value of cash flow from the investment, each cash flow must be discounted for the appropriate period, then all of the discounted cash flows added up.

EXAMPLE

Suppose an investment has the following cash flows:

Year 0 = (£100)
Year 1 = £30
Year 2 = £55
Year 3 = £65

If the opportunity cost of this investment is 9 per cent, the future cash flows must be discounted to make them comparable with the initial investment of £100:

$$\frac{£30}{1.09^1} + \frac{£55}{1.09^2} + \frac{£65}{1.09^3} = £124$$

The present value of the future cash flows discounted at 9 per cent is £124, which is greater than the present value invested (i.e. £100), so the investment will increase present wealth by £124 – £100 = £24.

In the above example, the figure of £24 is the NPV – and as long as the NPV of an investment is positive, it is worthwhile.

Discount rate: the cost of capital

The appropriate discount rate to use in NPV analysis is the rate of return that investors could get from an alternative investment of similar risk and growth opportunities. By making the proposed investment, the investor is losing the opportunity of earning the rate of return offered by the alternative investment, which is referred to as the *opportunity cost*. This is the minimum rate of return required by investors to compensate them for their opportunity cost and is called the *cost of capital*.

The capital used by an enterprise is often raised from different sources and the providers of the different types of capital have different required rates of return. It is therefore common to use a weighted average cost of capital as the discount, with the cost of each different type of capital being weighted according to the proportion of that type of capital in the capital structure of the enterprise. The rates of interest required by bank lenders would be components of the weighted average cost of capital.

It should be noted that when the rate of interest on borrowed capital is included in the weighted average cost of capital that is used as the discount rate, the interest payments should not also be included in the projected cash flows, because this would result in double counting of interest.

Advantages

The advantages of using NPV are several.

- It takes into account the time value of money.
- It considers all financial information relevant to the decision, for the entire period of the investment.

- It directly measures the prospective increase in the value of the firm and consequently the shareholders' wealth (maximisation of which is the firm's main objective).
- It is clear, unambiguous and simple to use.

7.3.2 The debt service coverage ratio

Investment appraisal using techniques such as discounted cash flow analysis is important to evaluate the overall viability of the venture that is being financed, since this directly impacts on the borrower's ability to repay the bank loan. In addition, lending banks also investigate the borrower's potential to maintain regular repayment of their debt obligations over the life of the loan. This is achieved using a measure known as the *debt service coverage ratio* (DSCR), which simply compares the projected net operating income for each year of the investment with the estimated debt repayment obligations for that year:

$$\text{DSCR} = \frac{\text{Net operating income}}{\text{Debt service obligations}}$$

Net operating income for this purpose is the net income *before* charging depreciation or any other non-cash items and also *before* charging any interest or any loan amortisation expenses. In other words, it is essentially the same annual cash flow that is used in standard discounted cash flow investment appraisal. Therefore, if a discounted cash flow investment appraisal is done, it is straightforward to calculate the DSCR using the investment appraisal cash flow estimates.

However, if only accounting profit statements, rather than cash flow estimates, have been projected, it would be necessary to adjust the accounting profits by adding back interest and depreciation or other non-cash items. This would provide an estimate of earnings before interest, depreciation and amortisation (EBIDA), which is generally a sufficient indicator of the net operating income available to service the debt obligations.

Since loan interest is a tax-deductible expense that has an impact on the taxation figure, a refinement that is sometimes suggested is to use earnings before interest, taxes, depreciation and amortisation (EBITDA) as the net operating income figure – in which case, the debt service obligations would also need to be adjusted to reflect the pre-tax provision for post-tax outlays. In most cases, this refinement does not add significantly to the quality of the loan evaluation, the use of EBIDA being sufficient to gain a reasonably accurate view of a borrower's potential to meet their debt service obligations.

The debt service obligations would include principal repayments, interest payments and lease rentals on finance leases.

7.4 CREDIT SCORING

Credit scoring models are developed by analysing statistics and picking out characteristics that are believed to relate to creditworthiness. A *credit score* is expressed as a number that is based on a statistical analysis of a person's current and past credit history, and is used by lenders to evaluate the creditworthiness of that person and the likelihood that the person will meet their debt obligations. Lenders use credit scores to determine who is eligible for a loan, what credit limit should be set and what interest rate should be charged. While credit reporting agencies such as Experian and Equifax adopt different credit scoring models, they are mostly based on components developed by Fair Isaac Credit Organization (FICO) to rate credit risk.

The credit score is determined by a complex formula that takes into account 100 or more factors. These factors are broadly weighted by FICO as summarised in Table 7.7.

Table 7.7 Components of a credit score

Component	Weighting
Payment history in relation to various accounts, such as credit cards and mortgage loans Credit events such as county court judgments (CCJs), lawsuits and insolvencies will have an adverse impact on the score.	35%
Amount of current indebtedness Having too many credit cards, for example, will have an adverse impact on the score.	30%
New credit The number of new credit accounts and the number credit checks that are run on the account will have an adverse impact on the score, based on the assumption that a borrower searching for more credit is a greater credit risk.	10%
Length of the credit history	15%
Type of credit	10%

A credit score assigned to an individual by a credit scoring organisation generally ranges between 300 and 850. The higher the score, the less risky the borrower, and vice versa. Generally, borrowers are classified as prime, below prime, or poor and unacceptable.

- Above 680: prime credit offered at competitive rates of interest
- Between 680 and 575: subprime credit offered at higher rates of interest
- Below 540: credit refused

Variables such as occupation, length of employment, length of residence, homeownership status and credit events will have an impact on the credit score. For example, bankruptcy may result in the deduction of 200 or more points from the credit score.

7.4.1 Advantages

- Credit scoring provides a consistent mathematical system to evaluate prospective and present borrowers. Each lender will have their own unique credit scoring models.

- The credit decision is simplified and the credit-granting process is expedited. Lenders are able to extend credit quickly and at competitive rates to borrowers with higher scores, while rejecting applicants with low scores. More time is available for re-evaluating borderline cases.
- Lenders are able to adopt a risk-based pricing system, charging interest rates that reflect the level of risk and probability of repayment.
- A machine-generated score based on statistical analysis is more likely to be free from bias.

7.4.2 Disadvantages

- Although mathematical, credit scoring systems can still be discriminatory, because they are based on criteria that rely on historic performance data and are set by credit risk committees' subjective judgement, which determines which factors should be considered and what weight should be assigned to these factors. Algorithms can also be programmed incorrectly.
- Lenders are not provided with much opportunity for using their credit appraisal skills and lending discretion.
- Borrowers with poor scores are required to pay high rates of interest to obtain credit or are unable to obtain credit at any cost. Such borrowers are often driven into the arms of illegal lenders, with resultant social costs.
- Some demographic groups may end up being disproportionately targeted with loans that charge predatory interest rates. Although the law might prohibit discrimination based on protected characteristics such as race, sex, national origin and religion, credit organisations might circumvent the rules by using proxy variables such as postcodes that might point to a preponderance of particular ethnic groups or religious affiliations, for example.
- People who have taken breaks in employment (for example to bring up children), part-time employees and the self-employed may find it difficult to obtain a good score.
- Just shopping around, e.g. for a better credit card, can have an adverse impact on the score because multiple enquiries show up on credit reference agency data and might be construed as potential multiple borrowing.
- Simply having a subprime loan may damage the credit score and therefore lead to borrowers having to resort to further subprime loans, trapping them in a vicious cycle.
- The unintended use of credit scores by other users, such as employers, utility providers and insurance companies, may deny certain products to individuals with poor scores and lead to unfair practices. For example, an individual's credit history might affect their car insurance premium even if their driving history is flawless.

- Credit reports can contain inaccuracies. Individuals with similar names or similar addresses can be lumped together erroneously. Individuals are entitled to complain and set the position right, but this can be a long, drawn-out process. Many individuals might not be aware of inaccuracies and may pay higher rates than they should be paying.
- There are flaws in the manner in which a credit scoring system is set up. For example, a thrifty individual with a complete absence of credit history might find it more difficult to obtain credit than an individual who is more prone to borrowing and spending.
- Scoring systems may not incorporate factors such as general economic conditions that might create difficulties for debt repayment across a range of borrower categories.
- Credit scoring is not fully transparent, despite the right of individuals to ascertain their credit score from a credit reference agency for the payment of a small fee.
- As pointed out by the chief executive of the Financial Conduct Authority (FCA):

> Credit reference agencies may have an incomplete picture of an individual's debt, as firms are not required to share data with all credit reference agencies and do not share data between themselves. This means that present debt levels and repayments can be understated.
>
> (Bailey, 2017)

7.5 CREDIT RATING AGENCIES

Credit rating agencies (CRAs) are organisations that award ratings for certain types of borrower, such as companies and national governments, and certain types of debt obligation that are traded in the secondary market. It should be noted that not all borrowers are rated by these agencies, including smaller borrowers and small or medium-sized enterprises (SMEs).

Credit ratings are the opinions offered by CRAs on the creditworthiness of a borrower, and on its ability and willingness to pay its debts. The ratings provide predictive opinions on the likelihood of the borrower repaying debt in a timely manner. Ratings can range from the highest credit quality of AAA through satisfactory credit quality to speculative or default. The United States' Standard & Poor's (S&P) and Moody's are among the world's top rating agencies. Other examples include Baycorp Advantage (Australia), Dominion Bond Rating Service (Canada) and Crisil (India).

The Basel Committee on Banking Supervision (BCBS) of the Bank for International Settlements (BIS) proposes the use of external credit assessments as the basis for risk-weighting credit exposures under its standardised approach for credit risk assessment.

7.5.1 Key factors in credit ratings

Credit ratings take into account both the financial and business risk profiles of a company, and involve the analysis of financial statements, the assessment of management strategies and the evaluation of a number of factors.

When analysing the financial risk profile, the CRA assesses the borrower's:

- financial characteristics, e.g.
  - capital structure and levels of debt,
  - debt service coverage,
  - cash flow,
  - liquidity, and
  - profitability;
- assessment of managerial strategies; and
- evaluation of company policy, e.g. dividend policy and borrowing policy.

When analysing the business risk profile, the CRA assesses the borrower's:

- industry characteristics;
- industry structure;
- industry risk and cyclicality; and
- competitive position within the industry, e.g. its marketing, technology, and efficiency.

7.5.2 Credit rating scales

Examples of rating scales are summarised in Table 7.8.

Table 7.8 Credit rating scales

Definitions	Moody's	S&P	Fitch
Prime/Maximum safety	Aaa	AAA	AAA
High grade/High quality	Aa1	AA+	AA+
	Aa2	AA	AA
	Aa3	AA–	AA–
Upper medium grade	A1	A+	A+
	A2	A	A
	A3	A–	A–
Lower medium grade	Baa1	BBB+	BBB+
	Baa2	BBB	BBB
	Baa3	BBB–	BBB–
Non-investment grade/Speculative	Ba1	BB+	BB+
	Ba2	BB	BB
	Ba3	BB–	BB–

Continued on next page

Table 7.8 Credit rating scales *cont.*

Definitions	Moody's	S&P	Fitch
Highly speculative	B1	B+	B+
	B2	B	B
	B3	B–	B–
Substantial risk/In poor standing	Caa1	CCC+	CCC+
	Caa2	CCC	CCC
	Caa3	CCC–	CCC–
Extremely speculative	Ca	CC	CC
Maybe in default	C		C
Default			DDD
			DD
		D	D

7.5.3 Advantages

The advantages of CRAs should include the following.

- They offer an independent and unbiased opinion on credit value.
- They increase accessibility to credit markets and the marketability of debt.
- They facilitate the pricing of debt.
- They facilitate benchmarking with similar entities.
- They improve transparency by reducing the information asymmetry between borrowers and lenders.
- They fuel an increase in investor confidence and this allows borrowers to have broader access to funds.
- The efficiency of credit or debt markets is enhanced.
- They are found to be useful by a range of users, e.g. banks, debt issuers, intermediaries, counterparties in contracts, investors, regulators, etc.

7.5.4 Disadvantages

Credit rating agencies have received much adverse publicity in recent times, for a number of reasons.

- The quality of their judgement has been questioned. They might need to be 'stricter and more probing' in their credit analysis (Cotis, 2007).
- They are subject to differing interpretations that are not always compatible with the intended objective of the rating.
- There can be issues relating to conflicts of interest.
  - They are paid by the companies that they rate and therefore may be inclined to be generous in the award of ratings.

  - They often offer help in structuring products that are required to be rated, 'playing both coach and referee in the debt game' (Levitt, 2007).
  - They can take on 'too familiar' a role with the management of the company, laying themselves open to undue influence.
- They have been accused of responding too slowly, e.g. Enron was rated investment grade up to four days before it went into bankruptcy, even though the rating agencies had been aware of its problems for a much longer period.
- They have been accused of laxity and of being unable to identify emerging problems.
- They have been accused of reacting inappropriately to the credit crisis and accelerating debt problems.
- They have been accused of being oligopolistic, reaping excessive profits, because of barriers to entering the rating agency business, which is itself reputation-based.
- They are reliant on the quality of the information available, and may not be able to detect deceit and fraud.

7.6 CONCLUSION

Loan evaluation is both an art and a science. The lender is able to use a number of tools, techniques and models, and also has recourse to the opinions of credit rating agencies. However, lending is dynamic; lending constraints arise endogenously, as well as exogenously, and there is no single evaluation technique that can ensure that debt repayment is perfectly enforced.

FURTHER READING

Porter, M. E. (1980) *Competitive strategy*, New York: Free Press.

Rouse, N. (2014) *Applied lending techniques*, 3rd edn, Cranbrook: Global Professional Publishing.

REVIEW QUESTIONS

1. What are the advantages and disadvantages of credit scoring?
2. Why have credit rating agencies been subject to negative publicity?

ACTIVITY

View the video at https://knowledge.insead.edu/strategy/cash-is-king-so-work-your-working-capital-1462 and identify strategies that a bank borrower might adopt for improving the management of working capital.

CASE STUDY A cancelled debt

Michelle Meadows, a childminder, and Tony, a sales representative, had been married for 22 years and had two daughters. They needed cash to refurbish their bathroom and borrowed £5,750 as a home improvement loan, at an annual interest rate of 34.9%, repayable over 15 years, with monthly payments of around £149. At the end of the loan term, they should have paid around £30,000, i.e. over five times the original sum borrowed.

The couple soon failed to make their repayments, and the impact of compounded interest and charges meant that their debt ballooned to £384,000. The lender took the Meadows to court for failing to keep up with repayments on their original home improvement loan and the borrowers faced the prospect of losing their home.

Judge Nigel Howarth, at Liverpool County Court, cancelled the debt, ruling that: 'Where the rate concerned is as high as 34.9 per cent, it seems to me that the combination of factors is so potentially exorbitant that it is grossly so and does grossly contravene the ordinary principles of fair dealing.' He continued, 'The reality of the situation is that the Meadows were very obviously desperate, as many people who seek non-status loans are, to pay for home improvements. The application of compound interest made the agreement like swimming against the tide that was coming in faster than the Meadows could swim. The agreement is bad and cannot be cured and that is the end.'

Said Tony Meadows: 'We're absolutely delighted. We have two girls and the worst thing for me was watching them go without things like holidays.'

(*Sources*: Hull, 2007, and Montagu-Smith, 2007)

CASE STUDY QUESTIONS

1. What was the amount of the loan that Tony and Michelle Meadows initially borrowed?
2. Why was a repayment schedule of £149 a month inadequate to repay the loan? (Explain your calculation.)
3. If there were no repayments made and charges are ignored, what would be the outstanding amount owed after 15 years? (Explain your calculation.)
4. What might be the lessons here for lenders?

Suggested answers can be found in Appendix A.

8

Security – general

LEARNING POINTS

This chapter considers the advantages and disadvantages of taking appropriate security, and the need to perfect security interest.

Learning areas include:

- the nature of security;
- the attributes of good security;
- the need to perfect security;
- clauses in charge forms; and
- the advantages and disadvantages of obtaining security.

8.1 INTRODUCTION

Security is what guards a loan against default. Securing a loan ensures that, in the event of a default, the loan will be repaid. Security obtained by a lender is a claim on the borrower and on the asset that is secured, and provides the bank with recourse should the borrower breach the terms of the loan. To be converted into security, an asset needs to be subjected to a charge in favour of the lender. The procedures for applying a charge to an asset will vary depending upon the nature of the asset.

The *primary security* for a loan is the borrower: the lender lends only if it considers the borrower to be creditworthy. *Creditworthiness* is a lender's measure of the likelihood that a borrower will meet their debt obligations. It involves both the willingness and the ability of a borrower to repay a loan. In addition to this primary security, the lender might wish to obtain assets owned by the borrower as a safeguard in the event of default on a loan. Assets so obtained as security for a loan are known simply as *security* or *collateral*, because they are obtained as a back-up in the event of the unwillingness or inability of a borrower to repay a loan. Accordingly, a loan is described as *collateralised* when it is secured by assets. A *clean* or *unsecured* loan is one that is not secured by any assets. The status of a loan is generally described in terms of the amount of security available; thus a loan can be secured, or unsecured, or partly secured. Following the Consumer Credit Act 1974, rule 60L of the Financial Services and Markets Act 2000 (Regulated Activities) (Amendment) (No. 2) Order 2013, SI 2013/1881, defines a security in relation to a consumer credit agreement as:

> . . . a mortgage, charge, pledge, bond, debenture, indemnity, guarantee, bill, note or other right provided by the borrower or . . . at the implied or express request of the borrower . . . to secure the carrying out of the obligations of the borrower . . . under the agreement.

Security can be given either *directly* by the borrower or by a *third party* who is willing to guarantee the repayment of the debt.

8.2 THE ATTRIBUTES OF GOOD SECURITY

The extent to which security is deemed to be desirable is determined by its value, as well as by factors relating to cost and administration (Willingham, 1997). The ideal security is one that has adequate and stable *value*, which is expected to rise over time, and which is easy (i.e. cost-effective and uncomplicated) to *measure* and monitor, *charge* or take, and *realise*.

From these four words is derived the initialism VMCR, which describes the framework used to evaluate different types of security for desirability.

8.2.1 Value

Good security should have a stable *value* that is expected to increase over time. Generally, the value of security in the form of land and property is considerable, and the value can be expected to rise over time, although crashes in property prices are also equally possible. A life policy may or may not be worth much when it has just commenced, but its value is likely to rise over time. The value of shares may or may not be considerable and it can rise, as well as fall.

8.2.2 Easy to measure and monitor

Some assets are comparatively simple to *measure*, while others are more difficult. Publicly quoted shares are easy to value simply by looking at a financial newspaper, but monitoring the value may be more time-consuming and costly, because it is liable to fluctuate every moment. Insurance policies can be instantly valued by asking the insurer. It may be more costly and difficult to value land, both in terms of the time taken and the accuracy of estimates; and some assets, such as art and jewellery, may need multiple independent valuations.

8.2.3 Easy to charge

Procedures for *charging* an asset vary with the nature of the asset. Insurance policies and shares are easy to charge, while the process of taking a charge on property is more time-consuming and expensive.

8.2.4 Easy to realise

Realisation is the process of converting a secured asset into cash towards settlement of the debt due. It is easy to sell shares and recoup the money on an insurance policy assigned in favour of the lender. However, it is more difficult to sell land and property quickly, and forced sales can lower the realisable value of these assets.

8.3 PERFECTING SECURITY INTEREST

An asset belonging to the borrower or a third party needs to be charged to the lender to enable the lender to use it as security. *Perfection* of security interest involves the taking of various steps to ensure that the lender's interest in the security becomes enforceable. Failure to properly perfect a security interest can be fatal to the interest of the holder of the security (Wernick, 1991).

Assets need to be charged in favour of the lender if the lender is to have a valid and enforceable security interest in them. Methods of perfecting security interest will vary with the type of security obtained and some of these types are discussed in Chapter 9.

A *charge* is the process whereby an asset is converted by the lender to a security for the repayment of debt. A charge is a contractual agreement, which will specify which assets are being taken as security, the circumstances in which the lender can dispose of the assets and the circumstances in which the borrower can regain full control over the assets.

Charges can take several forms.

8.3.1 Forms of charge

In a *legal charge*, title to the assets offered as security is transferred into the name of the lender. The lender assumes legal title to the assets subject to the right of the borrower to have the assets retransferred when the conditions of the debt and its repayment are met.

An *equitable charge* is a charge that arises according to natural justice, fairness or equity, notwithstanding any omission that might nullify a legal charge. For example, a legal charge that was never perfected or completed, but where the intention of the parties to the transaction was clear that the asset was being offered to the lender as security, would result in an equitable charge. Indeed, it has been held that the mere deposit of title documents gave rise to an equitable charge. While this is no longer true in relation to land in England, company shares can still be equitably mortgaged by deposit of share certificates. In *United Bank of Kuwait v Sahib* [1997] Ch 107, the Court of Appeal held that the English Law of Property (Miscellaneous Provisions) Act 1989 repealed the common law rules relating to the creation of equitable mortgages by deposit of title deeds. An equitable charge is therefore not as effective as a legal charge; it will be extinguished by a *bona fide* ('good faith') purchaser for value who did not have notice of the mortgage. Even if valid, the lender will need to seek the courts' approval for disposing the asset.

A *fixed charge* confers a right on the lender to have recourse to a particular asset in the event of the debtor's default and is enforceable by the power of sale of the assets so charged.

A *floating charge* is similar to a fixed charge, once it crystallises. Crystallisation might take place upon the commencement of liquidation proceedings against the debtor. However, prior to crystallisation, it 'floats', and covers assets such as stocks and goods over which the debtor continues to exercise physical control.

In a *pledge*, sometimes called a *bailment*, the borrower temporarily gives possession of property to the lender to provide assurance that the debt will be repaid. Pledges were used in old-fashioned 'lock and key' advances whereby the lender retained goods under lock and key, and took delivery of, and released, goods as and when required by the borrower to meet day-to-day operating requirements. They are still widely used by pawnbrokers, which continues to remain a regulated credit industry. A pledge does not confer a right to sale or disposal of property.

A *lien* is a right to retain physical possession of tangible assets as security for underlying obligations. In *Brandao v Barnett* (1846) 12 Cl & Fin 787, it was held that a *banker's lien* is a general lien on all instruments, such as cheques and bills, deposited with the bank as banker by a customer, unless there was an express or implied contract to the contrary.

Hypothecation is a form of security interest whereby the underlying assets are pledged by delivery of a document or other evidence of title, rather than by the actual delivery of the assets. A bill of lading that requires endorsement by a lender is an example of hypothecation of goods as security for a debt. The borrower is able to continue using the assets that are under lien to the lender.

8.3.2 Terms and conditions of charging security

The lender needs to make clear the terms and conditions under which a loan is extended to the borrower in such a way as to avoid any ambiguity in the interpretation of the clauses. There are some lenders who merely state on the application forms that 'terms and conditions are available on request' and do not take care to make these clear to the borrower. Such practices are fraught with danger and need to be avoided.

Clauses in the charge forms will be usually drawn up in consultation with legal practitioners, so that the clauses comply with legal and regulatory requirements, and facilitate the recovery of monies as and when they fall due for repayment. Lenders need to draw up the terms and conditions carefully, so that every eventuality is anticipated and the security becomes enforceable. Lenders also need to ensure that their terms and conditions do not violate the provisions of the Unfair Contract Terms Act 1977 and the Consumer Rights Act 2015, because any perceived contraventions might nullify the value of the security in the eyes of the law.

Some of the standard clauses in loan agreements and charge forms are as follows.

The *all monies clause* prevents release of title until all sums due have been paid. For example, a lender who has extended a mortgage against the security of a home will be able to retain title to the property until the borrower has repaid all dues, including any credit card and unsecured overdraft borrowings that might have been granted to the borrower. The mortgage of the property will thus extend to all debts of the borrower with the lender. To reiterate the right to the repayment of all monies, the agreement will also usually include a further clause specifically excluding the operation of section 93 of the Law of Property Act 1925, which restricts the consolidation of mortgages. These clauses will ensure that the borrower does not seek the release of some or part of the security on a partial repayment of the loan.

A *continuing security clause* indicates that the security continues to remain in force notwithstanding any interim payments made in satisfaction of the debt, until such time the liabilities are discharged in full, and that the security will not prejudice or be prejudiced by any other security that might be held by the lender. The effect of this clause is to prevent the rule in *Devaynes v Noble* (1816) 35 ER 781 (known as *Clayton's case*) from becoming operative. The borrower will be prevented from arguing that subsequent deposits had the effect of cancelling earlier debts.

An *after-acquired clause* covers subsequent acquisitions of assets by the borrower and includes such assets as security for an existing loan. For example, a borrower whose property is mortgaged under a loan with an after-acquired clause may purchase adjacent land for further development, but will be unable to raise a new mortgage, because the after-acquired land is captured as security for the existing mortgage.

A *repayment-on-demand clause* gives a lender the right of repayment on demand. The inclusion of a repayment-on-demand clause will exclude the delays envisaged by section 103 of the Law of Property Act 1925, which prescribes certain minimum time periods for exercising the right to realise security. By using this clause, lenders are able to reserve for themselves the right to proceed more quickly with the sale of charged property.

A *conclusive evidence clause* states that something is not open or liable to be questioned or challenged. For example, a document signed by the lender may be deemed to be conclusive evidence, as between the lender and guarantor, of the amount of the liability under the guarantee or mortgage. A conclusive evidence clause provides the lender with an expeditious way of proving the borrower's liability, particularly in circumstances in which the transactions are complex and proving each one will take much time and effort. The validity of conclusive evidence clauses has been upheld by courts on many occasions. In *Bache & Co. (London) Ltd v Banque Vernes et Commercials De Paris SA* [1973] 2 Lloyd's Rep 437, Lord Denning held that the commercial practice of inserting conclusive evidence clauses is 'only acceptable because the bankers or brokers who insert them are known to be honest and reliable men of business who are most unlikely to make a mistake'. In *Dobbs v National Bank of Australasia Ltd* (1935) 53 CLR 643, the High Court of Australia held that a clause providing that a certificate signed by the manager or acting manager of the office at which the debtor's account was kept should be conclusive evidence of his indebtedness at the date of the certificate.

A *successor clause* makes an agreement binding upon the parties, 'their successors, and assigns', regardless of whether the nature of such successors is changed by reorganisation, acquisition or reconstitution. For example, the use of such a clause would ensure that a building society's conversion to a bank will not adversely affect the status of a loan extended to a borrower while the bank was still a building society.

8.3.3 Independent legal advice (ILA)

It is good practice for a lender to confirm that a borrower has obtained independent legal advice prior to obtaining the borrower's signature on a charge form. To be independent, legal advice needs to come from a lawyer not associated with the other contracting party – the lender, in this case. A certificate of independent legal advice (CILA) is a document that attests that a person has received legal advice on a proposed contract from an independent lawyer not associated with the other contracting party. When a borrower receives independent legal advice about a loan contract, that borrower will be precluded from later claiming that they were not aware of what they were signing or the consequences of what they were signing.

Between two parties to a contract, that practice is all the more important, because one party might be deemed to be in a stronger position that might give rise to a situation in which the weaker party claims that the stronger party exerted an undue influence to their detriment. Between a banker and a borrower, the borrower will be the weaker party. In *Allcard v Skinner* (1887) 36 Ch D 145, it was held that where one party has obtained benefit by exercising undue influence, the contract will be set aside. Allegations of undue influence have been successfully upheld in courts in situations in which a wife had guaranteed loans extended to the husband and in which an elderly father had guaranteed advances to the son. It is therefore extremely important that lenders protect themselves against the charge of undue influence by insisting on and gaining evidence that the borrower and any guarantor has not only sought, but actually obtained, independent legal advice before signing any charge form.

8.4 THE DESIRABILITY OF TAKING SECURITY

Lenders need to be aware that security has disadvantages, as well as advantages.

8.4.1 Advantages

- Security reduces the risk caused by asymmetry of information and moral hazard (see Chapter 10) and serves as an incentive for borrowers to repay, thus reducing loan losses and increasing profits.
- Because security lowers credit default risk, i.e. protects the bank against losses in the event of credit default, the lender is able to charge lower interest, thereby easing the cost of capital for business and consumers. A quick comparison of interest rates charged for secured mortgages and unsecured credit cards will make this obvious.
- Security enables lenders to extend finance to certain high-risk borrowers who might otherwise not be eligible.

8.4.2 Disadvantages

- There is a possibility of losing customers if a lender insists on security. Borrowers might feel threatened and insecure, and move to other lenders or forms of lending that do not require security.
- The availability of security may lead to weakened lending standards on the basis of an assumption that any default can be mitigated by security, particularly if the value of that security is perceived as likely to increase over time. It has been argued that 'increasing collateral requirements could increase the riskiness of bank's loan portfolio' (Stiglitz and Weiss, 1981: 408), skewing the portfolio towards wealthier borrowers able to offer more security, who are likely to be less risk-averse.
- Taking security is time-consuming and often involves monitoring, re-evaluation and complicated paperwork.
- Taking security involves costs and these costs are generally passed on to the borrower, raising their overall borrowing costs. In some cases, such as property, these costs can be quite high.
- The retention of title (ROT) clause – sometimes also known as a Romalpa clause because of its appearance in *Aluminium Industrie Vaassen BV v Romalpa Aluminium Ltd* [1976] 1 WLR 676 – expressly provides for the retention of legal title to any goods that a seller might have handed over to the buyer until the goods are paid for. Thus some of the goods that a lender might consider to be available as security within the purview of a floating charge might, in fact, be beyond the reach of the lender, because the title to those goods might continue to vest with the seller.
- Problems might arise if it is difficult to identify the precise assets that are charged to the lender, particularly if they are mixed up with others that are not.
- When secured creditors are allowed to seize and sell key assets, any liquidator or trustee in bankruptcy loses the ability to sell off the business

as a going concern and may be forced to sell it on a break-up basis, reducing the amount available to creditors.

- Lenders might enforce their security and seek repossession of key assets too early, forcing into bankruptcy a company that might otherwise have recovered.
- It is argued that the general principle of most insolvency regimes is that creditors should be treated *pari passu*, i.e. equally, and that allowing secured creditors a preference to certain assets violates ethical principles in relation to distribution of assets under an insolvency.
- Taking security does not preclude loan losses. Legal and other reasons might reduce or remove the security that was deemed to be available in the event of a borrower's default. Undue influence, for example, has been cited by borrowers and guarantors to escape liability. Lenders who have sued borrowers for their security are known to have lost, incurring additional legal costs in the process.
- There might be other circumstances in which the lender loses more money because of obtaining security. For example, the liability of a lender who has financed a borrower subsequently found guilty of environmental pollution might be unlimited if the borrower is unable to meet the costs and goes into insolvency. The lender may end up incurring primary liability for contaminated land if it has control of the land in question, and if the lender enforces its security and takes possession of the property, it may also have liability to remediate as an owner or a knowing permitter of that contamination.

8.5 CONCLUSION

Duygan and Grant (2006) found that the propensity to fall into arrears or to default in the face of an adverse income shock was closely related to the punishment incurred by doing so, which in turn depended on the legal framework. The legal and mortgage systems in different countries can interact to produce different trade-offs between speed and full asset recovery.

It was found that in the United States, for example, when house prices were rising, many lenders' incentives were tilted more strongly in favour of lending on the basis of collateral rather than affordability. If it turned out that the borrower could not afford to repay the loan, the lender would access the collateral relatively quickly, the lender taking the view that it would be better to retrieve the collateral alone in a lower-cost process than to incur the legal costs of pursuing defaulting borrowers for any deficiency. Thus a lending sector with a collateral-based business model developed in the United States and elsewhere, where conditions were conducive to its growth. (Ellis, 2008).

It is, however, not advisable for lenders to rely only on security as the basis for granting credit. The borrower's creditworthiness is the primary security on which sound credit decisions need to be based. Recognising security alone as mitigating failings in credit, and ignoring fundamentals such as industry prospects, income and affordability, can be misleading and may lead to loan defaults and economic meltdown.

FURTHER READING

Roberts, G., and Keller, A. (2015) *Law relating to financial services*, Cranbrook: Global Professional Publishing.

Willingham, J. (1997) *International handbook of corporate finance*, London: Glenlake/Fitzroy Dearborn.

REVIEW QUESTIONS

1. Why do lenders take security?
2. What are the attributes of good security?
3. Why do lenders recommend that guarantors and borrowers should seek independent legal advice?
4. Examine some of the main clauses that are incorporated in bank charge forms.
5. What are the disadvantages of taking security?

ACTIVITY

Read the clauses in any charge form that you might have executed (e.g. in relation to a mortgage or car loan). Identify the clauses discussed in section 8.3.2 within the charge form.

CASE STUDY *West Bromwich Building Society v Wilkinson and another* [2005] UKHL 44

Mark and Lynne Wilkinson bought a house in Norfolk in October 1988, with the help of a loan from the West Bromwich Building Society, which lent them a sum of £35,895 against the mortgage of the property. The loan, with interest, was repayable by monthly instalments of about £480.

The Wilkinsons defaulted almost immediately, after paying only two instalments in 1989. On 25 July 1989, the building society obtained an order for possession, which was executed on 9 October 1989. The property market was, at that time, in decline and it was some time before the building society could negotiate a sale. More than a year later, on 14 November 1990, it sold the house for £34,000, leaving a shortfall of £23,921.92, representing arrears of interest and other charges.

After giving up possession, the Wilkinsons moved into other accommodation. They subsequently separated and lived at different addresses. The building society did not contact them for more than 12 years. However, in November 2002, it served the Wilkinsons with a claim for £46,865.99 and costs, which represented the shortfall on the sale in 1990 with accumulated interest. The Wilkinsons said that the building society's claim was barred by section 20(1) of the Limitation Act 1980 – a claim that the building society contested.

The Limitation Act 1980 provides timescales within which action may be taken for breaches of the law. For example, it provides that breaches of an ordinary contract are actionable for six years after the event, while breaches of a deed – such as a mortgage deed, in this case – are actionable for 12 years after the event:

> No action shall be brought to recover . . . any principal sum of money secured by a mortgage or other charge on property after the expiration of twelve years from the date on which the right to receive the money accrued.

In 2005, the House of Lords held that the building society's claim in this action, which was commenced on 12 November 2002, was time-barred under statute. The default by the borrowers in paying a monthly instalment had the result of making the entire loan outstandings become repayable and entitled the building society to sell the house. The lender had given a notice in writing requiring payment 'forthwith of the moneys hereby secured', and therefore the mortgage money outstanding had become due and payable by Mr and Mrs Wilkinson one month after they had made default in paying a monthly instalment. For the purposes of the Limitation Act 1980, time had begun to run well before 9 October 1989, when the Society took possession of the house with a view to its sale. Therefore the appeal by the building society was dismissed.

CASE STUDY QUESTIONS

1. What was the security obtained by West Bromwich Building Society when it extended a loan to the Wilkinsons in October 1988?
2. Examine possible reasons for the shortfall in the sale proceeds of the security in relation to the loan granted.
3. Why do you think the Limitation Act 1980 is so named?
4. What is the limitation period for a mortgage deed?
5. Why was the case considered to be time-barred under statute?
6. What are the lessons here for lenders?

Suggested answers can be found in Appendix A.

9

Security – specific forms

LEARNING POINTS

This chapter looks at how to apply the principles of security to various forms of assets.

Learning areas include:

- land and property;
- stocks and shares;
- life policies;
- guarantees; and
- debentures, incorporating fixed and floating charges.

9.1 INTRODUCTION

Security can take the form of:

- proprietary security, such as commercial or residential land and property, in which case the lender does not take possession of the asset and the borrower is able to continue to make use of it;
- possessory security, whereby the lender is able to take possession of the assets, such as accounts receivable or book debts and goods or stock lying in the borrower's premises;
- intangible security, over assets such as intellectual property and licence fees payable for the use of software, etc.;
- financial instruments, such as shares and bonds;
- insurance policies;
- third-party security, such as guarantees with or without security owned by the third party;
- choses in action, or security of which the lender is not in possession, but which can be demanded in law, such as deposits and credit balances held either with a lender or with other institutions, over which the lender can exercise a right; or
- debentures, which include fixed and/or floating charges.

We examine some of these forms of security in what follows.

9.2 LAND AND PROPERTY

9.2.1 Nature and types

The definition of *land* includes any buildings situated upon the land, particularly where parts of buildings at different levels are in different ownership as in the case of flats. The Land Registration Act 2002 and Land Registration Rules 2003, SI 2003/1417, came into force in the UK on 13 October 2003. The Act and Rules govern the role and practice of HM Land Registry, and provide a more complete picture of a title to land and the rights and interests affecting it. They also establish a framework for the development of electronic conveyancing.

The Land Registry records the ownership rights of freehold properties, as well as leasehold properties on which the lease has been granted for a term exceeding seven years, and guarantees title to registered estates and interests in land. *Registered land* is land that has been registered with HM Land Registry. *Unregistered land* is land that has not yet been registered with the Land Registry. The Land Charges Department of the Land Registry maintains a computerised record relating to charges on unregistered land. The registered purchaser's interest gets priority over all other interests.

Freehold title is a perpetual right to property, i.e. title that is subject to no time limit.

- *Absolute freehold title* evidences absolute title in freehold property subject to entries on the register and unregistered or overriding interests.
- In *possessory freehold title*, there is no documentary evidence of title and the title depends on adverse possession, which allows a person to obtain title to land by being in possession of the land for a specified period of time. It conveys no guarantee of title at the time of registration, but it can be upgraded into absolute title after being in possession as proprietor for 12 years.
- *Qualified freehold title* is subject to a fundamental defect.

Leasehold title is subject to specific time limits.

- *Absolute leasehold title* is similar to absolute freehold title, but it is time-limited and also subject to covenants in the lease.
- *Good leasehold title* is similar to absolute leasehold, but the right of the landlord to grant the lease is not guaranteed.
- *Possessory leasehold title* is similar to possessory freehold, but time-limited.
- *Qualified leasehold title* is similar to qualified freehold, but time-limited.

A *legal mortgage* is 'a charge by deed' whereby the lender gains sufficient rights over the property that it can realise it as security, e.g. take possession of the property or sell it. A legal mortgage will be recorded by the Land Registry. According to section 29 of the Land Registration Act 2002, a person acquiring a legal estate for valuable consideration as owner takes it subject to any notices on the charges register, any unregistered interests that override (formerly known as *overriding interests*) and, if the estate is a lease, subject to burdens or covenants incidental to the lease. A person, such as a spouse, who is in actual occupation of a property may acquire an overriding interest in the property even if such interest is not registered (*Williams and Glyn's Bank Ltd v Boland* [1981] AC 487). Since *Boland*, lenders generally take steps to ensure that the occupants of a property being mortgaged give their informed consent to the mortgage in writing.

In an *equitable mortgage*, the mortgagee obtains only an equitable interest. This may occur because the mortgagor has only an equitable interest or because all of the formalities required for a legal mortgage have not been completed.

Both legal and equitable mortgages are non-possessory security interests. Usually, the mortgagor will remain in possession of the mortgaged asset.

A prudent lender will obtain security that has absolute legal or absolute freehold title and reject other types of property for which title is not absolute.

9.2.2 Advantages

- Land is usually the most valuable asset that is available to a lender as security. Values tend to rise more quickly than inflation.
- Clear proprietary title can be obtained for registered land and it will be guaranteed by the Land Registry, subject to any defects, covenants, etc. The Land Registry is actively encouraging owners of unregistered land to register their properties.
- Land is usually the main asset of a borrower and serves as a powerful incentive to make repayment of debts secured by the asset.
- Because the security of land will be expected to considerably reduce the risk of default, the lender is able to charge lower interest, thereby easing the cost of borrowing for businesses and persons. A comparison of interest rates charged for secured mortgages and unsecured credit cards will make this obvious.
- There is always a demand for land because its supply is fixed.
- The value of domestic property is fairly easy to estimate by means of comparison with the sale prices of nearby properties in the neighbourhood. Sale prices of neighbouring properties are readily available from the Land Registry and also from other dedicated websites.
- For registered land, the title documentation is fairly simple, there being only one document of title: the *land certificate*.

9.2.3 Disadvantages

- There have been periods during which property prices have consistently fallen, wiping out any available equity and giving rise to the situation of *negative equity*, whereby the loan amount exceeds the value of the security.

- Taking a security interest in land is relatively time-consuming and involves complex documentation that will need to be examined by qualified solicitors or conveyancers.
- The costs of securing land are high. Valuation, legal and other costs will need to be incurred, but these will generally be passed on to the borrower.
- Realisation will be a slow process.
- Valuation of factory or other industrial premises may be particularly difficult. Valuation may not be accurate. Each property is different and comparisons with other properties may not be appropriate. No accurate, up-to-date prices are available, as in the case of shares or life policies.
- Valuation may prove to be inaccurate, but the lender may not be able to hold a professional valuer responsible for losses.
- For registered land, the title documentation is fairly complex, because all prior documentation needs to be verified.
- In certain circumstances, the creation of a second mortgage will have legal implications for the first mortgagee.

9.2.4 Second mortgages

A *second mortgage* is a security interest created in a property that is already subject to a first legal charge. The claim of the second mortgagee will rank subsequent to that of the first mortgagee, but above any subsequent mortgagees, such as a third mortgagee. In the event of sale of the property, the sale proceeds will be first used to pay off the outstanding first mortgage and the balance applied to subsequent charges in order of registration at the Land Registry.

Second mortgages allow borrowers to raise capital or release the equity in their property without having to remortgage – particularly when property prices are rising and available equity rises correspondingly. As long as sufficient equity is available in the property, a lender will be willing to extend advances against a second charge on the property.

In certain circumstances, a second mortgagee may find the security interest diluted if the first mortgagee is able to 'tack' advances granted subsequent to the second mortgage onto the original first mortgage, thus gaining priority over the second mortgagee in respect of subsequent advances. *Tacking* is the adding on of a loan given by a lender at a subsequent period to a loan granted earlier, so as to prevent an intermediate lender from gaining priority over the first lender in respect to the further advances granted by the first lender. The Law of Property Act 1925 abolished tacking, except as expressly allowed by section 94 of the Act, i.e. where the first mortgage 'imposes an obligation' on the first lender 'to make such further advances'. However, because lenders usually do not commit themselves to such further advances, the applicability of tacking in the case of second mortgages will be rare.

EXAMPLE

Tacking can be explained as follows.

- Lender A extends a loan against a first mortgage of property.
- Lender B extends a second loan against a second mortgage of the same property.

Lender B's claim will rank second to that of lender A, but prior to all subsequent mortgages.

If lender A then extends further advances against the same property, lender A's claim in relation to such further advances will rank subsequent to that of lender B, unless lender A can prove that the first loan granted carried an obligation to grant such further advances.

9.3 LIFE INSURANCE POLICIES

Insurance can be defined as protection against the risk of financial loss (Kapoor, Dlabay and Hughes, 2004). Insurance shifts risk from one party to another. Insurance refers to a financial arrangement under which the costs of unexpected losses are redistributed from those who suffer the losses to all of the members of an insurance pool. An *insurance company* or *insurer* is a financial intermediary that, for a price, promises to pay specified sums contingent on future events. The insurer provides protection in the form of a policy to cover a person's life, or property, or liability.

Insurance is a legally binding contract between the insured and the insurer, i.e. the *policyholder* and the insurance company. In return for the payment of premiums, the insurer indemnifies the insured against certain insurable risks. The *premium* is the price of insurance, paid in a lump sum or in instalments over a period of time. The premiums paid by members into the pool are calculated by the insurance company's loss prediction system.

Relevant statute law includes the Life Assurance Act 1774, the Policies of Assurance Act 1867, the Insurance Companies Act 1980, and the Financial Services and Markets Act 2000. Regulation of the insurance sector in the UK is vested with the Financial Conduct Authority (FCA) and Prudential Regulation Authority (PRA).

9.3.1 Some key concepts relating to credit and insurance

Key concepts such as 'moral hazard', 'adverse selection' and 'asymmetry of information' are relevant to the understanding of insurance as a form of security.

- *Moral hazard* is the risk that the presence of a contract will affect the behaviour of one or more parties (see Chapter 10).
- *Adverse selection* is the greater preference of higher-risk people to buy insurance, with the likelihood that higher-than-average levels of claims will become payable by the insurer.
- *Asymmetry of information* arises when one party to a transaction has more or better information than the other party.

9.3.2 The principles of insurance

The lender needs to be aware of the key principles of insurance while using insurance as a means of mitigating risk.

- *Contract of indemnity* The insurers agree to compensate in the event of loss such that the insured is left substantially in the same position financially after the loss as if the loss had not taken place at all. In other words, the insured cannot profit from a loss or damage.
- *Duty of utmost good faith* (uberrimae fidei) All material facts about an insured risk must be disclosed to the insurers at the time of completing the proposal form – or subsequently, if the facts change. The relationship between insurer and insured is characterised by a considerable asymmetry of information. Proven misrepresentation of material facts will render the insurance void.
- *Requirement of insurable interest* The insured must be so situated with regard to the matter insured as to benefit by its existence and sustain loss from its destruction, i.e. the insured must have an actual pecuniary interest in the subject matter of the insurance.
- *Principle of betterment* In the event of a claim and where the thing reinstated improves the insured's position, a financial payment is required of the insured. The betterment principle can be varied where the final compensation for loss is an agreed value beforehand or where the policy is based on an agreed replacement of new for old.
- *Principle of contribution* If more than one policy covers the same risk, it may not be possible for the insured to claim on both and make a gain. In this situation, each of the insurers involved would be required to contribute a proportionate amount of the loss.
- *Principle of subrogation* In the event of a claim and where the insurers have fully indemnified the insured, the insured's original interests can be taken over by the insurers.
- *Principle of average* The compensation paid will be averaged or reduced proportionally if a property was not insured to the full amount of its replacement cost. *Underinsurance* means that the replacement value of the property or the value of the contents has been understated on the proposal, thereby lowering the premiums paid.
- *Principle of proximate cause (*causa proxima*)* When a loss has effectively been brought about by two or more causes, the proximate (i.e. immediate and not remote) cause of the loss should be a peril that has been insured.
- *Mitigation of loss* In the event of some mishap, the insured must take all necessary steps to mitigate or minimise the loss that any prudent person would take in the circumstances. If the insured does not do so, the insurer can avoid the payment of loss attributable to the negligence. While the insured is bound to do the best for the insurer, the insured is not bound to do so at the risk to their life.

9.3.3 Nature and types

Life insurance is a form of personal insurance, whereas *property insurance* is a form of general insurance.

Life insurance provides personal protection, and includes life insurance (also known as *assurance*), health insurance, employment insurance and other related forms of insurance. In return for payment of premiums to an insurance company, usually monthly or annually, *life insurance* will pay a lump sum, or the *sum assured*, to dependants on death of a named person (the *assured*) during the term of the policy. Life insurance premiums will vary depending upon the sum assured, the term of the policy and individual lifestyle factors, such as age, occupation, gender, state of health, smoker/non-smoker, etc. Life insurance could cover a number of personal contingencies and includes the following types.

- *Term life insurance* provides life cover for a fixed term. It pays a lump sum on death of the assured during the term of the cover and could be decreasing term insurance or level term insurance. While such policies are often used to cover a mortgage, they have no cash value or surrender value and therefore are unsuitable as security.
- *Whole life insurance* pays a lump sum on the death of the assured. A payout is certain, because death is inevitable, and lenders are willing to take as security a policy that has sufficient surrender value.

9.3.4 The use of insurance in lending

The lender can make use of insurance in a variety of ways to mitigate credit risk.

- *Insurance of security* Where a loan is given to enable the borrower to purchase certain assets, such as land, buildings, cars, etc., these assets are insured, so that any damage to these assets is covered by insurance. The value of the security is thus protected against unforeseen loss.
- *Insurance taken out by the borrower in addition to, or in lieu of, security* The borrower may arrange for insurance either of their own volition or at the behest of the lender to safeguard the lender against potential losses. For example, the lender might require a borrower to take out life insurance or disability insurance, which will pay out to the creditor if the borrower suffers an accident or dies before the debt is repaid. A mortgage protection policy pays out if a mortgagor is in default.
- *Insurance taken out by the lender in addition to, or in lieu of, security* The lender may arrange for insurance via derivative and other products as a hedge against abnormal or unexpected credit losses.
- *Insurance policies as security* Insurance policies can, in themselves, constitute security against which loans are extended. For example, a life insurance policy on which premium has been paid for a number of years

could have accumulated a considerable amount of value, and this can serve as security for a loan. This use of life insurance policies in lending is considered next in greater detail.

9.3.5 Life policies as security

A life insurance policy is issued by an insurance company or insurer on the life of the assured in favour of a *beneficiary* who may or may not be the assured. *Assignment* refers to the practice of giving that benefit of the insurance policy to somebody else – in the case of a life policy as security, the lender. The assignment must be witnessed and signed in accordance with the Policies of Assurance Act 1867. The order in which notices of assignment are received by the insurer determines their priority (*Dearle v Hall* (1828) 3 Russ 1).

Certain life policies can be assigned in favour of a lender as security for loans; not all life policies are suitable as security for lending. Endowment policies are considered to be the most suitable. However, even among endowment policies, not all policies are suitable. To be considered suitable security, endowment policies need to meet the following criteria.

- The policy should have adequate surrender value. *Surrender value* is the amount receivable in the event of the surrender of the policy. If the policy has been taken out recently, not much premium would have been paid on it and so it will not have accumulated much surrender value. A policy will need to have been in force for some years for it to have accumulated a reasonable amount of surrender value.
- There should not be any restrictions for charging the policy.
- The policy should not be taken out in trust for specific beneficiaries who are unable to charge their interest in it. For example, a policy made out in favour of dependent children will not be suitable as security for a loan.
- The insurance company should be reputable and well established.
- The policy should be legally enforceable under the relevant law of the country.

9.3.6 Advantages

- Insurance policies are very easy to value. The surrender value of the policy will be readily available from the insurance company, on request.
- The value increases provided that the insurance premium is paid as stipulated.
- The procedure for taking a charge is relatively simple and easy. A legal assignment involves sending an assignment form signed by the borrower to the insurance company, which will notify the lender of having noted the assignment.

- Realisation is relatively straightforward.
- In the event of the borrower's death, the insurer's pay-out will go towards liquidating a part or whole of the debt.
- Legal mortgage of a policy has advantages.
  - It will take priority, provided that the lender retains the policy and the insurer confirms that there are no other known charges.
  - At the request of the lender, the insurer is bound to note the lender's security interest in the policy.
  - The lender will not require the agreement of the beneficiary of the policy to surrender or claim maturity proceeds.

9.3.7 Disadvantages

- Life policies are not always available as security for a number of reasons.
  - Many prospective borrowers have not taken out endowment policies.
  - An endowment policy might have already been charged by the provider of a mortgage and might not be available as security for a new loan.
  - Many insurance companies provide loans directly against their policies, reducing the lending opportunities for other lending organisations.
- Some policies cannot be charged, for example policies written in trust for a child.
- New policies have either no or only inadequate surrender value.
- The insurer is able to set off an earlier claim with the assured prior to receipt of notice of assignment.
- Because a contract for life insurance is a contract *uberrimae fidei* ('of utmost good faith'), any non-disclosure of material facts will render the policy void. Material facts will influence the premium amount to be determined and the decision as to whether the risk should be assumed. In *London Assurance v Mansel* (1879) 11 Ch D 363, non-disclosure of the refusal of life insurance by a number of other insurers was deemed to be a material fact. In *Lindenau v Desborough* (1828) 8 B & C 586, non-disclosure of doubts about the mental health of the assured was deemed to be a material fact because a mentally ill person might be more prone to suicide.
- Equitable mortgages of life policies have a number of disadvantages.
  - They are subject to prior equities.
  - The insurance company is not obliged to take note of any notice received from a lender.
  - The beneficiary of the policy needs to authorise the insurance company to pay the proceeds to the lender. If the beneficiary does not cooperate, the lender will have to go to court to realise the proceeds.

9.4 STOCKS AND SHARES

9.4.1 Nature and types

A *share of stock* represents a unit of ownership in the issuing company. There are two main types of stock: common and preferred.

- *Common stock*, or *ordinary shares*, confer on the owner voting rights, the right to a share in the earnings of the company and a claim on the company assets in the event of liquidation. Ordinary shareholders are the ultimate risk-bearers of a company and hence are known as *equity holders*, while ordinary shares are known as *equity*.
- *Preferred stock*, or *preference shares*, generally do not confer voting rights, but do involve the right to a prior claim on assets and earnings over ordinary shares. Preferred stock holders receive dividends before ordinary shareholders and have priority over ordinary shareholders in the event of company insolvency. Preferred stock is more like bonds or loans than shares, because the return is fixed and whatever profits remain go to the ordinary shareholders.

The market value of a share is influenced by a number of factors, such as the company's financial condition, its growth potential, and its earnings and dividend record, as well as external factors, such as the general state of the economy.

The main categories of common stock are as follows.

- *Blue-chip stocks* are high-quality stocks issued by well-established companies with many years of proven success and earnings growth. They tend to be a relatively safe form of security.
- *Income stocks* yield a higher-than-average dividend income. The value of such stocks is not likely to appreciate much, because a high proportion of the earnings is paid out as dividends.
- *Growth stocks* are expected to grow rapidly. Because profits are ploughed back into the business, the dividend yield may be low. The lender may find the value of the stock rising quickly if the company performs as expected.
- *Speculative stocks* may be issued by little known or newly formed companies, or they may be 'penny stocks', which have little or no value. This last category will not be considered suitable security by lenders.
- *Partly paid shares* are shares that have not yet been fully paid up and on which the company has a right to call for further or remaining payment(s).
- *Foreign shares* are shares in companies registered abroad and may or may not be expressed in foreign currency.
- *Shares in private companies* are not publicly quoted in the stock exchange and are not subject to the rigorous listing requirements of publicly quoted companies.

9.4.2 Advantages

- The value of stocks and shares tends to grow over time. Growth stocks, for example, which pay low or no dividends and reinvest company profits, can rise fairly quickly in value. As a whole, the stock market has had an upward trend in values, with years of gain generally outnumbering those of decline.
- Monitoring the value of stocks and shares traded on major exchanges is simple, because prices are readily available online and in the financial press.
- It is comparatively easy to take a charge over this form of security. In *Harrold v Plenty* [1901] 2 Ch 314, the mere deposit of share certificates was construed as having created an equitable charge for the lender. A legal charge created by transfer of shares in the lender's name gives complete control over the shares and enables the lender to sell the shares in the event of loan default. In *Deverges v Sandeman Clark & Co.* [1902] 1 Ch 579, it was held that the mortgagee has a power of sale that can be exercised if the borrower fails to repay by the due date or, where no due date is fixed, after a proper demand or notice has been given and a reasonable time has elapsed. Lenders usually keep shares in nominee accounts and have full power of sale should default occur. Provided that the lender is not aware of any defects in the title to the shares, a legal charge gives the lender priority over any prior equitable rights.
- Realisation is fairly straightforward. Stocks traded on major exchanges can be bought and sold quickly, and are easily at readily ascertainable prices and therefore highly liquid.

9.4.3 Disadvantages

- There is a risk that the value may fall over time. Companies may fail, stock prices may drop and the value of the security may disappear. Even if shares in general are performing well, shares in a single company may perform badly and the lender may see the value of the security diluted over time.
- Shares fluctuate in value and continuous monitoring of the share price will be required. The stock market can be very volatile and prone to sudden withdrawals of large amounts of funds by big players such as insurance companies, pension funds and international banks.
- The value of shares may be inflated owing to fraud or overstatement of values in the company books.
- The value of shares will be dependent upon a number of external factors over which neither the lender nor the borrower has much control, e.g. the condition of the market, the state of the company, speculative bids, ratings by credit rating agencies, etc.

- Unlike land and property, for which lenders are happy to lend up to 90 per cent or more of the value of the asset, a margin of at least 25–30 per cent is recommended in the case of shares (Willingham, 1997).
- While lenders may like to diversify risk by taking a number of different shares as security rather than only shares in a single company, such diversification will come at the cost of increased paperwork.
- The forced sale of a large stake in a company may depress the share price further. Realisation will also involve costs such as brokerage commissions.
- The restructuring of company shares may cause problems for the lender. For example, in the event of a rights issue, existing shareholders have the right to buy a specified number of new shares from the company at a specified (lower) price within a specified time frame. The right to buy new shares in the company may be rejected, accepted in full or accepted in part by each shareholder. Rights are often transferable, allowing the holder to sell them on the open market. Rights can be *renounceable* (sold separately from the share to other investors) or *non-renounceable* (shareholders must either take up the rights or let them lapse). Once the rights have lapsed, they no longer have any value. A lender who does not have a legal charge over shares may not be aware of the rights issue at all, and the value of the shares it holds as security will be reduced whether the borrower exercises the rights and acquires new shares that are not deposited as further security or the rights are allowed to lapse. Similarly, bonus shares that involve the issue of additional shares at no extra cost have the effect of lowering the market value of existing shares, while increasing the overall number of shares on issue. A lender who does not have a legal charge over shares may not be aware of the bonus issue and the value of the shares that it holds as security will be reduced if the borrower does not deposit the additional bonus shares received as additional security.
- If the share transfer form or letter are forged, the lender will lose the right to the shares taken as security. In *Sheffield Corporation v Barclay* [1905] AC 392, the signature of one of the transferors was forged. The company had to reimburse the person whose signature was forged and the bank had to reimburse the company for the implied wrongful warranty that the signature was genuine.
- Many companies require their directors to hold a certain minimum number of company shares to qualify them as directors. If the director were to execute a legal charge to a lender for transfer of such 'qualification' shares, that would lose the director their qualification to be on the board of the company.
- In some countries, such as the United States, there are regulations that stipulate a high margin or low loan-to-value (LTV) to prevent speculation in stocks using borrowed funds.

- The stock market is growing in complexity and opacity. Market turbulence can wipe out the value of a lender's security within a very short time.
- Unquoted shares will pose special problems. There may be restrictions on ownership and, consequently, if a need for sale arises, it may be difficult to find investors willing to buy. Unlike quoted shares, there will be difficulty in ascertaining current prices. Even if valuation is made by a comparison with similar quoted companies, the absence of ready quotations and valuation will deter potential buyers.
- Foreign shares may be subject to foreign law, as well as subject to currency risk resulting from fluctuation in the exchange rate.
- Partly paid shares will involve further payments by the shareholders as and when the company makes a call for such payments. There is a chance that such shares will become worthless if the call money is not paid up on time. If the lender has a legal charge on such shares, the lender will become liable for paying up on additional calls. Such calls will also be made when the company goes into liquidation, when the shares are not likely to be worth anything. Partly paid shares are therefore not recommended as security for lenders.

9.5 GUARANTEES

9.5.1 Nature and types

Guarantees are widely used by lenders. A guarantee is a promise or assurance offered by a third party to repay the lender if the borrower fails to repay the loan. Under section 4 of the Statute of Frauds 1677, a guarantee must normally be in writing and must be signed by or on behalf of the party acting as the guarantor. The guarantee does not need to be notarised or registered. Developments in case law mean that the guarantor is required to sign a document indicating that they have fully understood the legal significance of making a guarantee. While the guarantor has a right to know the extent of liability, the lender needs to take care that the duty of confidentiality to the borrower is not breached.

When the lender receives notice of the guarantor's death, mental incapacity or insolvency, it will be advisable to close the loan account and route future transactions through a new account to avoid the rule in *Devaynes v Noble* (1816) 35 ER 781 (known as *Clayton's case*) from becoming operative. In *Bradford Old Bank Ltd v Sutcliffe* [1918] 2 KB 833, the liability of a mentally incapacitated guarantor was deemed to be satisfied by subsequent credits because the account had not been closed when the guarantor became mentally incapable.

The guarantor who pays up on the borrower's default has the right of subrogation into the shoes of the lender, i.e. to assume the creditor's rights against the borrower who has defaulted. Many guarantees normally contain a clause that prevents the guarantor from standing in competition with the lender for the borrower's assets. In *Moschi v LEP Air Services Ltd* [1973] AC 331, it was held that the guarantor's liability arose only when the principal debtor defaulted.

Guarantees will therefore have to contain an indemnity clause that secures the liability of the guarantor even if the borrower escapes liability. The lender will generally incorporate suitable clauses in the guarantee document to ensure that they have *simultaneous recourse* against both the borrower and the guarantor, and can seek repayment from both or either to satisfy a debt. The lender can pursue the guarantor independently and is not bound to take action against the principal debtor first. Certain other types of guarantee may specify that the lender needs to exhaust the remedies available against the principal borrower *before having recourse* to the guarantor.

A guarantee will usually be *limited* to a specified amount and an assessment of the guarantor carried out to confirm their current, as well as future, estimated worth for the amount guaranteed. The practice of obtaining *unlimited* guarantee documents has been discouraged by law, as well as the unwillingness of potential guarantors to undertake unlimited liability.

A *discrete guarantee* covers a specific transaction. The amount of debt that needs to be guaranteed and the duration of the guarantee are specified at the outset. A *continuing guarantee* lasts for an indefinite period and covers a flow of transactions within a specified overall limit.

The guarantee itself can be secured or unsecured. When a guarantor offers tangible security (e.g. property or shares) to back the guarantee, it is described as *third-party security* in comparison with the *direct security* that a lender might obtain against a borrower's own assets.

Guarantees can be joint *or* several, or joint *and* several. Guarantees are generally drawn up as joint and several, meaning that each co-guarantor is liable for the whole of the sum guaranteed. If a lender proceeds initially against only one or some of the guarantors, the remaining guarantors will continue to be liable and can be sued at a subsequent date (Civil Liberty (Contribution) Act 1978). A lender needs to ensure that any loan is released only after all of the guarantors have signed the guarantee document. If a co-guarantor fails or refuses to sign a guarantee, prior signatories to the guarantee can escape liability on the grounds that they signed on the understanding that all signatures would be obtained (*National Provincial Bank of England v Brackenbury* (1906) 22 TLR 797).

Guarantees can be given for loans by different types of entity, including:

- between individuals, e.g. a parent for a child (the child may be too young or have inadequate assets), or a child for a parent (the parent may be too old or have inadequate assets), or one spouse for another, etc.;
- by a solicitor for a client;
- by a director for a company;
- by a parent company for a subsidiary or related company; or
- by a government or central bank for a state-owned borrower.

After the abolition of the *ultra vires* rule, the capacity of a limited company to give a guarantee is clearly accepted. A guarantee given by a company will be shown as an off-balance-sheet contingent liability, unless the liability is crystallised by the invocation of the guarantee.

The Infants Relief Act 1874 invalidated certain contracts made by minors and prohibited actions to enforce contracts ratified after majority. Under most circumstances, loan contracts with minors were therefore deemed to be void. In *Coutts & Co. v Browne-Lecky and others* [1947] KB 104, a guarantee by an adult of a minor's overdraft was held to be void because the principal debt was void. In *R v Wilson* (1879) 5 QBD 28, a minor was acquitted of leaving the country with the intention of defrauding creditors on the ground that, since the claim of the creditors rested on contracts declared 'absolutely void', the minor in fact had no creditors. However, after the Minors' Contracts Act 1987, the Infants Relief Act 1874 no longer invalidates certain contracts entered into by minors.

9.5.2 Advantages

- Guarantees offered by high-net-worth individuals can be valuable. Guarantees will be written to cover the value of the debt *plus* any accumulated interest and charges.
- The lender may enforce its rights under the guarantee without first trying to recover the debt from any pledged collateral (*HSBC Realty Credit Corp. (USA) v O'Neill*, 745 F.3d 564 (2014)).
- In case of bankruptcy of the borrower, the trustee in bankruptcy has no claim on third-party security.
- Valuation is comparatively straightforward. The lender regularly obtains status reports on the guarantor.
- A guarantee is very simple to take, involving only obtaining signatures on a document, and ensuring that the guarantor has the power and authority to execute the guarantee.
- A guarantor has a strong incentive to ensure that the borrower remains creditworthy and capable of repaying the loan, particularly when the guarantor has provided security to back the guarantee.

9.5.3 Disadvantages

- Unlike borrowers who expect that a loan will have to be repaid, guarantors do not expect to actually be in a position in which they are asked to pay for the debts of the borrower. While a borrower uses the loan to acquire assets and increase the potential to generate cash, the guarantor might need to sell assets, as well as reduce their own cash balances, to meet the obligations under a guarantee. They are therefore likely to vigorously resist any claim made by a lender.
- The guarantor's own finances may not be adequate to absorb the shock of having to repay a borrower's debt. Deterioration in the guarantor's financial position might invalidate the assumptions made at the time of assessment of the guarantor's worth. A guarantor may not be subject to

the same rigorous monitoring process as a borrower and the guarantor's financial position could have deteriorated, even to the point of insolvency, without the lender's knowledge.

- A guarantee by a company might be part of a complex arrangement whereby a cross-guarantee might be triggered when invoked.
- Some of the assets thought to be available against a guarantee might turn out to be removed or outside the scope of the guarantee.
- The guarantor might be a valued customer who the lender does not wish to alienate. In such circumstances, the lender might be reluctant to invoke the guarantee and lose the business provided by the guarantor.
- It is a general requirement that there should be sufficient legal 'consideration' for a guarantee. A guarantee must be backed by consideration unless it is executed as a deed or under seal. While certain situations, such as parental guarantee for a child's debt, do not require consideration to be proved, the lack of consideration in certain other situations might invalidate a guarantee. Where the consideration is further advances within an existing overdrawn account, the lender must prove that further advances were made (*Provincial Bank of Ireland v Donnell* [1932] 67 ILTR 142; *Bank of Montreal v Sperling Hotel Co. Ltd* 36 DLR (3d) 130) (1973).
- A guarantee may be negated on technicalities for not having been executed properly. Certain guarantees may be invalid from the outset, for example a company guaranteeing a loan made to a director of that company.
- Where a guarantor normally resides outside the country, the lending transaction might become subject to the jurisdiction of different laws.
- A borrower located in a different country might be able and willing to repay a debt, but prevented from repatriating the required funds by the central bank in that country. In such cases, a guarantor located outside the borrower's country may resist demands for payment with the argument that 'local payment' has been made by the borrower.
- A guarantee that requires the lender to first exhaust all remedies against the borrower can be administratively burdensome, time-consuming and costly.
- If the guarantee does not have the appropriate clauses, the lender may not be able to crystallise a claim on the guarantor's assets when the guarantor goes into insolvency, if the borrower continues to be financially sound and has not defaulted.
- Unless the guarantee document provides otherwise, the guarantor has an immediate right against the principal borrower when called to pay up under the guarantee (*Davies v Humphreys* (1840) 6 M & W 153). This will place the guarantor in direct competition with the lender for the borrower's assets.
- If there is a material variation in the loan account to which the guarantor's consent was not obtained, the guarantor will be discharged

from liability (*Ward v National Bank of New Zealand* (1883) 8 App Cas 755).

- The guarantor may be discharged if there is a change in the constitution or legal position of the parties, for example if the partner in a borrowing partnership firm dies or a borrowing company merges to form a new company (*Bradford Old Bank v Sutcliffe* [1918] 2 KB 833).
- Legal objections can prevent a lender from realising a guarantee. In certain situations in which the guarantor has signed a guarantee without fully understanding the consequences, the courts have held that the guarantor is not liable for any debt.
- A number of guarantors have pleaded that they signed the guarantee under 'undue influence' and have successfully escaped liability. For example, in both *Barclays Bank plc v O'Brien* [1994] 1 AC 180 and *Royal Bank of Scotland plc v Etridge (No. 2)* [2001] UKHL 44, the House of Lords acknowledged that the relationship between the debtor and the surety as man and wife was such that there may be an issue of undue influence. The lender should have been put on inquiry when taking the security and should have taken reasonable steps to ensure that the wife's agreement to stand surety had been properly obtained. If the lender cannot show that reasonable steps had been taken, the security cannot be enforced. Since *Etridge*, it is no longer sufficient only to seek a certificate from a solicitor that a spouse was independently advised of the risks taking when granting the security; new guidelines require a number of steps to be taken, including direct communication between the lender and the spouse or guarantor. Lenders need to set up appropriate internal procedures to ensure compliance with the law and seek legal advice as appropriate.

9.6 DEBENTURES – FIXED AND FLOATING CHARGES

9.6.1 Nature and types

The usage of the term *debenture* varies in different contexts and jurisdictions. An *unsecured debenture* is not secured by liens or pledges on specific assets, while a *secured debenture* is backed by assets. Here, a debenture is defined as a security interest that creates fixed and floating charges over all of the property of the borrower. A debenture secured by land and/or buildings is called a *mortgage debenture*. Debentures are used by governments and large companies to obtain funds.

A *fixed charge* identifies and secures existing specific assets such as land, buildings and machinery.

A *floating charge* is a security interest over – typically, but not necessarily – all of the assets of a company that 'floats' until crystallised, such crystallisation being usually triggered by a default by the borrower under the terms of the underlying loan documentation. A floating charge enables assets such as stock, debtors or receivables and cash that fluctuate over time to be caught as security. Floating charges cannot be created by individual persons or ordinary partnerships. *Re Yorkshire Woolcombers Association* [1903] 2 Ch 295 is generally cited as providing the most authoritative definition of a floating charge as a charge over a class of assets, both present and future, which class will be changing from time to time. Until the charge crystallises and attaches to the assets, the chargor may carry on using the assets in the ordinary course of business.

More recently, in *Re Spectrum Plus Ltd* [2005] UKHL 41, at [111], a floating charge was described as 'not finally appropriated as a security for the payment of the debt until the occurrence of some future event. In the meantime the chargor is left free to use the charged asset and to remove it from the security'.

9.6.2 Advantages of floating charges

- A floating charge enables the lender to take control over assets that are otherwise difficult to charge. The charge can cover goods in the process of manufacture, as well as future purchases.
- The procedure for creating a floating charge is fairly straightforward.
- A floating charge enables the lender to have priority of claim over unsecured creditors in the event of an insolvency (*Re Panama, New Zealand and Australian Royal Mail Co.* (1870) 5 Ch App 318).
- Floating charges are extremely flexible. From the lender's perspective, the security will cover each and every asset of the chargor. From the borrower's perspective, there is complete freedom to deal with the assets and dispose of them in the ordinary course of business.
- If necessary, the lender is able to crystallise the charge and then sell off the available assets. The Enterprise Act 2002 has enabled holders of floating charges to appoint an administrator simply by filing a notice of appointment at court, without a court application and hearing.
- The lender is also able to preserve the company as a going concern by appointing an administrator or administrative receiver to take over the management and control of the business with a view to discharging the debt out of income or selling off the entire business as a going concern. However, the ability of lenders who hold pre-existing floating charges to appoint an administrative receiver has been restricted under the Enterprise Act 2002.

9.6.3 Disadvantages of floating charges

- The valuation of assets covered by a floating charge is notoriously difficult. The price of goods may fluctuate, making valuation difficult.
- A floating charge cannot normally be enforced until it has crystallised. Because full control over the assets continues with the borrower prior to

any crystallisation, the assets may be irretrievably lost or may have fallen in value before realisation can take place.

- The costs of realisation will be high. Assets that have been caught by the crystallisation will have to be classified, stored, monitored and sold. Goods may be perishable and storage may be expensive. Goods may have been manufactured for a specific purpose and may not be in general demand if offered for sale. The lender might require the cooperation of the borrower for effecting a sale and such cooperation may not be forthcoming.
- The charge may be legally invalid if a business was insolvent when security was given.
- A floating charge and its crystallisation may generate adverse publicity to both the lender and the borrower.
- In the event of an insolvency, the lender's claim will rank behind holders of fixed security, such as a mortgage or fixed charge, and preferred creditors.
- A floating charge can be displaced by a subsequent fixed charge (*Church of England Building Society v Piskor* [1954] Ch 553).
- A third-party debt order (also known as a garnishee order in other jurisdictions) has priority over a floating charge prior to its crystallisation. Accordingly, the holder of the floating charge does not have any claim over any payment made to a garnishee prior to crystallisation. The existence of a floating charge does not defeat or prevent executions by judgment creditors (*Evans v Rival Granite Quarries Ltd* [1910] 2 KB 979).
- Another person can claim a right of set-off against goods covered by a floating charge even if they have notice of the floating charge, provided that the cross claim arises prior to crystallisation (*Biggerstaff v Rowatt's Wharf Ltd* [1896] 2 Ch 93).
- As regards security interests created before any crystallisation, a fixed charge has priority over an earlier floating charge. This holds good even if a holder of a subsequent fixed charge had notice of an earlier floating charge.
- Even after crystallisation, if the company creates a fixed charge over the charged assets, this subsequent fixed charge will have priority if the chargee (i.e. the holder of the new fixed charge) did not have notice of the crystallisation. Floating charges take effect in equity only and consequently are defeated by a *bona fide* purchaser for value without notice of the charge.
- Stock may be subject to retention of title (ROT) clauses and dispute over priority of contending claims.

9.7 THE REALISATION OF SECURITY

Realisation is the process whereby the assets taken as security for advances are converted to cash to repay a debt that is in default.

9.7.1 Action to be taken

The action to be taken by a lender in respect of realising available security will vary depending on the following factors.

- *The nature of the charge, e.g. whether it is legal or equitable* Generally, where a lender holds a legal charge, security can be realised without the need to obtain the consent of either the borrower or the courts, whereas in the case of an equitable charge, the courts will need to be approached to authorise any action related to realisation. In the US, a crucial element in any mortgage foreclosure proceeding is that the lender seeking foreclosure must demonstrate that it has standing to foreclose, which standing may be established by either an assignment or an equitable transfer of the mortgage (*McLean v JPMorgan Chase Bank NA*, 79 So.3d 170 (Fla. 4th DCA 2012)).
- *The nature of the security* We have considered the attractiveness of various forms of security in respect of ease of realisation throughout this chapter. For example, realising the proceeds of a life policy that has been legally assigned to a lender will simply involve the issue of a notice to the insurer to remit the proceeds of the policy in settlement of loan default. The realisation of land will take much more time and will involve a variety of processes such as valuation, advertisement, viewings, auction, conveyancing, etc.
- *The circumstances of the case* The lender also needs to recognise that each case will be different and that the circumstances of each case will need to be carefully considered before any decision is made to realise the security that has been charged to it.
- *The other legal remedies available* The lender will need to ensure that all other remedies against the borrower have been exhausted, and that proper procedures and legal requirements, such as reminders and notices of default, have been served. Some of the issues relating to recovery action are discussed further in Chapter 10.

9.7.2 Factors to be considered

The lender will need to carefully consider the various options available prior to the decision to realise the security. The issues that the lender will need to bear in mind will include:

- the possibility of 'nursing' the borrower back to health, so as to generate the revenues required to repay the debt;
- the possibility of selling the entire business as a going concern, rather than selling the break-up assets, which will be worth much less;
- its own position in relation to other creditors in the order of priority in the event of any insolvency;

- the costs of realisation, i.e. whether the realisation proceeds will be adequate to cover the costs plus at least a part of the debt due;
- the need to realise security in a commercially reasonable manner (*Smith v Firstbank Corp.*, WL 951377 (2013)), failure to do which will leave a lender vulnerable to litigation; and
- the likelihood of being able to realise the security successfully, which may depend upon legal and other factors, with an unsuccessful legal action resulting in, for example, additional costs without any attendant benefits, and which may also generate unfavourable publicity and customer animosity.

The various risks that form part of the risks of realisation also need to be evaluated carefully. While security serves to mitigate *credit risk*, it carries its own risks.

- *Collateral risk*, *recovery risk* (Bessis, 2002), or *realisation risk* (see Figure 9.1), refers to the combination of risks faced by a lender who needs to realise the security obtained towards repayment of debt.

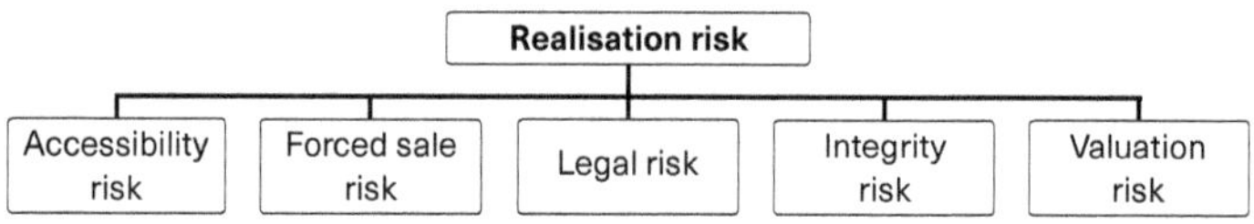

Figure 9.1 Realisation risk

- *Accessibility risk* is the risk that the assets secured to the lender may not be readily accessible to enable them to be seized and sold. Security such as bank deposits will be readily accessible, whereas mobile assets such as ships and planes could be difficult to seize. Aircraft can only be seized at airports, but if a plane flies within local airports abroad, it might be difficult to seize or even locate.
- *Integrity risk* is the risk that the assets seized by the lender with a view to their sale are damaged or have become defective. Assets can be damaged either inadvertently or deliberately, prior to or in the process of being seized.
- *Valuation risk* is the risk that the value of the assets is not readily ascertainable. Valuation will be dependent upon the existence of an active secondary market, the volatility in the market and market demand.
- *Forced sale risk* is the risk of loss of asset value as a result of the sale of assets under the constraints imposed by the lender or law. When a sale of property is carried out under the duress of law to satisfy debts incurred by the owner of the property, there may not be adequate opportunity to identify a buyer who is prepared to pay the reasonable value of the asset, resulting in the sale going ahead for a much-reduced price. Selling large amounts of assets at short notice will be particularly risky.

Legal risk, meanwhile, can arise as a result of disputes in law in a number of ways. Borrowers have successfully avoided giving up security by arguing that undue influence was exerted on the borrower or guarantor. As seen earlier, undue influence has been proven in certain circumstances to exist in cases of unequal bargaining power, e.g. between a husband and his wife (*National Westminster Bank plc v Morgan* [1985] AC 686; *Barclays Bank plc v O'Brien* [1994] 1 AC 180), and between an elderly parent and adult child (*Bullock v Lloyds Bank Ltd* [1955] Ch 317; *Avon Finance Co. Ltd v Bridger* [1985] 2 All ER 281).

The lender might be found guilty of *misrepresentation* if the lender was in possession of facts that should have given rise to a suspicion that the principal debtor was defrauding the guarantor and if it withheld these from the guarantor (*National Provincial Bank of England v Glanusk* [1913] 3 KB 335).

The defence of signing a document by *mistake,* i.e. *non est factum* ('not my act'), is available to those who were unable to understand the purpose of the document that was signed or those who signed a document that was not the document that was intended to be signed (*Foster v McKinnon* (1869) LR 4 CP 704).

The Enterprise Act 2002 is said to have encouraged a number of borrowers to avoid their debt obligations by resorting to *insolvency.* When a borrower goes into insolvency, any assets realised by the lender prior to insolvency might be subject to the risk of being considered as a preference and/or a transaction at undervalue.

Where a person or company transfers assets or pays a debt to a creditor shortly before going into insolvency, that payment or transfer can be set aside on the application of the trustee in bankruptcy or liquidator as a *preference.* For a transaction to be deemed to be a preference, it should be demonstrated that:

- the person or company was insolvent at the time the payment was made;
- the person or company went into insolvency within a specified 'relevant time' after making the payment; and
- the payment had the effect of putting the creditor in a better position than other unsecured creditors.

When a transaction is declared to be a preference, arrangements will be made for restoring the position as it would have been had that preference not been made. Sections 239 and 340 of the Insolvency Act 1986 describe the circumstances under which an unfair preference may be deemed to have been given by an insolvent company and individual respectively.

A transaction entered into by an individual or company which subsequently goes into insolvency can be deemed to be a transaction at *undervalue,* which the court can order to be set aside, provided that:

- the consideration received in the transaction, 'in money or money's worth', is significantly less than the value provided;
- the transaction was entered into during the 'relevant time' immediately prior to the bankruptcy; and

- at the time of the transaction, the borrower was unable to pay the debts as they fell due or became unable to pay its debts as they fell due as a result of the transaction.

In such circumstances, the court will arrange for restoring the position as it would have been had that transaction not been entered into. Sections 238 and 339 of the Insolvency Act 1986 describe the circumstances under which a transaction by an insolvent company and individual, respectively, may be deemed to be at an undervalue.

The 'relevant time' for preferential or undervalue transactions is laid down in sections 240 and 341, respectively, for a company and a person. In the case of a person, for example, for a preference that is not a transaction of undervalue, the 'relevant time' is two years if the beneficiary is an associate and six months in other cases.

Realisation of security is often costly, time-consuming and inefficient (Willingham, 1997). The realisation of security will involve the break-up or forced sale of the assets. The value of such assets will be less under such circumstances than if the asset had been sold as a going concern. Realisation of security should therefore be resorted to only when all other viable alternatives have failed.

There is a tendency among many lenders to readily grant credit facilities to prospective borrowers on the strength of the security available, without paying adequate attention to the viability of the loan proposal. It is important that lenders realise the dangers in this approach. Security is obtained as a back-up only and more as an incentive for the borrower to repay. It should always be remembered that the primary security is the borrower themselves and the borrower's activities need to generate the resources required for repayment of borrowings. Thus it will be the primary security, i.e. the borrower, rather than any security to which the lender will look for repayment. Sometimes, the very provision of security might be an indicator that default is likely to take place. It will be unwise to assume that the costs of default will be entirely compensated by obtaining security (Chant, 1970). Lenders are rarely able to recover both loan and costs by the realisation of security.

9.8 CONCLUSION

The lender is able to take a range of assets as security, including land and property, life policies, stocks and shares, guarantees, and debentures, incorporating fixed and floating charges.

- Land is valuable and the value generally rises over time, but it is relatively slow or difficult to measure, charge and realise.
- Life policies are easy to take, easy to monitor and relatively easy to realise, but not all policies will have sufficient value to be of use as security.

- Quoted stocks and shares are easy to charge, easy to value and easy to realise, but there is a possibility of dilution, or even disappearance, of value over time.
- Guarantees are relatively easy to measure and take, but more difficult to monitor and realise.
- Floating charges are relatively easy to take, but more difficult to measure, monitor and realise.

However, these are referred to as 'collateral' for a reason; the 'primary' security is always the borrower. Undue reliance by lenders on collateral security has often led to rapid credit growth and asset price bubbles, followed by sharp cyclical downturns, financial turmoil and loan defaults.

While the taking of security may serve as a good motivator for borrower repayment, that security alone cannot safeguard the lender's interests against defaults and loan losses.

FURTHER READING

Bessis, J. (2002) *Risk management in banking*, Chichester: John Wiley & Sons.

Roberts, G., and Keller, A. (2015) *Law relating to financial services*, Cranbrook: Global Professional Publishing.

Willingham, J. (1997) *International handbook of corporate finance*, London: Glenlake/Fitzroy Dearborn.

REVIEW QUESTIONS

1. Distinguish between proprietary security and possessory security.
2. What are the advantages and disadvantages of taking the following forms of security?
   - Land and property
   - Life insurance policies
   - Stocks and shares
   - Guarantees
3. Examine the nature of a floating charge. What are its advantages and disadvantages?
4. Examine the various components of realisation risk.
5. What are the implications of transactions at undervalue and preference for a lender in connection with the realisation of security?

ACTIVITY

Visit www.publications.parliament.uk/pa/ld199899/ldjudgmt/jd991021/barc.htm and read the transcript of *Barclays Bank plc v Boulter and Boulter* [1999] 4 All ER 513 in the House of Lords. Examine some of the issues raised about undue influence, misrepresentation and third-party guarantees.

CASE STUDY ***Barclays Bank plc v O'Brien*** **[1994] 1 AC 180**

Mr and Mrs O'Brien were husband and wife. The matrimonial home, situated at Farnham Lane in Slough, was in their joint names. Mr O'Brien was a chartered accountant and had an interest in a company called Heathrow Fabrications Ltd, which had an account with the Woolwich branch of Barclays Bank. In the first three months of 1987, the company frequently exceeded its overdraft facility of £40,000. Mr O'Brien told Mr Tucker, the manager of the Woolwich branch, that he was remortgaging the matrimonial home. The overdraft limit was raised at that stage to £60,000 for one month. Even though no additional security was provided, by 15 June 1987 the company's overdraft had risen to £98,000 and its cheques were being dishonoured.

On 22 June 1987, Mr O'Brien and Mr Tucker agreed: (a) that the company's overdraft limit would be raised to £135,000, reducing to £120,000 after three weeks; (b) that Mr O'Brien would guarantee the company's indebtedness; and (c) that Mr O'Brien's liability would be secured by a second charge on the matrimonial home.

The bank prepared the necessary security documents. They consisted of an unlimited guarantee by Mr O'Brien of the company's liability, and a legal charge, to be signed by both Mr and Mrs O'Brien, over the matrimonial home to secure any liability of Mr O'Brien to the bank. Mr Tucker arranged for the documents, together with a side letter, to be sent to the Burnham branch of the bank, for execution by Mr and Mrs O'Brien. In a covering memorandum, Mr Tucker asked the Burnham branch to advise the O'Briens as to the current level of the facilities, amounting to £107,000, and the projected increase to £135,000. The Burnham branch was also asked to ensure that the O'Briens were 'fully aware of the nature of the documentation to be signed and advised that if they are in any doubt they should contact their solicitors before signing'.

The Burnham branch, however, did not give Mrs O'Brien any explanation of the effect of the documents. No one suggested that she should take independent legal advice. She did not read the documents or the side letter. In July 1987, she signed the legal charge and side letter, and the bank clerk witnessed her signature. Mrs O'Brien was not given a copy of the guarantee.

Heathrow Fabrications Ltd struggled to survive and, by October 1987, its indebtedness to the bank was more than £154,000. In November 1987, demand was made on Mr O'Brien under his guarantee. When the demand was not met, the bank brought possession proceedings under the legal charge against Mr and Mrs O'Brien. Mrs O'Brien defended these proceedings by alleging that she was induced to execute the legal charge on the matrimonial home by the undue influence of Mr O'Brien and by his misrepresentation that the charge was to secure only £60,000, and that even this liability would be released in a short time, when the house was remortgaged.

The House of Lords found that the:

> . . . tenderness of the law towards married women is due to the fact that, even today, many wives repose confidence and trust in their husbands in relation to their financial affairs. The 'tenderness' shown by the law to married women is not based on the marriage ceremony but reflects the underlying risk of one cohabitee exploiting the emotional involvement and trust of the other.

However, the House of Lords also found that 'if the doctrine of notice is properly applied, there is no need for the introduction of a special equity in these types of cases'.

In the case of husband and wife living together, constructive notice would be presumed from the fact that the transaction was, on its face, not to the financial advantage of the wife. The bank should have been put on inquiry as to the circumstances in which Mrs O'Brien had agreed to stand as surety for the debt of her husband. Mrs O'Brien had signed the documents without any warning of the risks or any recommendation to take legal advice. The bank had constructive notice of the wrongful misrepresentation made by Mr O'Brien to Mrs O'Brien, but had failed to take 'reasonable steps'. Failure on the part of the lender to take these reasonable steps resulted in the obligations undertaken by Mrs O'Brien being set aside.

Following a similar case, *Royal Bank of Scotland plc v Etridge (No. 2)* [2001] UKHL 44, guidelines have been produced for solicitors acting in cases in which one party to a 'non-commercial' relationship – most commonly, but not exclusively, a wife – is standing as guarantor of the other party's business debts under which banks are required to follow even more rigorous procedures to ensure that issues relating to undue influence are avoided.

CASE STUDY QUESTIONS

1. What was the security obtained by Barclays Bank for the business loan given to Mr O'Brien's company?
2. What was the misrepresentation made by Mr O'Brien to Mrs O'Brien?
3. Was the lender's legal charge on the property set aside because of the 'tenderness of the law' towards wives?
4. How did the lender fail to take 'reasonable steps'?
5. What are the lessons here for lenders?

Suggested answers can be found in Appendix A.

10

The lending cycle – the monitoring and control process

LEARNING POINTS

This chapter looks at the life cycle of a lending facility after the credit-granting process has been completed, i.e. at loan monitoring and control procedures, and at the actions the lender may decide to take when the customer's ability to repay is under threat.

Learning areas include:

- monitoring and control, including information sources for review;
- early-warning signals;
- recovery action; and
- insolvency options.

10.1 THE NEED FOR MONITORING AND CONTROL

Lending is an activity that carries risk and appropriate follow up action is therefore required. There is a clear link between monitoring and profitability: on the one hand, monitoring involves costs and this reduces profits per loan; on the other hand, effective monitoring minimises credit losses. The monitoring and control of lending activities are essential, particularly because banks are subject to the problem of moral hazard (Carletti, Cerasi, and Daltung, 2007). *Moral hazard* is the risk that the borrower will act in an imprudent or reckless manner because the lender might have more to lose than the borrower.

The problem arises as a result of *agency conflict* between borrowers and lenders. When a lender makes a loan to a borrower, the lender is the *principal* and the borrower is the *agent* in a contract under which the agent is entrusted with loan capital to be used for an agreed purpose, then returned to the principal, together with interest at an agreed rate. Agency conflict arises in this relationship as a result of the conflicting self-interests of both principal and agent. Borrowers have better information about the performance of their own business than the lenders do, and this *asymmetry of information* between agent and principal makes it particularly difficult to manage the conflict of interest.

One example of such agency conflict is that a firm in difficulty will want to continue trading, but the bank will want to call in the loan(s). Because the owners of a borrowing firm can obtain private benefits from the firm as long as it is a going concern, they cannot be relied upon to act in best interests of other investors, such as lenders, when the value of the firm as a going concern falls below the liquidation value of the assets.

Another is that owners include intangible (but income-earning) human capital assets in their measure of value, which source of value is unavailable to creditors. Particularly in smaller firms, a major part of firm value can arise from the specialised skills of the owner-manager and their intimate knowledge of customers and suppliers; that value is not a reasonable basis for decision-making by lenders. Thus the owners may believe there is sufficient value in the firm for continuation even though the bank believes otherwise.

The owners' self-interest may distort their investment decision-making, as the following examples illustrate.

EXAMPLE

Owners with a low equity stake tend to take increasingly risky decisions.

Let us assume that the borrower's balance sheet looks as follows.

Table 10.1 Balance sheet

Assets		Liabilities	
Current assets	£30m	Bank overdraft	£50m
Fixed and non-current assets	£20m	Owner's equity	£0m
Total assets	**£50m**	**Total liabilities**	**£50m**

The bank can hope to recover the overdraft at least in part by means of foreclosure, but the owner can hope to recover their own capital only by continuing to run the business. Any upside gains from diverting the firm's cash to risky investments will benefit the owner, but not the bank (which will still get only a fixed interest on their loan). Downside losses will adversely affect the bank, but not the owner, who can walk away – particularly in the case of limited companies or limited liability partnerships, when owners who have already lost their investment have nothing to lose, but much to gain, by taking greater risk.

An owner with a low or negative equity position, however, may be reluctant to contribute equity.

Let us assume that the balance sheet has deteriorated yet further.

Table 10.2 Deteriorated balance sheet

Assets		Liabilities	
Current assets	£30m	Bank overdraft	£50m
Fixed and non-current assets	£10m	Owner's equity	(£10m)
Total assets	**£40m**	**Total liabilities**	**£40m**

The owner might be able to bring in £5 million of additional equity, the investment of which would generate additional cash of £10 million, thus taking the value of the firm's assets back to £50 million. The owner may fear, however, that the cash generated would be appropriated by the bank towards its overdraft, resulting in a zero return to the owner on their new equity investment – and hence the owner may be reluctant to invest any new equity.

Similarly, although reluctant to put money into a failing firm, owners may be quite happy to take money out. When their equity stake nears zero, it may benefit the owners to remove value from the firm by means of increased remuneration, siphoning of funds, etc., before formal liquidation.

To enable a firm in distress to continue running, the owners may try to conceal the true financial position by delaying, manipulating or simply not submitting financial statements, or by submitting overly optimistic business plans. Firms in financial distress are also tempted to raise additional debt from other sources, thereby increasing the risk of the original debt. Again, it is the original lender, rather than the owner, that has more to lose – particularly when the borrowing firm is a limited company or limited liability partnership.

Agency problems such as these can be particularly problematic when lending against liquid assets, because the security of creditors is inversely related to liquidity of the asset base – and highly liquid assets can be easily removed by owners prior to failure. Assets removed by the owners of firms in financial distress can also be used to set up competing businesses ('phoenix companies') to further dissipate creditor claims.

Loan accounts consequently need to be monitored so that the lender can:

- be fully aware of the up-to-date situation to ensure that the borrower is creditworthy and that borrowing remains within their capacity to repay;
- ensure that documentation and charges over security remain up to date;
- learn about potentially problematic activities, such as a borrower's gambling;
- detect adverse trends and potential problem loans as early as possible;
- ensure that legal and regulatory requirements are met;
- ensure that the loan is being used for the stated purpose;
- confirm the information provided by customer about income and outgoings;
- assess the overall condition and continued profitability of the loan portfolio;
- set aside provisions for loan losses; and
- enforce an appropriate credit environment within the lending organisation.

10.1.1 The credit-monitoring process and principles

The credit-granting process needs to be followed by the credit-monitoring and credit-recovery processes, as appropriate. These processes comprise a series of interdependent stages, as illustrated in Figure 10.1.

We looked at the key principles relating to the credit-granting process in Chapter 6. In Chapter 1, we saw that the key principles relating to the credit administration, measurement and monitoring processes require systems to be in place for:

- monitoring the condition of individual credits;
- determining the adequacy of provisions and reserves;

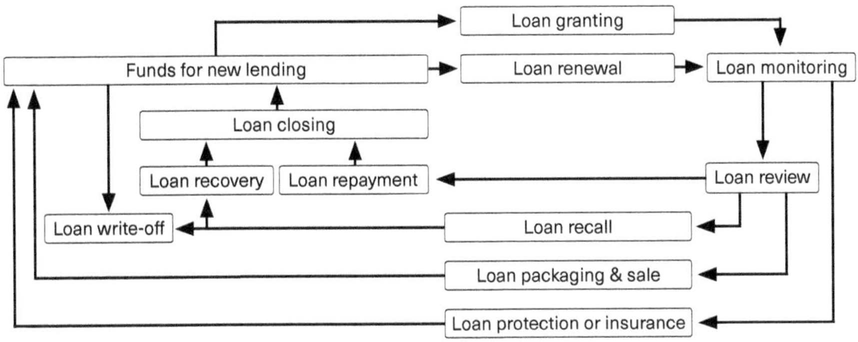

Figure 10.1 The lending cycle

- internal risk rating consistent with the nature, size and complexity of a lender's activities;
- obtaining adequate information on the composition of the credit portfolio;
- identifying any concentrations of risk;
- measuring the credit risk inherent in all on- and off-balance-sheet activities;
- forecasting changes in economic conditions; and
- assessing their credit risk exposures under stressful conditions.

The key principles relating to ensuring adequate controls over credit risk require systems to be in place for:

- assessing the lender's credit risk management processes on an ongoing basis;
- ensuring that credit exposures are within levels consistent with prudential standards and internal limits;
- establishing and enforcing internal controls for the prompt reporting of deviations from the norm;
- imparting appropriate training to staff; and
- taking prompt remedial action on deteriorating and problem credits.

10.2 INFORMATION SOURCES FOR REVIEW

Research has found that lenders' investments in both branch network density and human capital (personnel) contribute to their monitoring ability. Increased information flows enable lenders to monitor borrower activity and cash flows, thereby decreasing the amount of credit losses (Hyytinen and Toivanen, 2004). Sources of information are both internal and external (see Figure 10.2), and the information can be both hard and soft, as seen in Chapter 6.

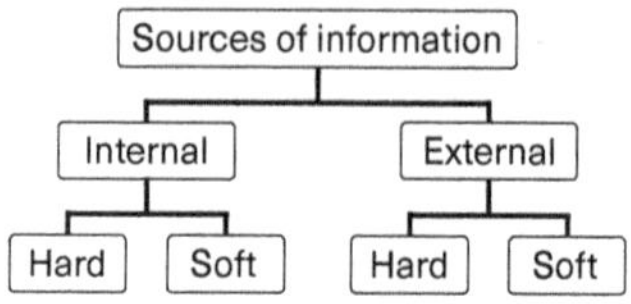

Figure 10.2 Sources of information for monitoring and control

10.2.1 Internal

Internal sources of *hard information* include:

- computer reports on borrower account information, such as balance trends;
- borrower account statements showing turnover, transactions and any extraordinary items;
- debit and credit vouchers showing details of any specific transactions; and
- banks' customer databases.

Internal sources of *soft information* can include bank staff – from head office or branches, or marketing, customer services and other departments – who interact with the borrower and personal interviews with the borrower.

10.2.2 External

External sources of *hard information* could include those available from the borrower, such as:

- audited financial statements and accounts;
- management accounts;
- sales forecasts;
- stock position;
- lists of pending advance orders;
- copies of quarterly tax returns; and
- value added tax (VAT), income tax and corporation tax returns.

External sources of hard information other than the borrower might include:

- governmental bodies, such as the Department for Business, Energy and Industrial Strategy (BEIS), the Office for National Statistics (ONS), etc.;
- non-governmental organisations (NGOs), such as the British Chambers of Commerce (BCC), the Finance and Leasing Association (FLA), etc.;
- commercial and semi-official sources, such as Dun & Bradstreet directories and Mintel;
- international organisations, such as the World Trade Organization (WTO);

- trade associations;
- newspapers and journals, such as the *Financial Times* and *The Economist*;
- libraries; and
- the Internet.

External sources of *soft information* could include telephone conversations and meetings between lender and borrower at the borrower's premises with management and staff employed by the borrower in functions including accounting and finance, operations, production, distribution, purchasing, sales and marketing, customer services, personnel, etc.

External sources may also include trade associations, such as the British Bankers' Association (BBA), the Association of British Insurers (ABI) and the FLA.

10.3 DETECTING PROBLEM LOANS

10.3.1 Early-warning signals

Detection of early-warning signals is part of the credit-monitoring process. Not all signals may be indicative of serious problems, but the simultaneous occurrence of several negative features calls for further investigation by the lender.

Early-warning signals include:

- a delay in the auditing or submission of financial statements, which could indicate a reluctance of the borrower to submit unfavourable financial results to the lender;
- deterioration in financial ratios and worrying trends in financial statements;
- cash flow problems, declining cash balances, and large increases in receivables, short-term debt, inventory and fixed assets;
- deteriorating relationships with trade suppliers;
- a decrease in inventory turnover and/or a decrease in receivables turnover;
- delays or an increase in accounts payable, including non-payment of short-term creditors by the end of the seasonal cycle;
- a decline in sales or unanticipated changes in demand as a result of obsolescence;
- reduced credits to the account and/or persistent overdrawing;
- a loss of key customers;
- lockouts, strikes or general deteriorations in labour relations;
- production and delivery problems;
- negative press reports;
- adverse environmental factors, including natural disasters;

- delayed payments of principal and interest;
- a decline in margins and an increase in loan-to-value (LTV) ratios;
- loan proceeds being used for unintended purposes;
- frequent turnover in management or other personnel;
- the expiry or cancellation of insurance policies;
- second charges on security filed against the borrower by other creditors;
- a notice of legal action against the borrower;
- a notice of tax liens or third-party debt orders against the borrower;
- a deterioration in the lender's rapport with the borrower, resulting from unexplained changes in the borrower's attitude or the reluctance of the borrower to communicate;
- the death or departure of key persons;
- health or marital and other personal problems among key persons;
- overcapitalisation and an inability to use available resources profitably; and/or
- overly rapid growth and potential overtrading.

Overcapitalisation is a situation in which the capital a business uses is excessive for its needs. It is characterised by excessive stocks, debtors and cash, leading to a low return on investment, and to long-term funds tied up in non-earning short-term assets.

Symptoms that might enable a lender to identify overcapitalisation include:

- liquidity that is too high, with increasing current and quick ratios;
- gearing that is too low, with a lower gearing ratio;
- too low a turnover to justify the investment in assets, resulting in idle cash and takeover threats;
- a drop in the ratio of sales to equity;
- a high ratio of fixed assets to working capital, which could indicate overinvestment in assets in anticipation of sales that did not materialise;
- inefficient working capital management; and/or
- excessive cash generation in relation to the availability of investment opportunities.

Overtrading refers to a situation in which turnover is increased without a matching increase in equity or other long-term sources of funds. As a result, a company that is earning good profits can run into a liquidity crisis and default on payment of its current liabilities. When a company is running profitably, such a crisis can overtake it without its managers even realising what is happening.

A simple example will demonstrate the concept of overtrading.

EXAMPLE

Mr Potter invests £2,500 in starting a business for buying and selling all-purpose grease. He buys a can of grease at £1 and sells it for £1.50, earning a profit margin of £0.50 (there are no other overheads). He keeps two months' stock purchased on one-month credit and sells on one-month credit. He retains all of his profits in the business.

Starting business in January, Mr Potter sells 1,000 cans in the first month, earning a profit of £500. Based on the above terms of doing business and with cash as the balancing figure, his balance sheet at the end of January would look like as follows.

Table 10.3 January (1,000 cans sold for a profit of £500)

Assets	£	Liabilities	£
Stock (2 months' inventory at cost)	2,000	Creditors (2 months' stock at cost bought on 1 month credit)	2,000
Receivables (1 month)	1,500	Owner's capital	2,500
Cash balance	1,500	Retained profit	500
Total assets	**5,000**	**Total liabilities and equity**	**5,000**

Next month, the turnover and profits both double.

At the end of February, Mr Potter's balance sheet looks as follows. (Once again, cash is the balancing figure.)

Table 10.4 February (2,000 cans sold for a profit of £1,000)

Assets	£	Liabilities	£
Stock (2 months' inventory at cost)	4,000	Creditors (2 months' stock at cost bought on 1 month credit)	4,000
Receivables (1 month)	3,000	Owner's capital	2,500
Cash balance	1,000	Retained profit	1,500
Total assets	**8,000**	**Total liabilities and equity**	**8,000**

During the month of March, sales and profits both double again.

Satisfied that his business is booming, Mr Potter heads off on holiday to Bermuda. However, before month end, he receives an email from his accountant saying: 'Return immediately. We have no cash to pay wages.'

The balance sheet at the end of March would look as follows.

Table 10.5 March (4,000 cans sold for a profit of £2,000)

Assets	£	Liabilities	£
Stock (2 months' inventory at cost)	8,000	Creditors (2 months' stock at cost bought on 1 month credit)	8,000
Receivables (1 month)	6,000	Owner's capital	2,500
Cash balance	0	Retained profit	3,500
Total assets	**14,000**	**Total liabilities and equity**	**14,000**

The terms of doing business have stayed exactly the same and all profits have been kept in the business – yet, despite both sales and profits doubling, the firm is facing a grave liquidity crisis.

This is the danger of overtrading: a firm can run out of cash to meet its current liabilities, even though it is apparently doing very well and earning big profits. It is the latter fact that can lull both borrower and lender into a state of complacency, only to be confronted by a liquidity crisis that can often spell failure of the business and default on the bank loans.

A scrutiny of the balance sheets in the above example will show that although the business was running profitably, its liquidity was declining: the current ratio had dropped from 2.5 (January), to 2 (February), to 1.75 (March). That the problem was caused by overtrading (increasing turnover without adequate infusion of equity) is shown by the movement of the ratio of sales to equity: from 0.5 (January), to 0.75 (February), to 1 (March).

In the situation faced by the firm in the example at the end of March, any bottleneck in the process of converting stocks or receivables into cash would result in pressure from creditors, causing disruption of supplies and making it necessary to borrow from one source to pay another. Even though current assets are substantially more than current liabilities, the firm has no ready cash. Although the firm could expect to collect the bulk of the receivables that have arisen out of sale contracts already completed, the conversion of stocks into cash would take place only through future sales, which would depend on variables such as market conditions, etc.

This is why the *quick ratio* or *acid test ratio* is often preferred as a better measure of a firm's real short-term solvency, which is calculated as

(Current assets – Inventory) ÷ Current liabilities

In the example, the quick ratio declined from 1.5 (January) to 0.75 (March).

It should be noted that overtrading is not the only cause of liquidity problems. Repayment of a loan without raising sufficient long-term funds for the repayment (either in the form of profit accruals or a fresh loan) can drain cash from the firm, creating the symptoms of overtrading. Excessive dividend payouts can result in depressing the equity and creating similar symptoms. The use of short-term sources of funds to finance long-term investments will shrink the net working capital (i.e. the surplus of current assets over current liabilities), resulting in identical symptoms. Moreover, it is not only physical increase in sales that can strain liquidity. In periods of high inflation, sales turnover and the corresponding working capital requirements can increase very sharply in nominal terms, resulting in the symptoms of overtrading.

Symptoms that might enable a lender to identify overtrading include:

- liquidity that is too low, with declining current and quick ratios;
- a decline in net working capital, which may even become negative;
- a decline in the ratio of debtors to creditors, with creditors being asked to wait longer before payment;
- gearing that is too high, with a higher gearing ratio;
- too high a turnover in relation to investment, resulting in cash shortages and liquidity crises;

- sharp increases in the ratio of sales to equity; and/or
- a severe shortage of cash.

Undercapitalisation is considered by both owners and official receivers to be the leading cause of insolvency (Hall and Young, 1991).

It is also important that there is in place a system of incentives that rewards *careful* lending. The best early-warning system will not work if no one wants to look or listen – a situation that has arisen when incentive systems are skewed in favour of loan quantity rather than loan quality.

10.3.2 Reasons for loan losses

Loan losses can arise when lending principles are not appropriately and adequately recognised nor incorporated in lending policies. Accordingly, it will be worth revisiting the lending principles at which we looked in Chapter 1, because failure to observe these principles can lead to loan losses.

The reasons for loan losses include:

- excessively lax loan covenants, perhaps because increased competition for loan customers has led to an easing of credit standards to obtain new business;
- encouraging borrowers to borrow more than they need or to falsify information on the application information or self-certify application details;
- lending to those who are clearly unable to afford the repayments;
- economic recession and business failure;
- excessively rigid loan covenants with which the borrower is unable to comply;
- a failure to arrange for the valuation of security;
- the overvaluation of security;
- lending against fictitious security;
- inadequate margins or excessive LTV;
- a failure to complete documentation;
- release of the loan prior to the completion of documentation;
- renewing a loan for increasing amounts, with no additional Security taken;
- repeatedly renewing a loan to cover unpaid interest;
- failure to analyse a borrower's cash flows;
- failure to review the condition of a loan frequently enough;
- loan officers who are too close to or too distant from the borrower;
- loan officers exceeding their discretionary powers or limits;
- loan officers who are too aggressive and dominating;
- lending in areas in which the lender lacks expertise;
- a loan being diverted to borrower's personal use and not applied for the purpose for which it was granted;
- no attempt to verify the purpose for which the loan was applied;

- failure to set out the repayment plan clearly;
- failure to ensure regular receipt of the borrower's financial statements;
- failure to follow established procedures;
- ignoring frequent overdrawing without investigating the reasons;
- making loans to a new business with inexperienced management;
- failure to get credit reports or to take note of negative credit reports;
- poor communication with the borrower;
- failure to inspect the borrower's business premises;
- failure to note early-warning signals; and/or
- failure to take quick recovery action when deterioration becomes obvious.

10.3.3 Control measures

In Chapter 6, we discussed measures for managing and controlling credit risk during the credit-granting process. In Chapters 7 and 8, we looked at ways of mitigating credit risk, such as security. We now look at the measures that might be adopted for monitoring and controlling credit risk *after* the credit-granting process.

There are many complex qualitative and quantitative models for measuring and controlling credit risk (Saunders and Cornett, 2006). A detailed discussion of these measures is outside the scope of this text, but they include:

- credit scoring models;
- risk-adjusted return on capital (RAROC) models, as pioneered by Bankers Trust (acquired by Deutsche Bank);
- CreditMetrics, as introduced by JPMorgan and others, as a value at risk (VAR) framework to apply to the valuation and risk of loans and bonds;
- the Credit Risk+ model developed by Credit Suisse;
- migration analysis – a method for measuring loan portfolio and concentration risk by tracking credit ratings of businesses in a particular sector or by other means;
- the KMV Portfolio Manager model, developed by KMV Corporation (owned by credit rating agency Moody's); and
- internal ratings-based (IRB) systems, as recommended by the Basel Committee on Banking Supervision (BCBS) of the Bank for International Settlements (BIS).

Modern methods of risk control are growing in complexity and sophistication. Artificial systems, such as artificial neural networks (ANNs), are used to measure and predict credit risk (Yang, Lib, and Xu, 2001).

Credit risk mitigation is the attempt to alleviate or reduce the potential adverse effects of credit risk by means of various techniques that reduce exposure to individual customers and transactions. Some examples of credit risk mitigation techniques include:

- taking security, such as cash, gold, land and other forms, as seen in the previous two chapters;

- taking guarantees and indemnities;
- on-balance-sheet netting of mutual claims or reciprocal cash balances between the bank and the counterparty; and
- credit derivatives.

A *credit derivative* is an arrangement that allows one party (the protection buyer or originator) to transfer the credit risk of a reference asset to one or more other parties (the protection seller). It is a financial contract with a pay-out linked to default or credit events, loan values, credit spreads, or credit ratings. Credit risk transfers have the potential to enhance the efficiency and stability of credit markets overall, and to improve the allocation of capital. They can also help to reduce the overall concentration of credit risk in financial systems by making it easier for non-bank institutions to take on the credit risks that banks have traditionally held. Some of the first-generation credit derivatives include total return swaps and credit default swaps. Some recent examples include the portfolio credit derivative and the basket default swap. The International Swaps and Derivatives Association (ISDA) has identified bankruptcy, failure to pay, repudiation and restructuring as some of the credit events that might trigger a pay-out on such a contract.

Loans can also be sold either outright to pension funds and other banks, or via securitised pools of mortgages. Consumer loans or commercial loans are offered for sale to secondary market investors. The trading of loans in the secondary loan market can be traced back to the early 1980s; the Loan Market Association (LMA), set up in London in December 1996, helped to further its development.

Securitisation is the conversion of loans into tradable assets, i.e. the packaging of debt in the form of securities and selling them off to investors. The sale of loans in the form of pooling mortgage-backed securities (MBSs) began in about 1970. Since then the market for MBSs and other asset-backed securities (ABSs) has grown in complexity and opacity.

The securitisation of loans has its advantages and disadvantages. Its advantages include increased liquidity, capital relief, the transfer of risk, and balance-sheet optimisation and an improved debt–equity ratio, leading to lower borrowing costs.

One of the disadvantages is that lenders can be tempted to lend too easily based on a misconception that they might repackage the debt and sell it off quickly to others in a short time after lending. Others include the following.

- Risk might not be borne by those most qualified and might have been passed on to those who least understand it.
- Some loans have been packaged and sold, and again repackaged and sold, to the extent that no one knows who is actually bearing the risk.
- There might be a cyclical decline in value when the economy goes through recessionary periods.
- Those who actually bear the risk might not be willing to accept that their assets have fallen in value. This creates uncertainty as to where the loss has crystallised.

10.4 THE STAGES OF RECOVERY

10.4.1 Recovery action

A good loan will be repaid with interest on its due date. A *non-performing loan* (NPL) is one on which interest payments or repayments of principal are not being made. A *bad debt* is one that appears to be unlikely to be repaid. Banks are required to set aside money to cover potential losses on loans, and they write off bad debt in their profit and loss account. Sometimes, banks may be able to sell off bad debts at a discount to specially established asset management companies.

A lender will need to take recovery action in respect of loans that are not repaid promptly. Recovery action will include the realisation of any security that the borrower might have provided.

As indicated in Figure 10.1, there will be a number of stages in the recovery action. First, the loan will have to be recalled or called up if it is not already in default as a result of non-observance of loan covenants. The lender might need to negotiate with the borrower to offer a moratorium on the debt or debt restructuring. Then, the lender will have to decide if the loan amount warrants legal action and the attendant costs. In the case of smaller amounts, the lender may find it more cost-effective simply to write off the loan amount after notifying the credit rating agencies of the default. In the case of larger amounts, the lender will want to initiate legal proceedings for the recovery of sums due. Such legal proceedings might ultimately result in the insolvency of the borrower.

Sometimes, lenders may wish to effect a debt rescue rather than insist on immediate repayment or force a foreclosure (US). Nursing a sick company back to health can be more beneficial than closing it. For lenders, receivership should be the last option. Irrecoverable debt can also be converted into equity or some form of convertible loan stock, thereby addressing weaknesses in capital structure.

10.4.2 Insolvency and liquidation

Insolvency is defined as a condition that arises when a borrower is unable to pay debts when they fall due for repayment.

The lender will need to prove that the borrower is unable to pay, or has no reasonable prospect of paying, the debts. The lender will also need to prove that it could have fairly or reasonably contemplated that it would have a claim for the monies, i.e. it must pass the 'fair contemplation' test (*Picerne Construction Corp. v Villas*, 244 Cal. App. 4th 1201 (2016)).

Once the lender has sent a petition to the court, a hearing takes place and an order is made if the court feels that this is the appropriate outcome. An official receiver is then appointed. The receiver will make an application to the court, claiming assets and any income that exceeds the amount needed by the bankrupt person to cover essential living costs for themselves and their family.

Liquidation is terminal for a company. It ceases to trade and the liquidator is left to dispose of the assets. The liquidator's objective is to maximise realisation from the sale of assets, collection of debts, etc., to pay a dividend to creditors, if at all possible. Directors are not liable for the debts of the company unless they have signed personal guarantees to that effect. The liquidator will also review the company's affairs with a view to reporting on the conduct of the directors. Any offences highlighted in the report may lead to directors being disqualified from acting in that capacity in the future.

Insolvency options

There are several options in the event of insolvency.

- *Compulsory liquidation* This ensues when a creditor has successfully presented a winding-up petition to the court. The official receiver is appointed. Any available assets will need to be realised and distributed. The process is much slower and more expensive than a creditors' voluntary liquidation.
- *Creditors' voluntary liquidation (CVL)* The decision to commence liquidation is voluntarily made by the directors or shareholders of a company. The shareholders nominate an insolvency practitioner as liquidator subject to the agreement of creditors at a creditors' meeting.
- *Administrative receivership* An administrative receiver can be appointed only by the holder of a valid floating charge and acts to achieve the best possible outcome for the charge holder. The administrative receiver deals only with assets covered by the security under which they are appointed. Changes in legislation, including under the Enterprise Act 2002, have introduced restrictions on the ability of lenders to appoint an administrative receiver under newer charges (i.e. those dated after 15 September 2003) and the appointment of an administrator by a charge holder is likely to be a more usual approach.
- *Administration order* An administrator will have a duty to all of the company's creditors, not only the holder(s) of any floating charge(s), irrespective of who appointed them. A business in trouble often seeks protection from creditor pressure, and the new regime introduced in September 2003 when the Enterprise Act 2002 came into force makes it much simpler and quicker for a company to enter administration, buying it time to get its affairs in order and to decide the best way forward. An administrator can be appointed in or out of court by either the directors, the holder of a floating charge or a creditor if they have concerns about the financial well-being of their customer. The administrator's role is to try to rescue the company if it is a going concern.
- *Company voluntary arrangement (CVA)* This is a contract between a company and its creditors that offers the creditors a better financial outcome than would be achieved in liquidation. The company may continue to trade – usually under the control of its directors – with a view to paying creditors either out of future profits, or from a more beneficial realisation of the company's assets, or both. The appointed insolvency

practitioner called in as supervisor monitors the company's performance to ensure that the terms of the proposal are complied with.

- *Informal arrangement* The lender may agree an alternative approach with the borrower aiming at the survival of the borrower or borrowing company, in whole or part, as a going concern.

Order of liquidation

There are strict rules of priority as regards the order in which creditors are paid in the event of insolvency and liquidation. Generally, the priority of claims on an insolvent *company*'s assets will be determined in the following order.

1. *Secured creditors* If a lender or other party holds a fixed and floating charge over the assets of the company (a debenture), then they will be entitled to realisations from 'fixed charge assets' first, such as freehold property, fixed plant and machinery, and realisations from investments. Book debts used to fall under this category, it being established in cases such as *Siebe Gorman & Co. Ltd v Barclays Bank Ltd* [1979] 2 Lloyd's Rep 142 that it is possible to obtain a fixed charge on book debts. However, the decision by the Privy Council in June 2001 in *Re Brumark Investments Ltd* [2001] UKPC 28 created uncertainty over whether this was the case and in June 2005, in *Re Spectrum Plus Ltd* [2005] UKHL 41, the House of Lords found that, under the terms of a debenture, the bank required the customer to pay debts into the account with the bank, but left the customer free to collect the debts in the normal course of business and to draw on the account for normal business purposes. This freedom to draw on the proceeds meant that the charge over book debts could not be categorised as fixed. The rulings imply that lenders now need to consider the administrative costs associated with securing a fixed charge over book debts rather than relying only on a floating charge.
2. *Expenses of liquidation* The costs of the liquidation are next met out of the company's remaining assets.
3. *Claims of preferential creditor* After the abolition of the preferential status of Crown creditors under the Enterprise Act 2002, in the vast majority of cases only employees for wages (up to £800 per person) and holiday pay rank ahead of the floating charge creditors.
4. *Floating charge* For floating charges created after 15 September 2003, the holders will have to give up a percentage of realisations to unsecured, non-preferential creditors.
5. *Debts that are neither preferential nor postponed* If there is anything left, the unsecured creditors are paid out *pari passu* (i.e. proportionately in accordance with their claims). These creditors include trade creditors, suppliers, customers, contractors and some staff claims, as well as HM Revenue & Customs (HMRC). Prior to 2003, HMRC was ranked as a preferential creditor, but the implementation of the Enterprise Act 2002 reduced their status to that of unsecured creditor for all forms of tax.

6. *Interest on debts*
7. *Claims of postponed creditors*, e.g. unauthorised investment business
8. *Surplus assets* These are distributed to the shareholders.

On 15 September 2003, the corporate provisions of the Enterprise Act 2002 came into effect, abolishing the rights of HMRC to establish preferential claims, which now ranks with trade creditors for any dividends. This means that creditors as a whole are more likely to receive a dividend in insolvencies than was previously the case.

The priority of claims on an insolvent *individual*'s assets will be determined in the following order.

1. Secured creditors
2. Expenses of the bankruptcy
3. Claims of preferential creditors
4. Debts that are neither preferential nor postponed
5. Interest on debt
6. Debts to postponed creditors, e.g. money owed to the spouse of the bankrupt at the date of the bankruptcy order
7. Surplus returned to the bankrupt

Insolvency entails advantages as well as disadvantages. The advantages include the following.

- There is a possibility that some recovery of funds will be possible by means of following a prescribed order of distribution of the bankrupt's assets.
- All creditors are dealt with equitably, as set out in the order of priority, as required by law.
- Creditors feel more comfortable when a trustee in bankruptcy or an insolvency practitioner is involved in the process.
- The process allows a full investigation of the borrower's affairs.
- Borrowers are likely to cooperate when the process is perceived as providing peace of mind as against the anxiety of being continually indebted.

The disadvantages include the following.

- If the lender has not secured a fixed charge against specific security, the chances of recovery recede.
- Insolvency proceedings involve additional costs, in the form of professional fees and the additional time involved in complying with statutory requirements.
- Borrowers are likely to resist when faced with the possibility of losing control over their assets, including their home, and also for various reasons including restrictions that might arise in relation to future credit, occupations and professions.

10.4.3 Loan write-off

Lenders need to provide for loan losses by debit to the profit and loss account. A portion of the profits is set aside in the form of provision for bad and doubtful debts. Any losses will have to be written off by debit to the provision for bad and doubtful debts account.

Ten years after the 2007–08 global financial crisis, fears loom again that a consumer borrowing binge and an unsustainable credit boom may lead to another credit crunch. Banks are now required to undertake annual stress-testing, and they are also required to submit detailed information about how they approve loans and how they assess the financial position of their riskiest borrowers. However, of particular concern are the increases in the size of some loans and the introductory '0%' rate on credit cards that has incentivised some borrowers to use credit card debt to fund their mortgage deposits – all in the context of wages and savings still in slow recovery after recession. In what has been dubbed the 'Debt Strikes Back' or 'The Return of the Regulator?' speech, the executive director of the Bank of England underlined the need to take continual measures 'to guard against the spiral of complacency by lenders' (Brazier, 2017).

10.5 CONCLUSION

Appraisal of a loan proposal and evaluation of borrower creditworthiness undertaken during the credit-granting process need to be followed up by monitoring and control on an ongoing basis. In *Royal Bank of Scotland plc v Etridge (No. 2)* [2001] UKHL 44, it was held that 'it is not necessary for the bank to play detective and to follow up any clue, however slight, which might indicate to them that the information provided was not scrupulously accurate', but it is incumbent on bank lenders to be alert to signals that may assist in the early detection of a problem loan.

Lenders have been frequently accused of an inability or unwillingness to spend the resources necessary to look beyond the short term. The 2007–08 global financial crisis has been held to illustrate the consequences of the costs of myopia for the bank lender, as well as for collective welfare. Whether or not myopia can be, in some sense, managed will have enormous implications for how bank lenders cope with the prospect of increasing global financial market volatility over the coming decades (Clark, 2011).

FURTHER READING

Carletti, E., Cerasi, V., and Daltung, S. (2007) 'Multiple-bank lending: diversification and free-riding in monitoring', *Journal of Financial Intermediation*, 16, 425–451.

Pond, K. (2017) 'The recovery of money', in *Retail banking*, 4th edn, Reading: Gosbrook, Chapter 12.

Saunders, A., and Cornett, M. M. (2006) *Financial institutions management: A risk management approach*, London: McGraw-Hill.

Yang, B., Lib, L. X., and Xu, H. J. J. (2001) 'An early warning system for loan risk assessment using artificial neural networks', *Knowledge-based Systems*, 14, 303–306.

REVIEW QUESTIONS

1. Identify some of the reasons for monitoring loan accounts.
2. Identify some of the internal and external sources of information that might be available for conducting loan reviews.
3. What are some of the early-warning signals of problem loans?
4. Examine some of the measures that might be adopted for controlling credit risk.
5. Identify the order of distribution in personal and corporate insolvency.

ACTIVITY

Visit www.bloomberg.com and http://www2.isda.org and browse for articles and links relating to bad loans and credit events.

CASE STUDY Is Fastgro Ltd overtrading?

Fastgro Ltd, a family-owned dealer in fertiliser products, appointed a full-time managing director two years ago, who overhauled the firm's marketing and working capital policies, resulting in a sharp growth in turnover. Because the growth is expected to continue, the managing director has approached the company's bank for an additional line of credit. In support of the application, he has submitted the following financial statements for the last two years.

Table 10.6 Income statements

	Year Y (£000s)	Year Z (£000s)
Sales	39,600	70,800
Opening stock	1,000	1,780
Plus Purchases	33,380	61,820
Less Closing stock	(1,780)	(3,400)
Cost of sales	*32,600*	*60,200*
Gross profit	7,000	10,600
Selling, general and administrative expenses	(5,200)	(8,300)
Net profit	1,800	2,300
Dividend	1,620	1,620
Retained profit	180	680

Table 10.7 Financial position statements

	Year Y (£000s)	Year Z (£000s)
Assets		
Current assets		
Cash	36	2
Trade debtors	2,304	4,480
Inventory	1,780	3,400
Total current assets	*4,120*	*7,882*
Net fixed assets	5,760	7,178
Total assets	**9,880**	**15,060**
Liabilities		
Current liabilities		
Trade creditors	1,800	5,200
Bank overdraft	900	2,000
Total current liabilities	*2,700*	*7,200*
Shareholders' funds		
Ordinary share capital	1,800	1,800
Reserves and surplus	5,380	6,060
Total equity	*7,180*	*7,860*
Total equity and liabilities	**9,880**	**15,060**

Reviewing the firm's performance, the managing director emphasised the effectiveness of his policies by pointing towards the impressive increase in turnover and also the big improvement in the cash conversion cycle. But, to the surprise of Fastgro's managing director, the bank has turned down the request for an increase in the overdraft facility on the grounds that the company is overtrading.

Fastgro's managing director has asked the bank's credit officer to explain the bank's decision in more detail.

CASE STUDY QUESTION

Discuss the bank's contention that Fastgro Ltd is overtrading, supporting your arguments by calculating the following ratios for the last two years.

- Net profit margin
- Ratio of sales to equity
- Current ratio
- Acid test (quick) ratio
- Net working capital
- Average age of inventory (inventory conversion period)
- Average collection period
- Average payment period
- Cash conversion cycle

Suggested answers can be found in Appendix A.

11

Islamic finance

LEARNING POINTS

This chapter considers the key aspects of Islamic finance and lending.

Learning areas include:

- modes of Islamic finance; and
- the special features of Islamic finance.

11.1 INTRODUCTION

The huge increase in wealth in many Islamic countries, particularly those in the Middle East, has led to a demand for banking and finance products that comply with Muslim religious law. Other emerging markets with large Muslim populations also contribute to the growth in demand.

London is established as the major centre for Islamic finance in the West. Five purely Islamic banks, one Shari'ah-compliant hedge fund manager and one Islamic insurance provider have been authorised by the UK's Financial Conduct Authority (FCA), and the UK has more than 20 banks that provide Islamic financial services – more than any other European country.

Estimates of the current size of the Islamic finance industry range from US$1.88 trillion to $2.1 trillion, with expectations of market size to be $3.4 trillion by end of 2018 (Naveed, 2015). Because of the size and geographical coverage of this market, it is important for lending bankers to understand the nature, structure, costing and risks of Islamic finance products.

The main underlying principle of Islamic finance is that profit should be earned only from trading activities that are approved under Shari'ah law.

- Since money is regarded as only a medium of exchange and not a tradable asset, all forms of interest (in Arabic, *riba*) are forbidden.
- Instead of interest on loans, providers of Islamic finance earn their return as a share of profits generated by the ventures they finance. Since this exposes them to greater risk, Islamic finance tends to be costlier than conventional loan capital.
- Islamic finance also prohibits speculation or gambling (*maisir*) and any form of uncertainty (*gharrar*).
- Islamic finance cannot be used to finance activities that are non-Shari'ah-compliant, such as gambling, prostitution, trading in alcohol, pork, pornography, etc.

Historically, disapproval of usury (the charging of interest) dates back to at least the time of Aristotle (384–323 BCE). Prohibitions on usury can be found in the ancient religious texts of Judaism, Christianity and, later, Islam. While Christians were forbidden to lend money at interest until the time of the Reformation in the 16th century, the prohibition on usury contained in the 7th-century Quran continues to be a fundamental principle of Islamic Shari'ah law today.

11.2 MODES OF ISLAMIC FINANCE

11.2.1 *Murabaha*

Murabaha is the most common mode of Islamic financing, under which the bank purchases the asset for cash and sells it to the customer at a profit (instead of lending, since interest – *riba* – is prohibited under Shari'ah law).

The key feature is that the transaction is not considered to be an interest-bearing loan, but the purchase and sale of an asset at a profit. The sequence of steps – i.e. the purchase of the asset from the vendor by the bank and subsequent sale of the asset by the bank to the buyer – is particularly important. There are two distinct sale contracts, one between the bank and the vendor, and another between the bank and the buyer. This is different from traditional trade financing under which there is generally a sale contract between the buyer and the seller, and a loan contract between the buyer and the bank.

The difference between *murabaha* and a standard bank loan is illustrated in Figure 11.1.

In practice, there will generally be a master financing agreement under which the bank provides the borrower with finance to take delivery of the goods directly from the supplier, following which the borrower pays the bank for the goods in deferred payment instalments that include a margin for the bank. Under traditional financing, this margin would be considered to be interest earned by the bank under a loan transaction. Under Islamic financing, the nature of the transaction is different, and this return is considered to be the bank's profit margin from buying the asset and selling it on.

Under section 47 of the Finance Act 2005, Islamic finance transactions come under the category of 'alternative finance arrangements'. For tax purposes, HM Revenue & Customs (HMRC) has created a 'level playing field' between 'conventional financial arrangements and ones that are differently structured but give an economically equivalent return' (www.hmrc.gov.uk). Instead of interest, the return is known as an *alternative finance return* – but, since it is economically equivalent to interest, the tax treatment in the hands of both the provider and user of finance is the same as for conventional loans. Therefore, as far as the impact of taxation on the cost of borrowing is concerned, there is no significant difference between Islamic finance and a conventional loan.

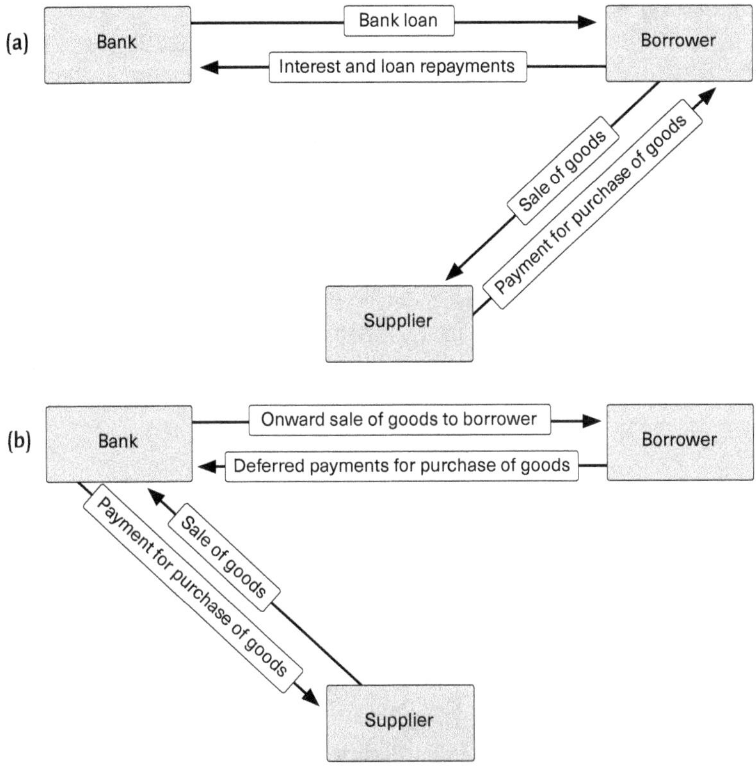

Figure 11.1 *Murabaha* finance and a standard bank loan compared: (a) a standard bank loan; (b) *murabaha* finance

Under the Finance Act 2005, the specific Islamic finance instrument known as *murabaha* is referred to as a 'purchase and sale arrangement'. According to HMRC:

> The difference between the sale price paid by the second purchaser and the purchase price of the first purchase equates in substance to the return on an investment of money at interest. A purchase and resale arrangement should, in accordance with GAAP [Generally Accepted Accounting Principles], be presented in the company accounts of the first and second purchasers in the same way as a conventional loan.
>
> At least one of the parties to the arrangement must be a financial institution . . . So the financial institution may be the party receiving or paying the alternative finance return, just as interest would be received by the bank as creditor or paid by the bank as debtor under conventional loans.
>
> (HMRC, 2017: section 44040)

11.2.2 *Tawarruq*

Tawarruq, which is also known as 'reverse murabaha' or 'monetisation', is the Islamic finance instrument that is used to obtain cash immediately. It is similar to the standard *murabaha* structure, but with an extra leg.

The standard part of the structure involves the bank buying the commodity from a goods supplier and selling it on to its customer on a deferred-payment basis. The extra step involves the customer selling on the commodity (usually back to the original goods supplier) against immediate cash payment – leaving the customer with cash in hand and a deferred-payment liability to the bank. In addition to credit risk in relation to the customer, the bank also takes on asset risk and third-party risk in relation to the supplier of the goods reneging on the agreement.

11.2.3 *Ijara*

Ijara is the term in Islamic finance for used for leasing, whereby an Islamic financier purchases the asset and leases it to the user for an agreed period. Lease rent is paid to the financier for the use of the asset over the agreed period.

A comparison of *murabaha* and *ijara* can be summarised as in Table 11.1.

Table 11.1 A comparison of *murabaha* and *ijara*

Murabaha	***Ijara***
Bank purchases asset and sells it to customer at profit	Bank purchases asset and leases it to customer for agreed period
Asset is paid for in deferred instalments over agreed period	Lease rent is paid for use of asset over agreed period
User of asset is owner of asset and has responsibility for maintenance, insurance, repair, etc.	Bank remains owner of asset, with responsibility for maintenance, insurance, repair, etc.

Ijara-wal-iqtina

Ijara-wal-iqtina is a similar arrangement to plain *ijara*, except that the customer is able to buy the asset at the end of the contract.

11.2.4 *Sukuk*

Islamic bond securities are called *sukuk*. They are unlike conventional bonds, in that *sukuk* certificates represent a proportionate interest in underlying assets and revenues rather than a proportionate share in loan capital. The proceeds of a *sukuk* issue are invested in an underlying asset, which is held in trust for the *sukuk* holders. Return on investment (ROI) for the *sukuk* investors is usually in the form of rental payments for use of the underlying asset. Like conventional bonds, *sukuk* are negotiable instruments that can be traded in the secondary market.

Under a typical *sukuk* arrangement, investors would buy *sukuk* (bond) certificates and the *sukuk* trustee would use their funds to purchase assets (most often, property). The user of the assets would make rental payments (not interest) to the *sukuk* trustee in return for the use of the assets over the agreed period; these payments are passed on to the *sukuk* investors.

Figure 11.2 depicts the structure of the *sukuk* transaction.

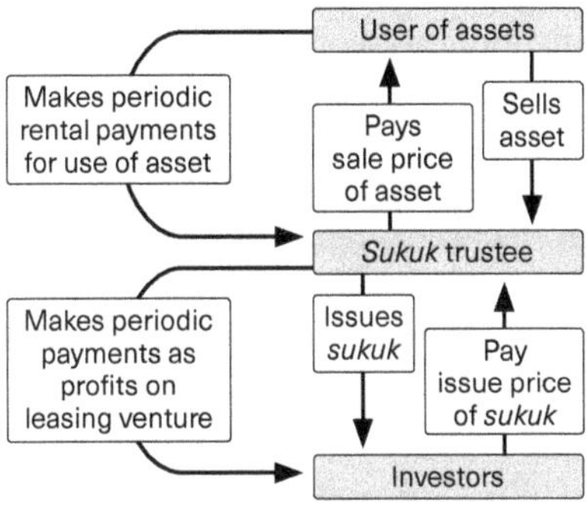

Figure 11.2 The structure of a *sukuk* transaction

Sukuk investors receive payments providing a fixed yield to maturity – either as a share of profits, or as rent on the assets *plus* repayment of the principal invested. The payments consist of a redemption payment plus 'additional payments'. According to HMRC: '"[A]dditional payments" are those payments to bond-holders that fulfil the function of interest on a conventional bond.' HMRC therefore treats the additional payments in the same way as interest on conventional loans.

Sukuk financing was in the news when the UK Treasury used these instruments to raise finance against prime government real estate in the Whitehall area (Elliott, 2016). A plan to relocate MPs to one of these buildings for the duration of a proposed refurbishment of the Houses of Parliament has met with resistance on the basis that the serving of alcohol in these buildings is prohibited under the terms of the *sukuk* agreement, because it is not in accordance with Shari'ah law.

11.3 SOME SPECIAL FEATURES OF ISLAMIC FINANCE

Some of the special features of Islamic finance can be summarised as follows.

- Islamic finance is less flexible than conventional finance as a result of Shari'ah law restrictions and the absence of cash lending, as well as general corporate lending.
- In addition to credit risk, the financier also tends to take on greater commercial risks.
- Asset risk is important – particularly real-estate risk.

- Compliance risk can be significant because non-compliance with Shari'ah law can have adverse consequences.
- Research findings in respect of the growth of Islamic finance methods show that the impact of fixed-income debt contracts could increase non-performing loans (NPLs) more than profit-and-loss-sharing contracts (Alandejani and Asutay, 2017).
- Islamic financial institutions and their customers were found to be more likely to opt for litigation in the event of a dispute (Oseni, Adewale, and Zain, 2016).
- Islamic finance was developed in the Middle East, where taxation is virtually non-existent; in other jurisdictions, the tax implications of Islamic finance products are engaging attention. Interest on traditional borrowing is charged before taxation, resulting in a reduction in its effective cost, as illustrated by the following example.

EXAMPLE

A business earns a profit of £60 on its capital investment of £100 in two different scenarios – one in which it is ungeared (the capital being entirely owner's equity) and the other in which it is geared (the capital being entirely borrowed at 10 per cent interest).

Assume too that the business is liable to pay tax at 20 per cent on its profits:

Table 11.2 Tax implications on forms of borrowing

	Ungeared firm	Geared firm
Capital employed	£100	£100
Profit before interest and tax (PBIT)	£60	£60
Interest @ 10%	£0	£10
Profit before tax	£60	£50
Tax @ 20%	£12	£10
Net profit	**£48**	**£40**

Even though the geared firm's profit is reduced by £10 as a result of having to pay interest on debt, its net profit is only £8 less than that of the ungeared firm. This is because of the tax saving from interest being charged before taxation, which results in the after-tax cost of debt being only 80 per cent of the before-tax cost, i.e.

$$0.80 \times 10 = 8\%$$

Of course this saving is available only to a taxpaying business – which is why firms that run into loss and stop paying tax (and therefore lose the tax saving) find that bank borrowing suddenly seems costlier than it used to!

The example illustrates that if the return on Islamic finance were treated as trading profit rather than interest – and hence charged after taxation – Islamic finance may be prohibitively expensive compared to the after-tax cost of standard borrowing. While the UK tax authority regards Islamic finance as alternative finance arrangements under which the returns paid to investors are tax-deductible in the same way as interest under conventional loans, it is one of the few jurisdictions to have done so. Because of differing approaches to the tax treatment of Islamic finance products, there is consequently a lack of consistency between countries.

11.4 CONCLUSION

The Islamic finance sector has developed a variety of instruments to comply with the ban on interest. Typically, Islamic banking seeks to structure interest as profit-sharing and Islamic financial institutions have devised a variety of structures using techniques, such as sale and leaseback, to get around the prohibition. There are types of Islamic finance product in which lenders are considered business partners or in which the lender essentially sells an asset to the borrower in exchange for a marked-up future repayment.

There is confusion over the legal protection offered to holders of Islamic finance products such as *sukuk*. In some cases in which *sukuk* issuers became insolvent, investors have found themselves competing with the general body of creditors rather than simply enforcing their right to take possession of the assets supporting the *sukuk*.

A recent statement by Dana Gas, a company based in the United Arab Emirates (UAE), that its own bonds issued a few years ago are no longer Shari'ah-compliant has sent shockwaves through the Islamic finance industry (see case study below). That non-compliance with Shari'ah law has been cited by a borrower as a reason to renege on pre-contracted debt has fuelled concerns relating to the lack of clearly articulated global standards in relation to Islamic finance products.

FURTHER READING

Ayub, M. (2007) *Understanding Islamic finance*, Chichester: John Wiley & Sons.

Hassan, M. K., Kayed, R., and Oseni, U. A. (2013) *Introduction to Islamic banking and finance: Principles and practice*, Harlow: Pearson Education.

International Shari'ah Research Academy for Islamic Finance (ISRA) (2016) *Islamic financial system: Principles and operations*, Kuala Lumpur: Pearson.

Kettell, B. (2010) *Islamic finance*, Chichester: John Wiley & Sons.

REVIEW QUESTIONS

1. Discuss some of the modes of Islamic finance.
2. Examine some of the special features of Islamic finance and how it differs from conventional finance.

ACTIVITIES

1. Peruse the HMRC Corporate Finance Manual at www.gov.uk/hmrc-internal-manuals/corporate-finance-manual, and search for and read the sections on 'Islamic finance' and 'Alternative finance'.
2. Visit the following websites and read about Islamic finance and its application:
   - http://aaoifi.com/?lang=en
   - www.globalislamicfinancemagazine.com
   - www.ifsb.org
   - www.irti.org
   - www.irtipms.org
   - www.isdb.org
   - www.islamic-bank.com
   - www.islamic-foundation.org.uk
   - www.isra.my
   - www.worldwaqf.org

CASE STUDY Borrower challenges the Shari'ah compliance of its *sukuk* bond

In *Dana Gas PJSC v Dana Gas Sukuk Ltd and others* [2017] EWHC 2340 (Comm), the English High Court decided that a claim brought by Dana Gas over whether a *mudarabah* agreement governed by the law of the UAE and a purchase undertaking governed by English law are valid and enforceable agreements will go to trial.

Dana Gas, a large regional independent natural gas company, listed in Abu Dhabi, entered into a production deal with Iraqi Kurdistan ten years ago. Now it is struggling to recover US$900 million it is owed by the autonomous region and the Egyptian government. It is therefore facing a liquidity squeeze and having difficulties meeting its own commitment to honour $700 million of Islamic bonds maturing in October 2017.

Dana wants to restructure the bonds which were deemed compliant in 2013. But Dana is seeking to have the *sukuk* declared invalid in a UAE court because it claims changes in the 'interpretation' of Islamic law mean the financial instruments are no longer Shari'ah-compliant.

Islamic law forbids the charging of interest so *Sukuk*, or Islamic bonds, are issued and backed by assets. Instead of lending the issuer money, the bond holder owns a nominal share in the asset on which the cash was spent. At maturity, the bond issuer buys the investor's share in the asset and receives an agreed share of the profit generated by the investment.

Shari'ah is a non-codified body of law underpinning Islam generally and Islamic finance as a product. Because it is not a codified body of law, it is capable of development and subjective interpretation, and there is no global standard for Shari'ah compliance. Some countries, such as Malaysia, have a central board overseeing Shari'ah compliance in financial services. Others, including the UAE, do not, leaving issuers and investors to rely on the guidance of a religious scholar or recognised Shari'ah advisor. Inevitably, opinions of the specialist scholars and advisors may vary, not least depending on which of the five Islamic schools of law that they belong to. A representative of the Islamic Development Bank says that some are 'now trying to revisit the standards to make them more Shari'ah-compliant'.

The *Dana Gas* case has shocked many in the Islamic finance market, but it is not entirely without precedent. In *The Investment Dar Company KSCC v Blom Developments Bank SAL* [2009] EWHC 3545 (Ch), The Investment Dar, a Kuwaiti investment company, argued in an English court that debt owed to Lebanese lender Blom Bank was not Shari'ah-compliant in the first place. The Court set aside that argument and viewed the transaction on its contractual terms. That case may be relevant for Dana because their *sukuk* are governed by English law, while the gas production assets behind the *sukuk* fall under UAE law.

Creditors are angry. If Shari'ah compliance were its only motive, nothing would prevent the borrower from issuing new *sukuk* with the same value. However, Dana is proposing to exchange the existing *sukuk* for a new Shari'ah-compliant security that would be less than half as profitable, so that the company can focus on 'cash preservation'.

Should Dana prevail, the biggest loser might be Islamic finance itself. The award might embolden other issuers, raising uncertainty for holders of all types of *sukuk*. Khalid Howladar of Acreditus, a Dubai-based advisory firm, says that no particular *sukuk* structure is 'immune to a challenge by someone really looking to find a discrepancy with Shari'ah'.

(Adapted from *The Economist*, 2017)

CASE STUDY QUESTIONS

1. Why is Dana Gas experiencing difficulty meeting its commitment to make payment in respect of US$700 million of Islamic bonds maturing in October 2017?
2. What reason has it cited for its wish to restructure the bonds?
3. Is there a global standard for Shari'ah compliance?
4. Is there a precedent for Dana's request?
5. How does a *sukuk* differ from the conventional bond?
6. Who might be the losers if Dana succeeds in having the bonds declared invalid in a UAE court?

Suggested answers can be found in Appendix A.

12

The impact of lending and social responsibility

LEARNING POINTS

This chapter assesses the impact of lending on the economy and society, and emphasises the need for responsible lending.

Learning areas include:

- the economic and social effects of lending;
- corporate social responsibility; and
- the importance of responsible lending.

12.1 THE ECONOMIC AND SOCIAL EFFECTS OF LENDING

Lending has far-reaching consequences: 'Systematic evidence over the last decade has documented a robust and positive relationship between finance and economic development' (Chakraborty and Ray, 2006: 2920). Lending can generate powerful economic and social effects that can be both beneficial and detrimental to society as a whole.

Lending can lead to huge economic and social benefits, including the following.

- Lending drives economic growth.
- Lending leads to more efficient allocation and utilisation of resources in the economy.
- Lending stimulates higher levels of saving: a part of the income earned from lending is used to reward savers who provide some of the funds required by lenders.
- Lending promotes liquidity, and makes available funds for investment and consumption.
- Lending improves the availability of funds to higher-risk ventures.
- Social lending makes funds available at low cost to disadvantaged sections of society.

Lending can also have detrimental effects on the economy. Irresponsible lending can encourage irresponsible borrowing, and there have been instances of borrowers being encouraged to overstate their income and to borrow more than they can afford to, because larger loans can lead to larger bonuses.

Lending also accentuates social inequalities. Perceived high-risk borrowers are charged higher rates of interest, trapping them with higher burdens of debt. In extreme circumstances, over-indebtedness can lead to depression and suicide.

Lending also accentuates business cycles, with the effect of business downturns becoming exacerbated by lending activity or inactivity. Indeed, lending has been found to be *procyclical*, i.e. there is a condition of positive correlation between lending and the overall state of the economy. It has been observed that lending often increases significantly during business cycle expansions and then falls considerably during subsequent downturns, sometimes leading to a severe shortfall in liquidity, described as a *credit crunch*.

These changes in lending are generally more than proportional to the changes in economic activity, suggesting that bank loan supply tends to accentuate the business cycle. Provision for bad debts and write-offs starts making its appearance towards the end of a period of expansion, and rises significantly during the downturn that follows, suggesting that lenders may take more risks during the expansion, but that it takes some time for the impact of these risks to be felt (Berger and Udell, 2004). This procyclicality is observed to be more marked in private banks rather than in state-owned banks; hence the latter are more likely to play a credit-smoothing role in developing economies, while the former are more likely to accentuate business cycles in developed economies (Micco and Panizza, 2006).

During his tenure as chair of the US Federal Reserve (the United States' central bank), Alan Greenspan (2001) observed that 'the worst loans are made at the top of the business cycle'; he also observed that, at the bottom of the cycle, 'the problem is not making bad loans . . . it is not making any loans, whether good or bad, to credit-worthy customers'. During boom times, both lenders and borrowers tend to make unrealistic assumptions that growth will continue forever. Psychologists have identified 'herd instinct' as a powerful force motivating human behaviour and there is growing evidence of herd behaviour within financial markets. Herd behaviour can emerge when aggressive lenders are valued by existing and potential employers, and consequently more cautious lenders are forced to become less conservative. Such competition-induced herd behaviour is liable to lead to periods during which lenders drive each other into strong credit expansions, which are succeeded by periods during which lenders are slowed down by losses from earlier lending. Thus herd behaviour introduces cyclical behaviour into the aggregate supply of credit, giving rise to inefficient credit cycles in the economy (Devenow and Welch, 1996; Röthelia, 2001).

12.2 RESPONSIBLE LENDING

To act responsibly is to act in a reliable and trustworthy manner, recognising a moral duty and accountability even where there are no specific legal obligations.

Acting responsibly implies assuming a duty to individuals and to society as a whole. *Responsible lending* covers a range of issues and practices: 'Responsible lending is more than just meeting the minimum legal requirements. It is also about driving forward best practice and treating customers fairly' (House of Commons Treasury Committee, 2003).

The requirements for responsible lending include the need to:

- take account of the consumer's ability to repay;
- keep adequate records to show that the lender has taken account of the consumer's ability to repay; and
- in the absence of evidence to the contrary, assume that repayments will be met from the consumer's main income.

A lender should, in fact, take into account more than the customer's ability to repay the credit. It should also take reasonable steps to assess the customer's ability to meet repayments in a sustainable manner without the customer incurring financial difficulties or experiencing significant adverse consequences. A lender must consider sufficient information to enable it to make a reasonable assessment and bear in mind that its assessment of the borrower must not be based primarily or solely on the value of any security provided by the borrower (FCA, 2017b).

Encouraging people to borrow what they want rather than to borrow what they can afford promotes an impression that borrowing is a glamorous and costless activity. Irresponsible lending, in the form of opaque pricing structures and misleading marketing methods, could lead to a situation of *over-indebtedness*. While there is no general agreement on what constitutes over-indebtedness, fears about over-indebtedness have been on the rise in recent years. A DTI Task Force on Over-indebtedness was set up in October 2000 to address concerns about consumer debt in the UK by considering ways of achieving more responsible lending and borrowing. The Task Force suggested the following definitions for households that are at a high risk of being in, or getting into, financial difficulty:

> **Over-indebtedness**
> - having four or more current credit commitments (7% of all households)
> - spending more than 25% of gross income (excluding mortgages) on consumer credit (5% of all households)
> - spending more than 50% of gross income (including mortgages) on consumer credit (6% of all households)
>
> (DTI Task Force on Tackling Over-indebtedness, 2003: 159)

The Money Advice Service (2016) has identified five key predictors of over-indebtedness as renting rather than owning a home, larger family sizes, single-parent family structures, low incomes (of below £10,000) and age (below

35 years old). Lenders will need to bear these indicators and predictors in mind, and recognise the dangers of over-indebtedness.

12.2.1 Lending practices inconsistent with responsible lending

In 2003, Citizens Advice identified seven key practices of credit card marketing that did not appear to be consistent with responsible lending practices:

> Marketing practices inconsistent with responsible lending
> (a) speed and ease of application
> (b) prominence given to very high credit limits
> (c) prominence given to very low interest rates for cards where the interest rate paid by the consumer is determined by risk
> (d) inducements to use the card
> (e) unsolicited mailshots for credit card cheques
> (f) important information in small print
> (g) indiscriminate targeting of direct mailshots
>
> (Citizens Advice, 2003)

Among the lending practices that have been recognised as inconsistent with responsible lending is a lack of transparency in charging systems, leading consumers to experience difficulty in deciding on best value. Such a lack of transparency in pricing obstructs effective competition and is against consumers' interest. Complex charging structures mean that understanding interest-rate calculations requires an unreasonable time and effort, while different interest calculation methods (e.g. in the date from which interest starts) can cause wide differences in the amount actually charged. Lack of transparency of the lending process means that the loan terms and conditions are not always clear.

Further commonplace poor lending practices include:

- the non-disclosure of fees, commission, inducements and other relevant information;
- excessive charges;
- inappropriate advice;
- unsolicited communications, e.g. cold calling;
- incentivising the sale of particular products;
- high-pressure selling techniques;
- automatically raising credit limits without carrying out internal and external credit checks, and without considering existing levels of indebtedness;
- reducing repayment instalments to unviable levels; and
- inadequate credit checking.

Another example is excessive loan-to-value (LTV) ratios. There is some evidence to show that the most successful loan recovery takes place when the LTV ratio is below 66 per cent (Mason, 2007: 11) – a condition that would have disqualified most of the subprime borrowers whose widespread defaults in the United States are said to have fuelled the 2007–08 global financial crisis.

Loan foreclosures (of the type to which many of those subprime borrowers were subject) are generally costly and time-consuming. The average time taken for mortgage foreclosure is estimated to be 18 months, costing approximately 20–25 per cent of the loan balance (Mason, 2007: 2).

Loan modification, e.g. reducing the repayments or extending the loan repayment period, may facilitate borrowers making a few payments and allow the lender to classify such loans as 'good' rather than 'bad' – but it masks the true level of credit exposure. The inclusion of such loans within the pool of performing loans distorts credit ratios and results in the skewed reporting of bad debts. Research suggests that modified loans suffer a 35–40 per cent default rate over the subsequent two years (Mason, 2007: 3).

Another poor practice among lenders is multiple re-aging, i.e the renewal of loans at increased levels to cover delinquent interest so that they can be reported as current, rather than delinquent, while *predatory lending* refers to lending to borrowers who cannot afford the repayments.

Less overtly, irresponsible lending can result simply from poor communication. The traditional banker, who might have cast a kindly eye on the difficulties faced by a borrower, been ready to listen to borrowers and rearrange loan terms if plausible reasons were adduced for delay in loan repayments, was perceived as a socially responsible individual. The modern lender is perceived as distant and unsympathetic.

12.2.2 Corporate social responsibility (CSR)

For the lending bank, responsible lending is only one aspect of its *corporate social responsibility* (CSR), whereby it takes account of the economic, social and environmental impacts of its operations, maximising the benefits and minimising the downsides. The UK government sees CSR as the 'actions that business can take, over and above compliance with minimum legal requirements, to address both its own competitive interests and the interests of wider society' (www.csr.gov.uk, quoted in Saeed, 2007: 7). Another definition speaks of the 'integration of an enterprise's social, environmental, ethical and philanthropic responsibilities towards society into its operations, processes and core business strategy in cooperation with relevant stakeholders' (Rasche, Morsing, and Moon, 2017: 6).

Corporate social responsibility contributes to competitive advantage by:

- enhancing the capacity to innovate;
- enhancing the corporate reputation that is a driver of customer satisfaction;
- enhancing internal and external relationships; and
- facilitating access to strategic assets, such as licences to operate.

12.2.3 The importance of responsible lending

Responsible lending is important not only from the point of view of the consumer, but also from that of the lender. From the lender's point of view, responsible lending can lead to significant benefits.

The perception of lenders as 'predators' and borrowers as 'struggling' does not do any good to the image of the lender. Responsible lending practices promote the image of the lender as trustworthy, and a better image can lead to a better competitive position. A lender who is perceived as responsible is seen to have a competitive advantage over others who are not.

It is obviously also in the lender's own interest to recover money lent, and responsible lending can result in better loan performance and recovery.

Responsible lending will therefore constitute a superior business model from which both lenders and borrowers can benefit in the long term.

12.3 RELATIONSHIP LENDING AND RESPONSIBLE LENDING

Lending can be transactional or based on an ongoing relationship. Responsible lending is more evident where the lending is relationship-based.

12.3.1 Transactional lending

A *transaction* consists of a trade of values between two parties – here, the lender and the borrower. *Transactional lending* generally comprises an arm's-length contract and strict adherence to contractual terms.

Within a transactional model, many lenders compete for the consumer's business and the consumer shops around with several lenders from among a limited number of products. There is little relationship between the two parties, with information flows significantly curtailed and a resulting reduced scope for flexibility.

Transactional lending is more commonplace in the United States and the UK than it is elsewhere in the world.

12.3.2 Relationship-based lending

Relationship-based lending is the process of creating, maintaining and enhancing strong, value-laden relationships with customers. It is based on a relational contract and spans an extended period of time, with the customer generally accessing a broad range of lending services from a single supplier.

Loan rates are usually established nominally at a spread above the base cost of funds and the focus of concern is the yield on the total activities.

A relationship lending strategy will involve multiple interactions and multiple lending products. A relationship lender will have an informational advantage over a non-relationship lender and therefore a relationship lending strategy is more likely to generate future lending opportunities (Bharath et al., 2007).

It is most evident in countries such as Japan and Germany, where there are cross-shareholdings between banks and non-financial corporations.

Moreover, relationship-based lending is likely to lead to responsible lending practices because the lender has more to lose by irresponsible lending.

12.4 CONCLUSION

Lending is an activity that has existed from time immemorial and it will be an activity that will continue into the foreseeable future. Over the centuries, lending has taken on many shapes, from pawnbroking, to cheque-cashing, to business lending, to credit derivatives. Lenders have alternatively taken on the hues of unscrupulous villains and benign saviours.

In *Bache & Co. (London) Ltd v Banque Vernes et Commerciale de Paris SA* [1973] 2 Lloyd's Rep 437, Lord Denning held that:

> [B]ankers or brokers . . . are known to be honest and reliable men of business who are most unlikely to make a mistake. Their standing is so high that their word is to be trusted. So much so that a notice of default given by a bank or a broker must be honoured.

Recent mis-selling scandals and stories of bank lenders profiting at the expense of their customers have altered this perception, giving rise to a vision of the dishonest, self-serving banker who takes advantage of vulnerable customers. There is a need to adopt instead a balanced view that recognises the lender's right to repayment, as well as the borrower's right to be treated fairly.

It is important that lenders should lend responsibly, because responsible lending provides the lender with ethical, as well as competitive, advantages. It is also important that lenders should lend cautiously and monitor meticulously, so that responsible consumers and shareholders – and taxpayers – do not have to pay too much to cover the losses from irresponsible borrowers.

Laws and codes have evolved over time to prevent irresponsible lending and to promote consumer protection. While laws were designed to protect unsophisticated borrowers from being exploited by unscrupulous moneylenders, they are capable of being used by unscrupulous borrowers to avoid paying their just debts to moneylenders (*Orakpo v Manson Investments Ltd* [1978] AC 95).

To lend justly and to ensure that just debts are repaid: this is the challenge for bank lenders now and in times to come.

FURTHER READING

Berger, A. N., and Udell, G. F. (2004) 'The institutional memory hypothesis and the procyclicality of bank lending behavior', *Journal of Financial Intermediation*, 13, 458–495.

Bharath, S., Dahiya, S., Saunders, A., and Srinivasan, A. (2007) 'So what do I get? The bank's view of lending relationships', *Journal of Financial Economics*, 85, 368–419.

Buckley, A. (2011) *Financial crisis: Causes, context and consequences*, Harlow: Pearson Education.

Financial Conduct Authority (FCA) (2017) *Consumer credit sourcebook*, available at www.handbook.fca.org.uk/handbook/CONC.pdf

REVIEW QUESTIONS

1. Identify some of the economic and social effects of lending.
2. What do you understand by 'responsible lending'?
3. What might be the criteria for over-indebtedness? How might lenders be contributing to the problem of over-indebtedness?
4. Identify some of the lending practices that might be described as inconsistent with responsible lending.
5. Why is it important to lend responsibly?

ACTIVITIES

1. Visit the following websites and search for 'corporate social responsibility':
   - www.csr.gov.uk
   - www.csreurope.org
   - www.fca.org.uk
2. Read the summary of the First Report of the Select Committee on Treasury, available at www.publications.parliament.uk/pa/cm200304/cmselect/cmtreasy/125/12503.htm, and identify issues that you think are inconsistent with responsible lending.

CASE STUDY Debt can cost lives

Britain's Streets of Debt

Marion McDonald found the body of her husband Mark on a railway line in January 2005. Although there was no suicide note, it appeared that he had committed suicide because of out-of-control debts, as the bank statements in his backpack indicated.

Jeannette Sharratt borrowed £2,500, but extortionate interest rates led to an increase of the debt to over £100,000. For 16 years she lived under the threat of repossession, but ultimately the courts ruled in her favour.

Gwen Colbourne, aged 72, had no assets and lived on a small pension but had three store cards, six credit cards and two loans.

(*Source*: BBC One, Britain's Streets of Debt, 5–9 June 2006)

Overdrawn Student Killed Himself Over £8,000 of Debt

Toby Thorn wrote a suicide note on the back of a bank letter demanding the repayment of his £3,000 overdraft. He was just 23 years old when he took his life after racking up the overdraft in addition to £5,000 of student debt.

(*Source*: Gore, 2012)

Manhattan Couple Jumped to their Death because of Mounting Financial Debt

The bodies of 53-year-old Glenn Scarpelli and his 50-year-old wife, Patricia, were found early in the morning on 28 July 2017 near Manhattan's Murray Hill neighbourhood. Suicide notes in their pockets indicated that they had jumped to their death because of mounting bills.

Scarpelli, a chiropractor, lived with his wife, 20-year-old daughter Isabella and 19-year-old son Joseph near Wall Street. The couple had travelled to Scarpelli's recently closed practice to jump from a 17-storey building.

According to the suicide notes, the couple were in 'financial peril' and asked that their children be taken care of. Public records showed that Glenn owed US$42,000 in unpaid taxes dating back to 2013, along with a $213,000 federal loan that had paid for his medical degree. Their two children had attended elite private schools.

(*Source*: *Vibe*, 2017)

CASE STUDY QUESTIONS

1. What is 'responsible lending'?
2. Identify any evidence of irresponsible lending in relation to the problems faced by these borrowers.
3. What might be the impact of irresponsible lending decisions?
4. What do lenders need to do to meet the responsible lending requirements of the UK's Financial Conduct Authority (FCA)?
5. What is the lesson here for lenders?

Suggested answers can be found in Appendix A.

Appendix A

Suggested answers to case study questions

CHAPTER 1

1. The root cause of the turmoil in the credit markets in 2007 appeared to be subprime lending, i.e. lending to individuals who were unlikely to meet their debt obligations.
2. 'Subprime lending' is lending to individuals who are not considered to be likely or easily able to repay their debt obligations, i.e. high-risk borrowers.
3. Northern Rock's strategy of borrowing short-term and lending long-term was highly profitable under conditions of credit boom – but when funds ran dry, the bank was pushed to the brink of insolvency. Profitability had run counter to liquidity requirements.
4. The impacts of poor lending decisions can include borrowers defaulting, banks accumulating bad debt and being pushed to the brink of insolvency, and the entire financial system experiencing a severe shortage of cash and loss of confidence.
5. The lessons here for lenders are that they need to carefully evaluate the quality of borrowers and their ability to meet interest payments prior to making any loans. Lenders need to perform a careful balancing act to meet the conflicting needs of profitability, liquidity and safety.

CHAPTER 2

1. Connected lender liability is a principle in terms of which credit card issuers are liable for payments for products and services between £100 and £30,000, individually and jointly with suppliers, if a consumer has a valid claim against the supplier for misrepresentation or breach of contract relating to goods or services bought with a credit card.
2. A valid claim will need to involve misrepresentation or breach of contract relating to goods or services bought with a credit card.
3. A lender who has provided a credit card to a UK borrower will be liable, along with the supplier, if the borrower used the card abroad to pay for goods and services that are deemed to be defective or misrepresented.

CHAPTER 3

1. A certificate of incorporation confirms the existence of a company, which is a separate entity independent from its members or shareholders.
2. A pre-incorporation debt is a debt that is incurred prior to the incorporation of a company, for which the company is therefore not liable.
3. No. A company is not able to ratify pre-incorporation debts after it has been duly incorporated.

4. If a lender has lent money to a company prior to its incorporation, the borrowing company will not be liable for the debts, but the individuals who purported to act as its agents will be personally liable.
5. The lesson for lenders that can be drawn from *Kelner v Baxter* is that they need to scrutinise the relevant company documentation and ensure that the company is duly incorporated before entering into any dealings with the company.

CHAPTER 4

1. The primary reason for the decline in LA Gear's sales in the 1990s is that the company failed to predict the change in fashion trends and to adapt its products to suit changing customer needs.
2. It is important that a lender has a good knowledge of the industry in which the borrower operates so that it can assess the company's asset quality. LA Gear, for example, collapsed and gave rise to losses for lenders despite strict loan covenants because not only the company, but also the lenders, failed to recognise the developments and emerging competition within the industry.
3. The company was able to survive for a number of years despite heavy losses by funding those losses with the sale of marketable assets. By managing its working capital and selling excess inventories, and despite strict loan covenants and large losses, the company LA Gear was able to survive for a considerable length of time largely because of the liquidity of its asset base.
4. A high degree of asset liquidity – particularly the ability to liquidate working capital – might enable a company to survive financial difficulties for a considerable length of time.

CHAPTER 5

1. Section 75 of the Consumer Credit Act 1974 establishes the principle of 'connected lender liability'.
2. Mr J alleged misrepresentation on the part of the seller of the watch.
3. No. It was found that no misrepresentation was involved.
4. No. Even if the transaction had happened in the UK, section 75 would not have applied.

CHAPTER 6

1. The two items of loan documentation that were found to have contradictory clauses in *Titford Property* were a loan agreement and a facility letter.
2. The loan agreement stated that the overdraft was payable on demand, while the facility letter indicated that the overdraft was provided for a period of 12 months.
3. The conclusion reached by both *Titford Property* and *Barnes* is that overdrafts are generally considered to have the attribute of being repayable on demand, but an express clause in a loan document can override this attribute.
4. The overdraft granted in *Titford* was held to be not repayable on demand because the facility letter stated that the overdraft was provided for a period of 12 months.
5. Lenders need to pay particular attention to the clauses in loan documents and ensure that there are no contradictions that might vitiate a claim for repayment.

CHAPTER 7

1. £5750.
2. 12 payments a year of £149 (£1788) does not cover the annual interest charged – 34.9 per cent of £5750 = £2007.
3. £512,680 – 15 years of compound interest at 34.9 per cent on £5750 is $5{,}750 \times 1.349^{15} = 512{,}680$.
4. The lessons for lenders are the need for careful evaluation of borrower intentions and creditworthiness, meticulous monitoring of loans before they become irrecoverable, and avoidance of what might be construed as usurious rates of interest and unfair contract terms.

CHAPTER 8

1. The security obtained by West Bromwich Building Society was the house in Norfolk, which the Wilkinsons purchased in October 1988.
2. Possible reasons for the shortfall in the sale proceeds of the security could be the decline in the property market at that time, the poor condition or location of the property (as indicated by the time taken to negotiate a sale) and the risk of loss in asset value in a forced sale.
3. The Limitation Act 1980 is so named because it provides time limits within which action may be taken for breaches of the law.
4. The limitation period for a mortgage deed is 12 years.
5. The case was considered to be time-barred under statute because more than 12 years had elapsed after the loan became repayable in 1989 before the building society commenced legal action (in 2002).
6. Lenders need to carefully monitor loan accounts and take prompt remedial action to ensure that their claim is not invalidated by the operation of the Limitation Act 1980. Lenders need to recognise that obtaining security does not necessarily preclude them from incurring loan losses.

CHAPTER 9

1. The security obtained by Barclays Bank for the business loan given to Mr O'Brien's company was the guarantee of Mr O'Brien, secured by a legal charge, signed by Mr and Mrs O'Brien, over their matrimonial home situated at Farnham Lane in Slough.
2. Mr O'Brien misrepresented to Mrs O'Brien that the charge was to secure only £60,000 and that even this liability would be released in a short time, when the house was remortgaged. In reality, the current level of the facilities granted to the company amounted to £107,000 and this was projected to increase to £135,000.
3. The lender's legal charge on the property was not set aside because of the 'tenderness of the law' towards wives. It was found that, in such cases, there was no need for any special treatment to wives if the doctrine of notice were properly applied.
4. The lender had constructive notice of the wrongful misrepresentation made by Mr O'Brien to Mrs O'Brien, but had failed to take 'reasonable steps' to make Mrs O'Brien 'fully aware of the nature of the documentation to be signed'. The Burnham branch of Barclays Bank did not give Mrs O'Brien any explanation of the effect of the documents. No one suggested that she

should take independent legal advice. She did not read the documents or the accompanying side letter. She was not even given a copy of the guarantee.

5. There are a number of lessons here for lenders.
   - A lender needs to be aware of the circumstances in which guarantees are signed and to take reasonable steps, as required by the law, to ensure that obligations are not avoided by guarantors on account of undue influence.
   - The availability of security should not cloud the lender's ability to judge the viability of a business proposition.
   - Security is only a fall-back arrangement and should not be deemed to be the primary source of repayment.

CHAPTER 10

The managing director is correct in highlighting the impressive increase in turnover. However, calculation of key working capital ratios indicates a worsening liquidity position.

Table 10.8 Key working capital ratios for Fastgro Ltd

Ratio	Formula	Year Y (£000s)	Year Z (£000s)
Net profit margin (%)	$\frac{\textit{Net profit}}{\textit{Sales}} \times 100$	$\frac{£1,800}{£39,600} \times 100 = \mathbf{4.55\%}$	$\frac{£2,300}{£70,800} \times 100 = \mathbf{3.25\%}$
Sales to equity	$\frac{\textit{Sales}}{\textit{Total equity}}$	$\frac{£39,600}{£7,180} = \mathbf{5.52}$	$\frac{£70,800}{£7,860} = \mathbf{9.01}$
Current ratio	$\frac{\textit{Total current assets}}{\textit{Total current liabilities}}$	$\frac{£4,120}{£2,700} = \mathbf{1.53}$	$\frac{£7,882}{£7,200} = \mathbf{1.09}$
Acid test (quick ratio)	$\frac{\textit{Total current assets} - \textit{Closing stock}}{\textit{Total current liabilities}}$	$\frac{£4,120 - £1,780}{£2,700} = \mathbf{0.87}$	$\frac{£7,882 - £3,400}{£7,200} = \mathbf{0.62}$
Net working capital	*Total current assets – Total current liabilities*	£4,120 – £2,700 = **£1,420**	£7,882 – £7,200 = **£682**
Inventory conversion period (i.e. days sales in inventory)	$\frac{\textit{Total current liabilities}}{\textit{Cost of sales}} \times 365$	$\frac{£1,780}{£32,600} \times 365 = \mathbf{19.9\ days}$	$\frac{£3,400}{£60,200} \times 365 = \mathbf{20.6\ days}$
Average collection period	$\frac{\textit{Trade debtors}}{\textit{Cost of sales}} \times 365$	$\frac{£2,304}{£39,600} \times 365 = \mathbf{21.2\ days}$	$\frac{£4,480}{£70,800} \times 365 = \mathbf{23.1\ days}$
Average payment period	$\frac{\textit{Trade creditors}}{\textit{Purchases}} \times 365$	$\frac{£1,800}{£33,380} \times 365 = \mathbf{19.7\ days}$	$\frac{£5,200}{£61,820} \times 365 = \mathbf{30.7\ days}$
Cash conversion cycle	$\frac{\textit{Closing stock}}{\textit{Cost of sales}} \times 365 + \frac{\textit{Debtors}}{\textit{Sales}} \times 365 - \frac{\textit{Creditors}}{\textit{Purchases}} \times 365$	19.9 + 21.2 – 19.7 = **21.4 days**	20.6 + 23.1 – 30.7 = **13 days**

This can be assessed as follows.

- Although profits have increased in absolute terms, net profit margin has declined, possibly as a result of increased selling expenses (including discounts).
- The ratio of sales to equity indicates that equity investment has not kept pace with the increase in sales. (Note that an increase in this ratio could either indicate more efficient utilisation of capital *or* working capital stringency.)
- The declining liquidity ratios and net working capital position are classic indicators of overtrading, indicating that the current assets may soon be insufficient to cover the company's maturing obligations.
- The big increase in creditor days (payables deferral period) is a cause for concern, because loss of supplier goodwill could result in delays or difficulties in obtaining timely supplies.
- A low cash conversion cycle can be either an indication of efficient working capital management or a sign of a very tight liquidity position. The latter seems to be the case here, because the reduction is not as a result of better current asset management (both inventory conversion period and average collection period show an increase), but rather as a result of delay in payment of creditors.

Referring to the second and last points, note that financial ratio analysis should be done with care, looking at the overall picture. Ideally, ratios of other similar companies, or industry average ratios, should be scrutinised for comparison.

Given the financial situation of the firm, the bank is unlikely to increase its exposure unless more long-term funds are brought in to improve the net working capital.

- The kneejerk solution is to take more trade credit and bank overdraft finance – but this is likely to be only a short-term fix that ultimately exacerbates the situation and worsens the liquidity crisis.
- Better short-term solutions would be either to restrict the growth in turnover to manageable proportions or to improve working capital management so that the investment in current assets required to support the level of sales is reduced (i.e. better inventory control, credit policy and debt collection).
- The long-term solution is to provide more long-term funds for working capital purposes, i.e. to improve the net working capital position of the firm.

CHAPTER 11

1. Dana Gas is experiencing difficulty meeting its commitment to make payment in respect of US$700 million of Islamic bonds maturing in October 2017 because it is struggling to recover the US$900 million it is owed by the Iraqi Kurdistan and the Egyptian government, and is therefore facing a liquidity squeeze, making it difficult for it to meet its own repayment obligations.
2. Dana has said that it wants to restructure the bonds because it has received legal advice that the bonds are no longer Shari'ah-compliant. Although the bonds were deemed compliant in 2013, Dana is seeking to have the *sukuk* declared invalid in a UAE court because it claims changes in the 'interpretation' of Islamic law means the financial instruments are no longer Shari'ah-compliant.

3. There is no global standard for Shari'ah compliance. Some countries, such as Malaysia, have a central board overseeing Shari'ah compliance in financial services. Others, including the UAE, do not, leaving issuers and investors to rely on the guidance of a religious scholar or recognised Shari'ah adviser. Inevitably, opinions of the specialist scholars and advisors on issues may vary, not least depending on which of the five Islamic schools of law that they belong to.
4. There is precedent for the *Dana Gas* case. In *The Investment Dar Company KSCC v Blom Developments Bank SAL* [2009] EWHC 3545 (Ch), The Investment Dar (TID), a Kuwaiti investment company, argued that debt owed to Lebanese lender Blom Bank was not Shari'ah-compliant in the first place. In the present case, Dana does not dispute that the debt was initially Shari'ah-compliant, but argues that it has since become non-compliant as a result of developments in the interpretation of Islamic financial instruments.
5. Islamic law forbids the charging of interest. *Sukuk*, Islamic bonds, are issued and backed by assets. Instead of lending the issuer money, the bond holder owns a nominal share in the asset on which the cash was spent. At maturity, the bond issuer buys the investor's share in the asset and receives an agreed share of the profit generated by the investment.
6. Dana's creditors would be the losers if Dana succeeds in having the bonds declared invalid in a UAE court. The biggest loser might be Islamic finance itself, because such a declaration is likely to embolden other issuers, raising uncertainty for holders of all types of *sukuk*.

CHAPTER 12

1. Responsible lending covers a range of issues and practices that are about more than meeting minimum legal requirements, but cover best practice and treating customers. It includes the need to take account of the consumer's ability to repay and, in the absence of evidence to the contrary, assuming that repayments will be met from the consumer's main income.
2. The evidence of irresponsible lending in relation to the problems faced by these borrowers includes evidence of lending without regard to the consumers' ability to repay, extortionate rates of interest and a failure to assume that repayments will be met from the consumer's main income in the absence of evidence to the contrary.
3. Irresponsible lending decisions can lead to a loss of income for the lender, in the form of legal costs and lost income, and a poor image for the lender – but, most importantly, a loss of consumer lives.
4. To meet the responsible lending requirements of the UK's Financial Conduct Authority (FCA), lenders need to:
   - take account of the consumer's ability to repay;
   - keep adequate records to show that they have taken account of the consumer's ability to repay; and
   - in the absence of evidence to the contrary, assume that repayments will be met from the consumer's main income.
5. It is important that lenders should lend responsibly, because responsible lending provides the lender with ethical, as well as competitive, advantages – and reduces the risk of the most serious consequences: depression and suicide among over-indebted consumers.

Table of cases

Allcard v Skinner (1887) 36 Ch D 145 ... 125
Aluminium Industrie Vaassen BV v Romalpa Aluminium Ltd [1976] 1 WLR 676 ... 126
Asset Land Investment Plc v Financial Conduct Authority [2016] UKSC 17 ... 33
Avon Finance Co. Ltd v Bridger [1985] 2 All ER 281 ... 151
Bache & Co. (London) Ltd v Banque Vernes et Commercials De Paris SA [1973] 2 Lloyd's Rep 437 ... 124, 190
Barclays Bank plc v Boulter and Boulter [1999] 4 All ER 513 ... 153
Barclays Bank plc v O'Brien [1994] 1 AC 180 ... 146, 151, 154–55
Biggerstaff v Rowatt's Wharf Ltd [1896] 2 Ch 93 ... 148
Bradford Old Bank Ltd v Sutcliffe [1918] 2 KB 833 ... 142, 146
Brandao v Barnett (1846) 12 Cl & Fin 787 ... 123
Brumark Investments Ltd, Re [2001] UKPC 28 ... 71, 170
Buckingham and Co. v London and Midland Bank (1895) 12 TLR 70 ... 68
Bullock v Lloyds Bank Ltd [1955] Ch 317 ... 151
Church of England Building Society v Piskor [1954] Ch 553 ... 148
Coutts & Co. v Browne-Lecky and others [1947] KB 104 ... 38, 144
Cuthbert v Robarts Lubbock and Co. [1909] 2 Ch 226 ... 65
Dana Gas PJSC v Dana Gas Sukuk Ltd and others [2017] EWHC 2340 (Comm) ... 182–83, 198
Davies v Humphreys (1840) 6 M & W 153 ... 145
Dearle v Hall (1828) 3 Russ 1 Dearle v Hall (1828) 3 Russ 1 ... 137
Devaynes v Noble (1816) 35 ER 781 (Clayton's case) ... 40, 65, 124, 142
Deverges v Sandeman Clark & Co. [1902] 1 Ch 579 ... 140
Evans v Rival Granite Quarries Ltd [1910] 2 KB 979148
Foster v McKinnon (1869) LR 4 CP 704 ... 151
Garnett v M'Kewan (1872) LR 8 Ex 10 ... 66
Harrold v Plenty [1901] 2 Ch 31 ... 140
Investment Dar Company KSCC, The v Blom Developments Bank SAL [2009] EWHC 3545 (Ch) ... 183, 198
Joachimson v Swiss Bank Corporation [1921] 3 KB 110 ... 66
Kelner v Baxter (1866) LR 2 CP 174 ... 47, 194
Lindenau v Desborough (1828) 8 B & C 586 ... 138
London Assurance v Mansel (1879) 11 Ch D 363 ... 138
Moschi v LEP Air Services Ltd [1973] AC 331 ... 143
National Provincial Bank of England v Brackenbury (1906) 22 TLR 797 ... 143
National Provincial Bank of England v Glanusk [1913] 3 KB 33 ... 151
National Westminster Bank plc v Morgan [1985] AC 686 ... 151
Nottingham Permanent Benefit Building Society v Thurstan [1903] AC 6 ... 39

Office of Fair Trading v Lloyds Bank plc and others [2006] EWCA Civ 268; [2007] UKHL 48 .... 24, 36
Orakpo v Manson Investments Ltd [1978] AC 95 190
Panama, New Zealand and Australian Royal Mail Co., Re (1870) 5 Ch App 318 147
Produce Marketing Consortium Ltd (No. 2), Re [1989] 5 BCC 569 43
Provincial Bank of Ireland v Donnell [1932] 67 ILTR 142 145
R v Wilson (1879) 5 QBD 28 144
R.A. Cripps and Son Ltd v Wickenden [1973] 1 WLR 944 66
Rouse v Bradford Banking Co. [1894] AC 586 66
Royal Bank of Scotland plc v Etridge (No. 2) [2001] UKHL 44 .... 146, 155, 172
Royal Bank of Scotland v Christie (1841) 8 Cl & Fin 214 40
Salomon v Salomon & Co. Ltd [1897] AC 22 42
Sheffield Corporation v Barclay [1905] AC 392 141
Siebe Gorman & Co. Ltd v Barclays Bank Ltd [1979] 2 Lloyd's Rep 142 170
Spectrum Plus Ltd, Re [2005] UKHL 41 .... 147, 170
Titford Property v Cannon Street Acceptances Ltd, unreported, 22 May 1975 .... 99, 100, 194
United Bank of Kuwait v Sahib [1997] Ch 107 122
United Dominions Trust Ltd v Kirkwood [1966] 2 QB 431 2,
Ward v National Bank of New Zealand (1883) 8 App Cas 755, PC 146
West Bromwich Building Society v Wilkinson and another [2005] UKHL 44 128–29
William C. Leitch Brothers Ltd, Re [1932] 2 Ch 7 43
Williams and Glyn's Bank Ltd v Barnes [1981] Com LR 205 .... 68, 99, 100, 194
Williams and Glyn's Bank Ltd v Boland [1981] AC 487 132
Yorkshire Woolcombers Association, Re [1903] 2 Ch 295 147
Yourell v Hibernian Bank Ltd [1918] AC 372 5

AUSTRALIA

Dobbs v National Bank of Australasia Ltd (1935) 53 CLR 643 125

CANADA

Bank of Montreal v Sperling Hotel Co. Ltd 36 DLR (3d) 130 (1973) 145

UNITED STATES

HSBC Realty Credit Corp. (USA) v O'Neill, 745 F.3d 564 (2014) 144
McLean v JPMorgan Chase Bank NA, 79 So.3d 170 (Fla. 4th DCA 2012) 149
Picerne Construction Corp. v Villas, 244 Cal. App. 4th 1201 (2016) 168
Smith v Firstbank Corp., WL 951377 (2013) 150

Table of statutes

Bank of England Act 1998
  Pt III 22
Banking and Financial Services Act 1994 23
Banking and Financial Services Act 2017 .... 23, 34
Charities Act 2007 45
Charities Act 2011
  s 3 45
Civil Liberty (Contribution) Act 1978 143
Companies Act 2006 .... 42, 43
  s 1(1) 42
Companies Acts 42, 44, 46
Companies (Audit, Investigations and Community Enterprise) Act 2004 44
Consumer Credit Act 1974 .... 23, 24, 25, 120
  s 10 65
  s 11 67
  s 75 .... 24, 36, 71, 83, 194
Consumer Credit Act 2006 .... 23, 24, 25
Consumer Rights Act 2015 .... 34, 123
Data Protection Act 1998 26
Data Protection Act 2018 26
Deregulation Act 2015 25
Enterprise Act 2002 .... 147, 151, 169, 170, 171
Enterprise Act 2016 25
Family Law Reform Act 1969 38
Finance Act 2005
  s 47 176
Financial Services Act 2012 .... 23, 34
Financial Services and Markets Act 2000 (FSMA) 22, 23, 25, 33, 34, 134
Financial Services (Banking Reform) Act 2013 .... 23, 34
Infants Relief Act 1874 144
Insolvency Act 1986 .... 25, 42
  s 238 152
  s 239 151
  s 240 152
  s 339 152
  s 340 151
  s 341 152
Insolvency Act 2000 25

Insurance Companies Act 1980 134
Land Registration Act 2002 131
s 29 132
Law of Property Act 1925 133
s 93 124
s 94 133
s 103 124
Law of Property (Miscellaneous Provisions) Act 1989 122
Life Assurance Act 1774 134
Limitation Act 1980 .... 129, 195
s 20(1) 128–29
Limited Liability Partnership Act 2000 41
Limited Partnerships Act 1907 41
Minors' Contracts Act 1987 144
s 2(b) 38
Partnerships Act 1890 39
s 1(1) 39
Policies of Assurance Act 1867 .... 134, 137
Small Business, Enterprise and Employment Act 2015 .... 25, 26
Statute of Frauds 1677
s 4142
Trustee Act 2000 45
Trusts of Land and Appointment of Trustees Act 1996 (TOLATA) 45
Unfair Contract Terms Act 1977 .... 33, 123
s 11(1) 33

UNITED STATES

Foreign Account Tax Compliance Act of 2010 (FATCA) 22
Wall Street Reform and Consumer Protection Act of 2010
(Dodd–Frank Act) 22
§619 22

Table of statutory instruments

Financial Services and Markets Act 2000 (Regulated Activities) (Amendment) (No. 2) Order 2013, SI 2013/1881
r 60L ... 120
Insolvency Rules 2017, SI 2017/369 ... 25
Land Registration Rules 2003, SI 2003/1417 ... 131
Unfair Terms in Consumer Contracts Regulations 1999, SI 1999/2083 ... 34
reg 5(1) ... 34
Sch 1, Pt 1 ... 34

Table of European legislation

DIRECTIVES

Capital Requirements Directive IV (CRD IV) *See also* Directive 2013/36/EU; Regulation 575/2013 ....21, 22

Directive 2004/39/EC of the European Parliament and of the Council of 21 April 2004 on markets in financial instruments amending Council Directives 85/611/EEC and 93/6/EEC and Directive 2000/12/EC of the European Parliament and of the Council and repealing Council Directive 93/22/EEC (Markets in Financial Instruments Directive, or MiFID) 22

Directive 2013/36/EU of the European Parliament and of the Council of 26 June 2013 on access to the activity of credit institutions and the prudential supervision of credit institutions and investment firms, amending Directive 2002/87/EC and repealing Directives 2006/48/EC and 2006/49/EC (Capital Requirements Directive, or CRD), OJ L 176/338, 27 June 2013 22

Directive 2014/65/EU of the European Parliament and of the Council of 15 May 2014 on markets in financial instruments and amending Directive 2002/92/EC and Directive 2011/61/EU (MiFID II), OJ L 173/349, 12 June 2014 22

REGULATIONS

Regulation (EU) No 575/2013 of the European Parliament and of the Council of 26 June 2013 on prudential requirements for credit institutions and investment firms and amending Regulation (EU) No 648/2012 (Capital Requirements Regulation, or CRR), OJ L 176/1, 27 June 2013 22

Regulation (EU) No 600/2014 of the European Parliament and of the Council of 15 May 2014 on markets in financial instruments and amending Regulation (EU) No 648/2012 (Markets in Financial Instruments Regulation, or MiFIR), OJ L 173/84, 12 June 2014 22

Regulation (EU) 2016/679 of the European Parliament and of the Council of 27 April 2016 on the protection of natural persons with regard to the processing of personal data and on the free movement of such data, and repealing Directive 95/46/EC (General Data Protection Regulation, or GDPR), OJ L 119/1, 4 May 2016 26

References

Alandejani, M., and Asutay, M. (2017) 'Nonperforming loans in the GCC banking sectors: does the Islamic finance matter?', *Research in International Business and Finance*, 42, 832–854.

Arora, A. (2014) *Banking law*, Harlow: Pearson Education.

Ayub, M. (2007) *Understanding Islamic finance*, Chichester: John Wiley & Sons.

Bailey, A. (2017) 'Responsible lending is essential to protect the vulnerable', *The Times*, 31 July.

Barth, J. R., Caprio, G., and Levine, R. (2007) *Rethinking bank regulation: Till angels govern*, Cambridge: Cambridge University Press.

Basel Committee on Banking Supervision (BCBS) (2000) *Principles for the management of credit risk*, available at www.bis.org/publ/bcbs75.pdf

Berger, A. N., and Udell, G. F. (2004) 'The institutional memory hypothesis and the procyclicality of bank lending behavior', *Journal of Financial Intermediation*, 13, 458–495.

Bessis, J. (2002) *Risk management in banking*, Chichester: John Wiley & Sons.

Bharath, S., Dahiya, S., Saunders, A., and Srinivasan, A. (2007) 'So what do I get? The bank's view of lending relationships', *Journal of Financial Economics*, 85, 368–419.

Brazier, A. (2017) ' "Debt strikes back" or "the return of the regulator"?', Speech delivered at the University of Liverpool, Institute for Risk and Uncertainty, 24 July, available at www.bankofengland.co.uk/publications/Documents/speeches/2017/speech992.pdf

Buckley, A. (2011) *Financial crisis: Causes, context and consequences*, Harlow: Pearson Education.

Carletti, E., Cerasi, V., and Daltung, S. (2007) 'Multiple-bank lending: diversification and free-riding in monitoring', *Journal of Financial Intermediation*, 16, 425–451.

Caouette, J. B., Altman, E. I., Narayanan, P., and Nimmo, R. (2008) *Managing credit risk: The great challenge for global financial markets*, 2nd edn, Chichester: John Wiley & Sons.

Chakraborty, S., and Ray, T. (2006) 'The development and structure of financial systems', *Journal of Economic Dynamics and Control*, 31, 2920–2956.

Chant, J. F. (1970) 'Security, default allowances, and risk preference', *Quarterly Journal of Economics*, 84, 688–695.

CIC Regulator (Office of the Regulator of Community Interest Companies) (2016) *Information Pack*, available at www.gov.uk/government/uploads/system/uploads/attachment_data/file/605429/13-783-community-interest-companies-information-pack.pdf

Citizens Advice (2003) cited in House of Commons Treasury Committee (2003) *Transparency of Credit Card Charges*. First Report of Session 2003–04, Vol. I, available at https://publications.parliament.uk/pa/cm200304/cmselect/cmtreasy/125/12506.htm#n202

Citizens Advice (2015) '1 million mortgage holders have no plan on how to repay', press release, 4 September, available at www.citizensadvice.org.uk/about-us/how-citizens-advice-works/media/press-releases/1-million-mortgage-holders-have-no-plan-on-how-to-repay/

Clark, G. L. (2011) 'Myopia and the global financial crisis: context-specific reasoning, market structure, and institutional governance', *Dialogues in Human Geography*, 1 March.

Cotis, J.-P. (2007) quoted in Spencer, M., 'EU says role of credit rating agencies needs to be clearer', 5 September, available at www.marketwatch.com/story/eu-says-role-of-credit-rating-agencies-needs-to-be-clearer

Crook, J. N., Edelman, D. B., and Thomas, L. C. (2007) 'Recent developments in consumer credit risk assessment', *European Journal of Operational Research*, 183, 1447–1465.

Cruickshank, D. (2000) *Competition in UK banking: A report to the Chancellor of the Exchequer*, London: HMSO.

Davies, H., and Green, D. (2013) *Global financial regulation: The essential guide*, Chichester: John Wiley & Sons.

Davis, K. (2013) 'Regulatory reform post the global financial crisis: an overview', available at www.apec.org.au/docs/11_con_gfc/regulatory%20reform%20post%20gfc-%20overview%20paper.pdf

DeAngelo, H., DeAngelo, L., and Wruck, K. H. (2002) 'Asset liquidity, debt covenants, and managerial discretion in financial distress: the collapse of LA Gear', *Journal of Financial Economics*, 64, 3–34.

Department of Trade and Industry (DTI) Task Force on Tackling Over-indebtedness (2003) *Second report of the Task Force on Tackling Over-indebtedness*, London: HMSO.

Devenow, A., and Welch, I. (1996) 'Rational herding in financial economics', *European Economic Review*, 40, 603–615.

Duygan, B., and Grant, C. (2006) 'Households debt and arrears: what role do institutions play?', available at http://citeseerx.ist.psu.edu/viewdoc/download?doi=10.1.1.432.4351&rep=rep1&type=pdf

Economist, The (2017) 'The infant Islamic-bond industry faces a crisis', 29 June.

Edmonds, T. (2013) *The Independent Commission on Banking: Final report*, London: HMSO.

Elliott, F. (2016) 'Islamic rule will leave MPs gasping', *The Times*, 29 January.

Ellis, L. (2008) 'The housing meltdown: why did it happen in the United States?', Bank of International Settlements (BIS) Working Paper No. 259, September.

Ellison, A., Collard, S., and Forster, R. (2006) *Illegal lending in the UK: Research report*, London: DTI.

Financial Conduct Authority (FCA) (2014) 'PRIN 2.1 The Principles', available at www.handbook.fca.org.uk/handbook/PRIN/2/1.html

Financial Conduct Authority (FCA) (2016a) 'Fair treatment of customers', available at www.fca.org.uk/firms/fair-treatment-customers

Financial Conduct Authority (FCA) (2016b) 'Risk management', available at www.fca.org.uk/about/supervision/risk-management

Financial Conduct Authority (FCA) (2017a) 'GC17/6: Proposals on staff incentives and performance management in consumer credit firms', available at www.fca.org.uk/publications/guidance-consultations/gc17-6-proposals-staff-incentives-and-performance-management

Financial Conduct Authority (FCA) (2017b) *Consumer credit sourcebook*, available at www.handbook.fca.org.uk/handbook/CONC.pdf

Financial Ombudsman Service (FOS) (2003) 'Credit cards: equal liability under section 75 of the Consumer Credit Act 1974', Ombudsman News, available at www.financial-ombudsman.org.uk/publications/ombudsman-news/31/creditcards-31.htm

Financial Services Authority (FSA) (2011) *The Financial Conduct Authority approach to regulation*, available at www.fsa.gov.uk/pubs/events/fca_approach.pdf

Florez-Lopeza, R. (2007) 'Modelling of insurers' rating determinants: an application of machine learning techniques and statistical models', *European Journal of Operational Research*, 183, 1488–1512.

García-Céspedes, R., and Moreno, M. (2017) 'An approximate multi-period Vasicek credit risk model', *Journal of Banking and Finance*, 81, 105–113.

Gonzalez, L., and James, C. (2007) 'Banks and bubbles: how good are bankers at spotting winners?', *Journal of Financial Economics*, 86, 40–70.

Gore, A. (2012) 'Overdrawn student killed himself over just £8,000 of debt and left a suicide note written on the back of a letter from his bank', *MailOnline*, 3 December, available at www.dailymail.co.uk/news/article-2242259/Student-Toby-Thorn-killed-just-8-000-debt-wrote-suicide-note-BANK-letter.html

Greenspan, A. (2001) 'The financial safety net', Speech delivered to Chicago Bank Structure Conference, 10 May, available at www.federalreserve.gov/boarddocs/speeches/2001/20010510/default.htm

Hall, G., and Young, B. (1991) 'Factors associated with insolvency amongst small firms', *International Small Business Journal*, 9, 54–63.

Hassan, M. K., Kayed, R., and Oseni, U. A. (2013) *Introduction to Islamic banking and finance: Principles and practice*, Harlow: Pearson Education.

Heaney, V. (2007) 'A repackaged crisis', *Financial World*, October, 14–16.

Heaney, V. (2017) 'Mortgages: a serpent underfoot', *Financial World*, June/July.

Heffernan, S. A. (2002) 'How do UK financial institutions really price their products?', *Journal of Banking and Finance*, 26, 1997–2016.

Hempel, G. H., and Simonson, D. G. (1999) *Bank management*, Chichester: John Wiley & Sons.

Her Majesty's Revenue and Customs (HMRC) (2017) *Corporate finance manual*, available at www.gov.uk/hmrc-internal-manuals/corporate-finance-manual

House of Commons Treasury Committee (2003) *Transparency of credit card charges: First report of Session 2003–04*, available at https://publications.parliament.uk/pa/cm200304/cmselect/cmtreasy/125/125.pdf

Hull, L. (2004) '£5,750 loan grew to £384,000', ThisisMoney.co.uk, 26 October, available at http://www.thisismoney.co.uk/money/news/article-1584500/1635750-loan-grew-to-163384000.html

Hyytinen, A., and Toivanen, O. (2004) 'Monitoring and market power in credit markets', *International Journal of Industrial Organization*, 22, 269–288.

ICO (Information Commissioner's Office) (2018) Guide to the General Data Protection Regulation (GDPR). Wilmslow: ICO, available at https://ico.org.uk/for-organisations/guide-to-the-general-data-protection-regulation-gdpr/

International Shari'ah Research Academy for Islamic Finance (ISRA) (2016) *Islamic financial system: Principles and operations*, Kuala Lumpur: Pearson.

Kapoor, J., Dlabay, L., and Hughes, R. (2004) *Personal finance*, London: McGraw-Hill Irwin.

Kettell, B. (2010) *Islamic finance*, Chichester: John Wiley & Sons.

Levitt, A. (2007) 'Conflicts and the credit crunch', *Wall Street Journal*, 7 September.

Macintyre, E. (2016) *Business law*, Harlow: Pearson Education.

Marriott, P., Edwards, J. R., and Mellett, H. (2012) *Introduction to accounting*, London: Sage.

Mason, J. R. (2007) 'Mortgage loan modification: promises and pitfalls', available at https://judiciary.house.gov/_files/hearings/pdf/Mason_Attach101202.pdf

Mateut, S., Bougheas, S., and Mizen, P. (2006) 'Trade credit, bank lending and monetary policy transmission', *European Economic Review*, 50, 603–629.

Matthews, K., and Thompson, J. (2005) *The economics of banking*, Chichester: John Wiley & Sons.

Matthews, K., Murinde, V., and Zhaoc, T. (2007) 'Competitive conditions among the major British banks', *Journal of Banking and Finance*, 31, 2025–2042.

Micco, A., and Panizza, U. (2006) 'Bank ownership and lending behavior', *Economics Letters*, 93, 248–254.

Money Advice Service (2016) *A picture of over-indebtedness*, available at www.moneyadviceservice.org.uk/en/corporate/a-picture-of-over-indebtedness

Montagu-Smith, N. (2007) 'Judge cancels £384,000 debt over £5,750 loan', *The Telegraph*, 29 October, available at www.telegraph.co.uk/news/1475315/Judge-cancels-384000-debt-over-5750-loan.html

Naveed (2015) 'The size of the Islamic finance market', 21 May, available at www.islamicfinance.com/2015/05/size-islamic-finance-industry/

Oseni, U. A., Adewale, A., and Zain, N. R. B. M. (2016) 'Customers' perceptions of the dispute resolution clauses in Islamic finance contracts in Malaysia', *Review of Financial Economics*, 31, 89–98.

Pike, R., and Neale, B. (2006) *Corporate finance and investment*, London: Prentice Hall/Financial Times.

Pilbeam, K. (2010) *Finance and financial markets*, 3rd edn, London: Palgrave Macmillan.

Pond, K. (2017) *Retail banking*, 4th edn, Reading: Gosbrook.

Porter, M. E. (1980) *Competitive strategy*, New York: Free Press.

Prudential Regulation Authority (PRA) (2017) *Refining the PRA's Pillar 2A capital framework*, Consultation Paper CP3/17, available at www.bankofengland.co.uk/pra/Documents/publications/cp/2017/cp317.pdf

Rasche, A., Morsing, M., and Moon, J. (eds) (2017) *Corporate social responsibility: Strategy, communication, governance*, Cambridge: Cambridge University Press.

Riches, S., Allen, V., and Keenan D. J. (2013) *Keenan and Riches' business law*, Harlow: Pearson Education.

Riding, A. L., and Haines, G. (2001) 'Loan guarantees: costs of default and benefits to small firms', *Journal of Business Venturing*, 16, 595–512.

Roberts, G., and Keller, A. (2015) *Law relating to financial services*, Cranbrook: Global Professional Publishing.

Röthelia, T. F. (2001) 'Competition, herd behavior, and credit cycles: evidence from major Swiss Banks', *Journal of Economics and Business*, 53, 585–592.

Rouse, N. (2014) *Applied lending techniques*, 3rd edn, Cranbrook: Global Professional Publishing.

Ruhnka, J. C., and Young, J. E. (1987) 'A venture capital model of the development process for new ventures', *Journal of Business Venturing*, 2, 167–184.

Ruhnka, J. C., and Young, J. E. (1991) 'Some hypotheses about risk in venture capital investing', *Journal of Business Venturing*, 6, 115–133.

Saeed, U. (2007) *Corporate social responsibility: Analysis of current practices in selected companies and recommendations*, MSc thesis, Royal Institute of Technology, Stockholm.

Sathye, M., Bartle, J., Vincent, M., and Boffey, R. (2003) *Credit analysis and lending management*, Chichester: John Wiley & Sons.

Saunders, A., and Allen, L. (2010) *Credit risk management: In and out of the financial crisis*, 3rd edn, Hoboken, NJ: John Wiley & Sons.

Saunders, A., and Cornett, M. M. (2006) *Financial institutions management: A risk management approach*, London: McGraw-Hill.

Saxby, S. (2006) 'Court of Appeal increases UK consumer protection for overseas credit purchases', *Computer Law and Security Report*, 22, 181–182.

Smith, T. (1996) *Accounting for growth*, London: Random House.

Stiglitz, J. E., and Weiss, A. (1981) 'Credit rationing in markets with imperfect information', *American Economic Review*, 71, 393–410.

Taylor, M. (2007) 'Basel travel bag', *Financial World*, July/August.

van der Veer, K. J. M., and Hoeberichts, M. M. (2016) 'The level effect of bank lending standards on business lending', *Journal of Banking and Finance*, 66, 79–88.

Vibe (2017) 'A Manhattan couple jumped to their death because of mounting financial debt', 29 July, available at www.vibe.com/2017/07/couple-commits-suicide-financial-debt/

Wernick, A. S. (1991) 'How to perfect security interest in software', *Computer Law and Security Report*, 7, 61–62.

Willingham, J. (1997) *International handbook of corporate finance*, London: Glenlake/Fitzroy Dearborn.

Wilson, H. (1979) *The financing of small firms: Interim report of the Committee to Review the Functioning of the Financial Institutions*, London: HMSO.

Yang, B., Lib, L. X., and Xu, H. J. J. (2001) 'An early warning system for loan risk assessment using artificial neural networks', *Knowledge-based Systems*, 14, 303–306.

Index

Page numbers in italics indicate figures or tables.

accessibility risk 150, *150*
Accounting for Growth (Smith) 95
accounting standards 77–8, 81–2, 95
activity ratios 89
administration order 169
administrative receivership 169
adverse selection 134
agency conflict 156–8
alternative dispute resolution (ADR) 25
alternative finance arrangements 176, 181
annual equivalent rate (AER) 5
annual percentage rate (APR) 5
asset turnover ratios 89
Asset-backed Finance Association (ABFA) 30
asset-based lending (ABL) 71
assets
  in the balance sheet *61, 88, 89, 104, 157, 163*
  current 55–6, 57, 60, 104–7, *107*
  fixed 58–9, 75–6, 89
  intangible 157
  loans as 4, *5*, 6, 8
  surplus 171
  and working capital requirements 104–7
assignment of insurance policy 137
asymmetry of information 117, 126, 134, 135, 156
automation, and credit cards 71

bad debt 168
bailment of security 123
balance sheet 6, *61*, 88–9, *88*, 104–5, *104, 157, 163*
balance sheet equation *89*, 105
Bank for International Settlements (BIS) 6, 27, 115, 166
bank loans *see* loans
Bank of England 5, 16, *20*, 22, 172
  Financial Policy Committee (FPC) 20, *20*
Bank Rate 5
Bankers Trust 166
Banking and Financial Services Acts (1994 and 2017) 23, 34
Banking Code (UK) 29
banking codes 29–30
bankruptcy 144, 171
Barclays Bank 17, 154–5
Basel Accords 6, 8, 21–2, 27–9, 34
Basel Committee on Banking Supervision (BCBS) 6, 12, 27, 115, 166
Baycorp Advantage (Australia) 115
beneficiary of life insurance 137–8
bills 72
blue-chip stocks 139
board of directors 13
bonus issues of shares 141
borrower types 37–46
  companies 42–4
  granted overdrafts 65
  and lending categories 2–3
  need to understand 37–8, 46
  partnerships 39–42
  personal 38–9
  unincorporated associations 45–6
borrowers
  as agents 156
  definition *5*

lenders as 4
as primary security 85–6, 120, 127–8, 152–3
self-interest 157–8
borrower-specific credit risk 8
Brexit, and the 'single passport' 21
bridging loans 49–50
British and Irish Ombudsman Association (BIOA) 31–2
British Bankers Association (BBA) 30
British Business Bank 80–1
BT *61, 91*
building societies 4
buildings *see* land and property
Business Banking Code (UK) 29
business cycles 185
business expansion loans 54–5
business finance 53–60, 90–1
business performance and prospects 88
business risk 91–4, 115
buy-to-let borrowers 52

CAMPARI loan evaluation framework *101–2*
Canada 16
capital
in the balance sheet 88–9, *89*
cost of 111–12
debt 90–4
human 157, 159
overcapitalisation 162
requirements 6, 21–2, 27–9, 34, 104–7, *107*, 164
share 44, 79–80, 90
structure 6, 91–4
undercapitalisation 165
venture 53–4
working 48, *48*, 55–8, 60, 104–7, *107*, 164
capital adequacy 27
capital allowances 76, 77–8
Capital One 4
Capital Requirements Directives (CRDs) (EU) 21–2
capped interest 5
cash flows 88, 108–12
cash operating cycle 105–7, *105*
CCCPARTS loan evaluation framework *102*
central bank, as lender of last resort (LOLR) 9
charge
over shares 140
of security 121, 122–5
charging systems 187
Charities Act (2011) 45
Charity Commission 45
cheap credit 2
checking accounts 65
checklists for loan evaluation 101–3
choses in action 130
Citizens Advice 187
Civil Liberty (Contribution) Act (1978) 143
clean loans 85, 120
clubs 45
codes of practice 29–31
collateral 120, 150
collateralised debt/loan obligations (CDOs/CLOs) 6
commercial lending 2, 3, 4
Committee to Review the Functioning of the Financial Institutions 80
common stock 139
community interest companies (CIC) 44
companies 42–4
Companies (Audit, Investigations and Community Enterprise) Act (2004) 44
Companies Act (2006) 42–3
company voluntary arrangement (CVA) 169–70
Competition and Markets Authority (CMA) 21
complaints procedures 32
compliance risk (of Islamic finance) 180
compound interest 5

compulsory liquidation 169
concealment 158
connected lender liability 24, 35–6
Consumer Credit Acts (1974 and 2006) 23–5, 36, 65, 67, 120
consumer credit scoring processes 27–8
consumer finance 48–53
consumer protection 24
Consumer Rights Act (2015) 34, 123
contagion risk 9
contractual terms 33–4
control measures 14, 166–7
corporate social responsibility (CSR) 188
costs
  of capital 111–12
  of security 126
Council of Mortgage Lenders (CML) 30
countries 4
country risk 9
creative accounting 95
credit
  analysis 88
  availability 1, *63*
  cheap 2
  fixed *63*, 64
  instalment 64
  loan as the creation of 4
  repayment or recovery process *84*
  revolving *63*, 64, 65
credit agreements 24
credit cards 4, 24, 35–6, 69–71, 82–3, 172, 187
credit crunch 2, 6, 16–17, 172, 185
credit derivative 167
credit market 2–4
credit rating agencies (CRAs) 115–18
credit ratings 115–16, *116–17*
credit risk *see also* risk
  appropriate environment for 13
  consumer 27–8
  control measures 14, 166–7
  definition 15
  of Islamic finance 179
  in lending 8–10
  management 8–10, *11*, 12–15
  mitigation 166–7
Credit Risk+ 166
credit scoring 112–15, *113*, 166
Credit Suisse 166
credit-granting process 13, *84*, 85, *85*
CreditMetrics 166
credit-monitoring process 13–14, *84*
  and control measures 14, 166–7
  detecting problem loans 161–7
  information sources for review 159–61, *160*
  need for 156–8, 172
  and principles 158–9
  and stages of recovery 168–72
creditor 4, *5*
creditor repayment rate 89
creditors' voluntary liquidation (CVL) 169
creditworthiness 67, 115, 120, 127–8
Crisil (India) 115
currency risk 9
current accounts 64–5
current assets 55–6, 57, 60, 104–7, *107*
current ratios *61*, 90
customer interviews 87
customers 32–4, 37–8

Dana Gas 181–3
Data Protection Act 1998 26
Data Protection Act 2018 26
data regulation 26–7
debentures 130, 146–8, 170
debt capital 90–4
debt service coverage ratio (DSCR) 112
debt-equity ratio 90
debtor 4, *5*
debtor finance 71
debtor recovery rate 89
default risk 8, 85–6, 126, 152
Denning, Lord 2

Deregulation Act (2015) 25
Deutsche Bank 166
direct debits 65
directors' shares 141
discount rate, and evaluation of term loans 111–12
diversification of risk 141
dividend cover 90
dividends 80
Dodd–Frank Act (2010) (US) 22, *22*
Dominon Bond Rating Service (Canada) 115
drawee/drawer (buyer/seller) 72
dual regulatory models 19
duty of utmost good faith (*uberrimae fidei*) 135, 138

early warning signals (of problem loans) 161–6
earnings before interest, depreciation and amortisation (EBIDA) 112
earnings before interest, taxes, depreciation and amortisation (EBITDA) 112
earnings per share (EPS) 90
economic effects 184–5
effective annual rate (EAR) 5
endowment policies 137–8
Enterprise Acts (2002 and 2016) 25, 147, 151, 169, 170–1
Enterprise Finance Guarantee (EFG) 80–1
Equifax 112
equitable charge 122–3, 149
equitable mortgages 132, 138
equities *see* shares (owned capital)
equity finance 79–80
equity holders 139
equity release products 69
European Central Bank (ECB) 21
European Commission 21
European Union 21–2
Experian 112
external information 87, 160–1

factoring 73–5
Fair Isaac Credit Organization (FICO) *112*
fair treatment of customers initiative 32–3, 34
family businesses 80
Family Law Reform Act (1969) 38
fees
  credit cards 70–1
  factoring 74
  hire purchase 76
  leasing 78
  lending 5
  loan 68
  overdraft 65, 66, 67
Finance Act (2005) 176–7
finance lease 77
Financial CHOICE Act (2017) (US) 22
Financial Conduct Authority (FCA) 7, *20*, 21, 23, 26, 29, 32–3, 37, 87, 115, 134, 175
  Banking Conduct of Business sourcebook (BCOBS) 67
  Handbook 32
  Principles for Businesses 33
financial disintermediation 6
Financial Fraud Action UK 30
financial institutions 6
financial intermediation 6
financial market 2
Financial Ombudsman Service (FOS) 23, 25, 26, 31, 34
financial risk 91–4, 115
Financial Services Act (2012) 23, 34
Financial Services Action Plan (FSAP) 21
Financial Services and Markets Act (2000) 22–3, 25, 33, 34, 120, 134
Financial Services and Markets Tribunal 23
Financial Services Authority (FSA) 22–3
Financial Services (Banking Reform) Act (2013) 23, 34

financial statements *174*
  interpreting 88–94
  limitations of 94–6
'first in, first out' approach 65–6
fixed asset turnover 89
fixed assets 58–9, 75–9, 89
fixed charges 123, 146, 148
fixed credit *63*, 64, 67
fixed interest 5
floating charges 123, 146–8, 153, 170
forced sale risk 150, *150*
forecast for the future loan evaluation framework *103*
Foreign Account Tax Compliance Act (2010) (FATCA) (US) 22
foreign shares 139, 142
forgery 141
fraud 43, 87
freehold title 131
further advances 97–8
future value (FV) 109–11

gearing
  acceptable level of 93–4
  definition 6
  financial 92–3, *92*
  high 90
  and leasing 77
  and mortgages 93
  operating 91–3
  ratios 90–1, *91*
  and taxation 93
General Data Protection Regulation (GDPR) 26
Germany 190
global financial crisis 2007-08 3, 6, 9, 22, 172
globalisation 10
going concern 147
government 46
Greenspan, Alan 185
gross profit margin 89
growth stocks 139, 140
guarantees 142–6, 153
guarantors 142–3

Halifax 51
hard information 86, 160
hard-core debt 65
hedge funds 4
herd behaviour 185
high-risk loans 69
hire purchase 75–6
Hirst, Damien 11
home improvement loans 49
Houses of Parliament refurbishment 179
HSBC 17
human capital 157, 159
hypothecation of security 123

ijara (leasing) 178, *178*
ijara-wal-iqtina 178
illegal lending 3
incentives 86–7
income statement *see* profit and loss account
income stocks 139
indemnity 135, 143
Independent Commission on Banking (ICB) 23
Independent Insurance 43
independent legal advice (ILA) 125
individuals 38, 171
inequality 185
Infants Relief Act (1874) 144
informal arrangement 170
information
  asymmetry of 117, 126, 134, 135, 156
  and credit-monitoring process 159–61, *160*
  and risk 126
  supporting loan application 86–8
insolvency 25
  definition 168
  and floating charge 148
  and guarantees 145
  of individuals 171
  options 169–70
  payments in the event of 91
  and realisation of security 151–2

risk 27
and security 127
stages of recovery 168, 169–70
and *sukuk* (bond securities) 181
undercapitalisation as cause of 165
Insolvency Acts (1986 and 2000) 25, 151–2
Insolvency Rules (2017) 25
instalment credit 64
insurance 68, 130, 134, 136–7 *see also* life insurance
Insurance Companies Act (1980) 134
insurers 134
intangible assets 157
intangible security 130
integrity risk 150, *150*
interest
cover 90
from credit cards 70–1
definition 5
forbidden in Islamic finance 175–6
and hire purchase 76
and insolvent individuals 171
loan 68, 112
and order of liquidation 171
overdraft 65, 66, 67
perfecting security 122–5
interest rate risk 9
interest rates 69, 78
interest-only products 69
internal information 87, 160
internal ratings-based (IRB) systems 8–9, 166
International Accounting Standard (IAS) 16 95
International Accounting Standards Board (IASB) 81–2
International Financial Reporting Standards (IFRS) 78, 81–2
International Swaps and Derivatives Association (ISDA) 167
Internet 35–6
investment appraisal of term loans 108–12
investment banks 3–4
investor ratios 90
invoice discounting 71–3
invoices 72
irresponsible lending 184, 186, 188
Islamic finance 175–6, 181
modes of 176–9
size of industry 175
special features 179–81

Japan 190
JP Morgan Chase 3, 166

KMV Portfolio Manager model 166
knowledge of the past loan evaluation framework *102*

LA Gear 62
land and property
advantages and disadvantages 132–3
definition 131
and realisation of security 149
as security 131–4, 152
Land Registration Act (2002) 131–2
Land Registration Rules (2003) SI 2003/1417 131
Law of Property Act (1925) 124, 133
lead generation *85*
leasehold title 131
leasing 75–9
Leeds Building Society 51
legal charge 122, 149
legal mortgage 131–2
legal risk *150*, 151
legislation
supranational 27–9
in the UK 22–7
lender of last resort (LOLR) 9
lenders 4, *5*, 156, 190
lending concepts 1–12, 15
benefits 184
categories 2–4
definition 4–6, 15
detrimental effects 184–5

economic and social effects 184–5, 190
importance 1–2
market overview 2–4
objectives 11–12, *12*
relationship lending 189–90
responsible lending 185–9
risk and return 6–11
lending cycle *159*
credit-granting process 84–6, 98
further advances 97–8
loan application and supporting information 86–96
loan documentation and covenants 96–7
monitoring and control process 172
detecting problem loans 161–7
information sources for review 159–61
need for 156–9
stages of recovery 168–72
lending decision errors 1
lending environment trends 18–19
lending fees 5–6
lending growth 2
lending market 2–4, 10
lending objectives 11–12, *12*, 15
lending practices 187–8
lending principles 12–15
lending purposes 48, *48*, 60
business finance 53–60
consumer finance 48–53
lending services 3–4
lending standards 2
lending types 63–4, *63*, 81–2
credit cards 69–71
factoring 73–5
hire purchase 75–6
invoice discounting 71–3
leasing 77–9
loans 67–9
other forms 79–81
overdrafts 64–7
leverage 6, 90
liabilities
in the balance sheet 88, *88*, *89*, *104*, *157*, *163*, *174*
current 55–6, *61*, 90, 104, 105, 107, 164
loans as 4, *5*
and working capital requirements 104–7
lien of security 123
Life Assurance Act (1774) 134
life insurance 134–8, 149, 152
limited companies 43, 143–4
Limited Liability Partnership Act (2000) 41–2
limited liability partnerships (LLP) 41–2
limited partnerships 41
Limited Partnerships Act (1907) 41
liquidation 168–71
liquidity 11, *12*, 184, 185
liquidity ratios 90
litigation 180
Lloyds Bank 36
Lloyds TSB 16
loan application *85*
and interpreting financial statements 88–94
and limitations of financial statements 94–6
and supporting information 86–8
loan commitments *63*, 64, 65, 67
loan consolidation 98
loan covenants 96–7
loan documentation 96
loan evaluation *85*, 118
credit rating agencies 115–18
credit scoring 112–15
frameworks 101–3
term lending requirements 108–12
tools and techniques 101–4
working capital requirements 104–7
Loan Market Association (LMA) 167
loan modification 188
loan prices 2, 187
loan types *see* lending types

loanable funds 2
loans
  as assets 6
  decisions on *85*
  definition 4–6, *5*
  evaluation of requirement 108–12
  foreclosures 188
  interest 112
  losses 165–6, 172
  murabaha (finance) 176–7, *177*
  problem 161–7
  securitisation of 167
  types of. *see* lending types
  write-off 172
loan-to-value (LTV) ratios 187–8
London 175
London Inter-bank Offered Rate (LIBOR) 5, 30
long-term finance
  in the balance sheet *88*, *89*
  and forms of lending 77
  and investment appraisal 108
  and problem loans 162, 164
  purposes of 48, *48*, 59–60
  and working capital requirements 104–7, *107*
loss
  loan 165–6, 172
  mitigation of 135
  unexpected 9

mainstream lending 2–4
Markets in Financial Instruments Directives (MiFIDs) (EU) 22
merchant acquirer 70
Metro Bank 3
migration analysis 166
minors 38–9, 144
Minors' Contracts Act (1987) 38–9, 144
misrepresentation 151
mistake (*non est factum*) ('not my act') 151
mitigation of loss 135
monetisation *see tawarruq* (monetisation)
Money Advice Service (2016) 186
Moody's 115
moral hazard 86, 126, 134, 156
more principles-based regulation (MPBR) 32–3
mortgage debenture 146
mortgages
  asset-backed 6
  from building societies 4
  and debentures 146
  equitable 132, 138
  and gearing 93
  high-risk types 69
  legal 131–2
  lending purposes 50–3
  second 133–4
  subprime 6, 16, 187–8
multiple re-aging 188
murabaha (finance) 176–7, *177*, *178*

National Property Buyers 53
Nationwide 4, 51
negative equity 133
net present value (NPV), for investment appraisal 108–12
net profit margin 89
net working capital 104–5
new ventures, loans for 53–4
non-performing loan (NPL) 168, 180
non-possessory security interests 132
Northern Rock 11, 16, 93
not-for-profit lending 2

obligor 4
off-balance sheet financing 6, 75, 77, 143–4
Office of Fair Trading (OFT) 24, 36
ombudsmen 31–2
operating gearing 91–3
operating lease 77
opportunity costs 110, 111
ordinary shares 90, 139
overcapitalisation 162
overdrafts 64–7, 108

overriding interests 132
overtrading 162–5, *163*, *173*, *174*

PARSER loan evaluation framework *102*
partly paid stocks 139, 142
partnerships 39–42
Partnerships Act (1890) 39–40
pawnbrokers 123
payment protection insurance (PPI) 30, 69
Payments UK 30
Pensions Ombudsman 31–2
personal borrowers 38–9
PESTLE analysis 104
pledge of security 123
Policies of Assurance Act (1867) 134, 137
policyholders, insurance 134
Porter's Five Forces (for loan evaluation) 104, *104*
portfolio risk 8
postponed creditors 171
predatory lending 188
preference shares 90, 139
preference transaction 151–2
preferential creditors 170–1
preferred stock 139
premium, as price of insurance 134
present value (PV) 109–11
price-earnings ratio (PE) 90
prices *see* loan prices
primary security, borrower as 85–6, 120, 127–8, 152–3
principal 5, 156
principles
- of credit risk management 12–15
- definition 12
- of insurance 135

private companies 42, 44, 139
private equity firms 4
probability
- of default 9
- as element of risk 7

problem loans 161–7
procyclicality 185
profit and loss account 88, *173*
profitability 11, *12*, 156
profitability ratios 89
property *see* land and property
property insurance 136
Property Rescue 53
Prudential Regulation Authority (PRA) 20, *20*, 23, 134
public companies 42, 44
purchase and sale arrangement, *murabaha* as a 177

quick ratios 90, 164

ratios 90
- for business and financial risk 91–4
- limitations of 94–6
- quick 90, 164
- using 89–91

realisation
- and floating charge 148
- risk 150, *150*
- of security 121, 122, 148–52
- of stocks 140

receivership, administrative 169
recognition, lack of 10
recovery risk 150
recovery stages 168–72
redistribution 10
regulation
- codes of practice 29–31
- consumer rights and complaints procedures 32
- framework 18–29, 34
- global process 19
- importance of 18
- national models 19–22
- ombudsmen 31–2
- treating customers fairly 32–4

relationship-based lending 189–90
repackaging 10
reserves *89*
responsible lending 185–9, 190
retail banks 3

retention of title (ROT) clause 126, 148
return
  impact of variability *93*
  and risk 6, 91–3
  trade-off with risk 10–11
return on capital employed (ROCE) 89
return on equity (ROE) 90
return on investment (ROI) ratios 77, 178–9
reverse *murabaha* (monetisation) *see tawarruq* (monetisation)
revolving credit *63*, 64, 65, 70
rights issues 141
ring-fencing 3, 23
risk *see also* credit risk
  business 91–4, 115
  default 85–6, 152
  definition 7–8, 15
  of discounted invoices 72
  and equity finance 80
  of factoring 75
  financial 91–4, 115
  of guarantees 144–6
  and hire purchase 76
  insolvency 27
  of Islamic finance 175, 179, 180
  of leasing 78
  legal 151
  in lending 8–10
  of loans 69
  and overdrafts 67
  and realisation of security 150, *150*
  and return 6, 91–3
  and security 126
  of stocks and shares 140–2
  trade-off with return 10–11
risk-adjusted return on capital (RAROC) models, as control measure 166
Royal Bank of Scotland (RBS) 16, 81

safety, as a lending objective 11, *12*
sale-and-leaseback scheme 53
savings, stimulated by lending 184
second mortgages 133–4
secondary loan markets 167
secured creditors 170, 171
secured debenture 146
secured loan *63*, 64, 85
securitisation 6, 167
security 120–1, 127–8
  advantages and disadvantages 125–7
  attributes of good 121–2
  borrowers as primary 85–6, 120, 127–8, 152–3
  desirability of taking 125–7
  insurance as 136–7
  insurance of 136
  and lending type *63*
  life insurance as 137–8
  perfecting interest 122–5
  specific forms 130, 152–3
    debentures 146–8
    guarantees 142–6
    land and property 131–4
    life insurance policies 134–8
    realisation 148–52
    stocks and shares 139–42
self-certification products 69
self-interest 157–8, *157*
senior management 13
severity, as element of risk 7
shares (owned capital) 44, 79–80, 90–1, 139, 140, 141, 142
Shari'ah law restrictions 175–6, 179–81
short-term finance
  and forms of lending 72, 77
  overdraft as 65, 108
  and problem loans 161–2, 164
  purposes of 48, *48*, 56–60, 68
  and working capital requirements 104, 105–7, *107*
simple interest 5
single-payment loans 64
Small Business, Enterprise and Employment Act (2015) 25–6
small or medium-sized enterprises (SMEs) 80–1

social effects of lending 184–5
social lending 2, 184
societies 45
soft information 86, 160–1
sole traders 39
sovereign borrowers 46
sovereign states 4
specialist lenders 3
speculative stocks 139
spot loan *63*, 64, 67
stand-alone risk 8
Standard & Poor's (S&P) 115
standard deviation 7
standard variable rate (SVR) 5
Standards of Lending Practice 30–1, 34, 77
standing orders 65
statement of financial position *see* balance sheet
Statements of Standard Accounting Practice (SSAP) 77
Statute of Frauds (1677) 142
stock markets 142
stock turnover 89
stocks and shares
  advantages and disadvantages 140–2
  as security 139–42, 153
stress-testing 172
subprime lending 16–17
subprime mortgages 6, 16, 69, 187–8
subrogation 39, 135, 143
sukuk (bond securities) 178–9, *179*, 181–3
supervisors 14
supply and demand of loanable funds 2
supranational regulation 27–9
surplus assets 171
surrender value 137
SWOT analysis 103–4, *103*
syndicated loan 64
systematic credit risk 8
systemic risk 9

tacking of loans 133–4
tawarruq (monetisation) 178
tax trading 78
taxation
  and gearing 93
  and Islamic finance 176–7, 180–1
  and loan interest 112
technology 10
term life insurance 136
term loans *see* loans
third-party security 130, 143
time value of money concept 108–9, 112
timing
  of credit card repayment 70
  of invoice discounting 72
  and lending type *63*
  of loan repayment 67–8
  of overdraft payment 66, 67
trade-off theory of capital structure 94
transaction 189
transactional lending 189
transparency, lack of 10, 187
tripartite regulatory models 19
Trump administration 22
trusts 45–6
turnover growth (fall) 89
twin peaks' systems regulatory model 19, 20–1, *20*

UBS AG 16
UK Cards Association 30
UK Finance 30
uncertainty
  as element of risk 7
  prohibited in Islamic finance 175
  and risk-return trade-off 10–11
undercapitalisation, and problem loans 165
undervalue transaction 151–2
undue influence 145, 151
unexpected loss 9
Unfair Contract Terms Act (1977) 33–4, 123

unified regulatory model 19
unincorporated associations 45–6
United Kingdom
annual percentage rate (APR) 5
banks 11
Department for Business, Energy and Industrial Strategy (BEIS) 25
DTI Task Force on Over-indebtedness 186
HM Land Registry 131, 132, 133
HM Revenue & Customs 170–1, 176–7, 179
HM Treasury *20*, 23
regulation 20–1, *20*
specific legislation 22–7
transactional lending 189
United States
annual percentage rate (APR) 5
collateral-based business model 127
regulation 22
share regulations 141
subprime mortgages 187–8
transactional lending 189
unlimited companies 43
unquoted shares 142
unregistered land 131
unsecured creditors 170
unsecured debenture 146
unsecured loan *63*, 64, 65, 67, 85, 120

valuation risk 150, *150*
value, measure, charge, realise (VMCR) 121
value of security 121
variability 7, 91–2, *93*
variable interest 5
venture capital 53–4

Wall Street Reform and Consumer Protection Act (2010) (known as the Dodd–Frank Act) 22, *22*
whole life insurance 136
wholesale banks 4
wholesale funds 11
window-dressing 95
working capital 48, *48*, 55–8, 60, *61*, 104–7, *107*, 164
wrongful trading 43

zopa.com 2

www.ingramcontent.com/pod-product-compliance
Lightning Source LLC
LaVergne TN
LVHW011758200926
848484LV00003B/735